WJEC Vocational Award

Hospitality and Catering

Level 1/2

Anita Tull
Alison Palmer

Illuminate Publishing

Contents

Unit 2: Hospitality and Catering in action

You will find suggested answers to Activities, Practice questions and Stretch and challenge activities from the book, online:

www.illuminatepublishing.com/hosp&cateranswers

Introduction

This student textbook has been especially written for the WJEC Vocational Award in Hospitality and Catering Level 1/2 qualification that you are taking, and it matches the course specification produced by WJEC.

The aim of the Vocational Award in Hospitality and Catering course

The course has been designed with the aim of enabling you to gain a good foundation of knowledge, understanding and skills that are required by the Hospitality and Catering industry, which is a major employer of people in the UK and other countries. You will have the opportunity to develop a variety of skills, including food preparation and cooking skills, organisation, time management, planning, communication and problem solving.

Success in this course will enable you to progress on to further training if you decide to choose a career in this industry.

The course is made up of two units:

Unit 1: The Hospitality and Catering Industry
Unit 2: Hospitality and Catering in Action.

To pass the course, you must complete the assessments for both units (see chart below).

In **Unit 1** you will learn about:

- All the different parts of the Hospitality and Catering industry
- Different types of hospitality and catering establishments and job roles
- Different types of hospitality and catering provision for particular situations
- Front of house and kitchen operations
- The needs and requirements of customers
- What makes hospitality and catering businesses successful
- Issues related to nutrition and food safety.

In **Unit 2** you will apply your learning in order to:

- Plan, prepare, cook and serve a variety of nutritional dishes, in a safe and hygienic manner, that are suitable for different situations and customer needs and requirements.

Unit 1	40%	For the online e-assessment you will need to gain knowledge of all parts of the industry and be able to propose new hospitality and catering provision for a particular location. You should be able to identify different types of establishment and job roles to determine the best option.	You will use your knowledge gained over the course to determine how the proposed hospitality and catering provision will operate efficiently, legally and financially viably whilst meeting the needs of their potential customers.
The Hospitality and Catering Industry *External assessment: Online e-assessment*			

Unit 2	60%	This unit is based around a given brief in which you will need to complete all the Assessment Criteria; this will form your coursework, along with a practical assessment. You will use your knowledge gained over the course to carry out	preparation, cooking and present nutritional dishes. You will apply knowledge gained of different types of provision and kitchen and front of house operations in Unit 1, as well as personal safety in their preparation.
Hospitality and Catering in Action *Internal assessment: Controlled Assessment Task*			

Understanding the terminology and grading

Learning Outcomes (LOs)

These are the topic skills and knowledge you should be able to demonstrate when you have completed your course.

Assessment Criteria (ACs)

These are the Learning Outcomes, broken down into criteria against which your learning will be assessed and graded. They are a means of checking your knowledge and understanding. Each AC has a number, AC2.1, AC2.2, etc. You will see this numbering used throughout the book, which makes it clear which AC each section of the book is covering.

Unit	Learning Outcomes	Assessment Criteria	Marks	%
1	LO1 Understand the environment in which hospitality and catering providers operate	AC1.1 Describe the structure of the Hospitality and Catering industry	15–28	17%–32%
		AC1.2 Analyse job requirements within the Hospitality and Catering industry		
		AC1.3 Describe working conditions of different job roles across the Hospitality and Catering industry		
		AC1.4 Explain factors affecting the success of Hospitality and Catering providers		

Marks

You will see how many marks are available in the assessment for each LO.

%

The the percentage of the total marks available for the LO.

Learning Outcomes	Assessment Criteria	Content
The learner will:	*The learner can:*	
LO1 Understand the environment in which hospitality and catering providers operate	AC1.1 Describe the structure of the **Hospitality and Catering industry**	**Hospitality and Catering industry** • Types of provider • Types of service • Commercial establishments • Non-commercial catering establishments • Services provided • Suppliers • Where hospitality is provided at non-catering venues • Standards and ratings • Job roles within the industry (management, kitchen brigade, front of house, housekeeping, administration)

Content

This is what should be covered in each AC. Any of this content could appear in the assessments. The content for all the AC are covered in this textbook to make sure you are prepared.

How to work out your overall grade

This qualification is graded as Level 1 Pass, Level 2 Pass, Level 2 Merit, Level 2 Distinction or Level 2 Distinction*. You will be awarded a grade for each unit you complete, and these grades will be converted into marks that will then give you an overall, final grade.

So, for example, if you receive a **L2 Merit** for your Unit 2 coursework, this is worth **9** points (see table right).

In order to make sure you receive an *overall grade* of **L2 Merit** you would need to make sure you achieve an additional 6 points in your Unit 1 e-assessment to take your overall points score to **15** (see table right).

If you only achieve **2** points in your Unit 2 e-assessment then you would end up with an *overall grade* of **L2 Pass**, even though you had a Merit grade for Unit 2 coursework.

Unit	Points per unit			
	Level 1 Pass	**Level 2 Pass**	**Level 2 Merit**	**Level 2 Distinction**
Unit 1	2	4	6	8
Unit 2	3	6	9	12

Overall grading points	
Level 1 Pass	5–8
Level 2 Pass	9–13
Level 2 Merit	14–17
Level 2 Distinction	18–19
Level 2 Distinction*	20

If you receive a L2 Distinction for Unit 2 (12 points) and L2 Merit for Unit 1 (6 points) the you would have 18 points and an overall grade of L2 Distinction.

You can only achieve a L2 Distinction* by achieving Distinction in both units.

If you do not achieve the minimum points required for a L1 Pass in both units your overall grade will be Unclassified.

For more grading information please refer to the WJEC specification.

How to use this book

The book is set out in the same order as the units in the course specification, which is divided into these sections:

UNIT 1: Learning Outcomes	Assessment Criteria	Chapter
LO1 Understand the environment in which hospitality and catering providers operate	AC1.1 Describe the structure of the Hospitality and Catering industry	1
	AC1.2 Analyse job requirements within the Hospitality and Catering industry	2
	AC1.3 Describe working conditions of different job roles across the Hospitality and Catering industry	2
	AC1.4 Explain factors affecting the success of hospitality and catering providers	3
LO2 Understand how hospitality and catering provision operates	AC2.1 Describe the operation of the kitchen	4
	AC2.2 Describe the operation of front of house	5
	AC2.3 Explain how hospitality and catering provision meet customer requirements	6
LO3 Understand how hospitality and catering provision meets health and safety requirements	AC3.1 Describe personal safety responsibilities in the workplace	7
	AC3.2 Identify risks to personal safety in hospitality and catering	8
	AC3.3 Recommend personal safety control measures for hospitality and catering provision	8
LO4 Know how food can cause ill health	AC4.1 Describe food-related causes of ill health	9, 10
	AC4.2 Describe the role and responsibilities of the Environmental Health Officer (EHO)	12
	AC4.3 Describe food safety legislation	11
	AC4.4 Describe common types of food poisoning	9
	AC4.5 Describe the symptoms of food-induced ill health	9, 10
LO5 Be able to propose a hospitality and catering provision to meet specific requirements	AC5.1 Review options for hospitality and catering provision	13
	AC5.2 Recommend options for hospitality provision	13

UNIT 2: Learning Outcomes	Assessment Criteria	Chapter
LO1 Understand the importance of nutrition when planning menus	AC1.1 Describe functions of nutrients in the human body	15
	AC1.2 Compare nutritional needs of specific groups	16
	AC1.3 Explain characteristics of unsatisfactory nutritional intake	17
	AC1.4 Explain how cooking methods impact on nutritional value	18
LO2 Understand menu planning	AC2.1 Explain factors to consider when proposing dishes for menus	19
	AC2.2 Explain how dishes on a menu address environmental issues	20
	AC2.3 Explain how menu dishes meet customer needs	21
	AC2.4 Plan production of dishes for a menu	22
LO3 Be able to cook dishes	AC3.1 Use techniques in preparation of commodities	24, 27
	AC3.2 Assure quality of commodities to be used in food preparation	23, 27
	AC3.3 Use techniques in cooking of commodities	25, 27
	AC3.4 Complete dishes using presentation techniques	26, 27
	AC3.5 Use food safety practices	23, 24, 26, 27

Features to help you

Throughout the book, there are a number of features to help you to study and progress through the course, which are shown below

AC1.2

Assessment Criteria: flagged throughout so it is clear which AC is being covered.

Activity

Activities: a range of activities are given throughout the book. They are designed to help you learn a topic more thoroughly and practise answering questions.

Case study

Case study: these are activities that ask you questions about people or situations you might come across in hospitality and catering.

Did you know?

Did you know?: these are short pieces of information about aspects of the Hospitality and Catering industry that are included for interest and to further explain a topic.

Key terms

Key terms: these give you the definitions of the key terminology (words) in each of the topics that you need to know and use.

Photographs and drawings: there are many of these throughout the book. They are included to help you further understand and visualise a topic.

Practice questions

Practice questions: these are end-of-topic questions, written in different styles and with a range of command words. They are designed to give you opportunities throughout the course to practise and improve your techniques for answering questions.

Put it into practice

Put it into practice: these are activities that involve practising your cooking skills, whilst at the same time reinforcing what you have learned in a topic.

Recipes: a variety of recipes, related to particular commodities, are provided in Chapter 27. Each recipe gives the ingredients and method for making it. You will find at the beginning of each recipe, a chart showing the commodities, techniques and cooking methods used.

Scenario

Scenario: these are activities that use realistic situations/proposals/problems that occur in hospitality and catering. You are asked to consider and make suggestions as to how these situations would be dealt with and/or, suggest an appropriate option for hospitality and catering provision, and/or suggest solutions to the problems presented.

Stretch and challenge

Stretch and challenge activities: these are activities/questions in which you will need to find out more about a topic and practise being able to answer questions at a higher level, showing your detailed knowledge and understanding.

Good luck on your course. We hope that you will enjoy learning about Hospitality and Catering and will develop your skills and confidence as you progress through the course and possibly on to further training and a career in this industry.

What will I learn?

The Hospitality and Catering industry is one of the largest employers in the UK. In this chapter, you will learn about the structure of the industry and the wide range of jobs and services it provides.

You will also learn about how the industry is rated according to different sets of standards, e.g. food hygiene, services provided, sustainability and environmental practices.

Key terms

- Caterer – a business or person who arranges the preparation, delivery and presentation of food for clients

- Catering – providing a food and beverage service to people in a particular location

- Establishment – a place where a business or organisation operates from

- Hospitality – the business of providing people with accommodation, meals and drinks in a variety of places away from their home

The structure of the Hospitality and Catering industry (AC1.1)

The Hospitality and Catering industry is very large and varied.

There are many job roles within it that require different sets of skills to make the industry effective and successful.

The Hospitality and Catering industry also relies on other outside agencies, businesses and people **(suppliers)** to supply it with the things it needs, e.g. food commodities, drinks, cleaning materials, tableware, agency staff, equipment, furniture, uniforms, laundering services, waste disposal, floral displays, etc.

Catering

Catering services are provided by:

- **Contract food service catering businesses (large and small),** caterers who supply businesses and establishments such as airlines, hospitals, schools, care homes and some private functions in hotels. The food is usually prepared in a central place and then delivered to the establishments. They may also supply food to places that do not have catering facilities, such as historical houses, museums, community halls, sports venues, for events such as parties, anniversaries, wedding receptions, open-air concerts and sports events.

- **In-house catering staff,** who work in the kitchen, which is a permanent part of the establishment.

The following table shows the different types of food service systems that are operated by the catering sector to provide customers with food. Food is served to customers in a variety of different ways (systems), depending on the establishment where the food is eaten.

Types of food service system

Counter service

Cafeteria – all the types of food and drink on sale are displayed at a long counter. Customers move along the counter with a tray and choose what they want, then queue up to pay at the end. Used in schools, some restaurants and cafes.

Free-flow – different types of food and drinks are displayed at different counters. Customers take their trays and choose what they want from different counters then pay at a central till.

Multi-point – different types of food and drinks are displayed and paid for at separate counters.

Buffet service – food is displayed in containers at an open counter or a central serving station. Customers pick up a plate or bowl and help themselves to food and drinks.

Some foods may be served to customers, e.g. fish, meat, poultry. Often used in hotels for breakfast and in 'all-you-can-eat' restaurants that charge a fixed price per person for a meal.

Fast food – foods and drinks are displayed on a menu behind the counter or on an outside screen/poster at a drive-through outlet. The customer places their order and pays at a sales point at the counter, or from a communication point at a drive-through fast food outlet.

Seated counter service – customers sit at the counter on stools and are served their food. Used in places such as sushi bars, stations and airports.

Carvery service – roasted meat joints are displayed on a counter and carved for customers by a chef. Customers help themselves to vegetables, sauces, etc.

Customers can see what is available and its price and can easily choose what they want.

Customers have to queue to pay before they can eat the food.

Queueing may take longer at busy times.

The food can be eaten in the establishment or taken away.

Table service

Waiters and waitresses (waiting staff) take food orders and serve customers who are seated at a table.

A large restaurant or pub will divide the customer tables into areas. These areas are called 'stations'. Each member of waiting staff is allocated to a station to ensure that all customers are served in good time.

For large banquets or special occasions, such as wedding receptions, waiting staff are put into teams, each of which serves a specific group of people throughout the meal.

Food is generally more expensive when served this way, in order to pay the wages of the waiting staff.

Gueridon system (also called trolley or moveable service)

This is used in restaurants for cooking, or preparing for **service**, some food, e.g. a steak, Caesar salad, flambéed bananas, from a special trolley at a customer's table.

Cooking food at the table for customers is a form of entertainment and adds excitement and drama to the meal. It is often carried out by one of the waiting staff.

Transport catering system

Trains: long-distance trains usually have dining carriages for sit-down meals or takeaway cafeteria food available. Mobile food and drinks trolleys are also used to deliver directly to travellers throughout the train.

Aeroplanes: on long-haul flights, customers are given one or two meals that have been made by contract food service caterers and delivered to the flight either frozen or cook-chilled. Customers may be able to pre-order their choice of cuisine (e.g. vegetarian, vegan, gluten-free, oriental) before their flight – this helps the airline to plan their catering. Meals are heated in the aeroplane kitchens and delivered to passengers by flight attendants.

Ships: cruise ships will have a variety of food service options available, including table and counter service. Ferries will usually have cafeteria service.

All forms of transport are limited as to what they can take on board, so planning their catering carefully is really important. They need to include some food options for different customer needs and requirements, e.g. gluten-free, vegetarian, Kosher, etc.

Vending system

Vending machines provide hot and cold drinks, snacks and meals.

They need to have a person or team of people in charge of regularly maintaining and re-stocking them.

These are used in many large organisations and establishments to cater for different requirements.

A vending machine in Japan selling meals

The following table shows the different types of hospitality and catering establishments, the clients they cater for, the services they provide and the job roles in each. The table is divided into the two main **sectors** (parts) in the Hospitality and Catering industry:

The commercial sector, where a business (e.g. a restaurant, hotel, sports stadium, travel company) **aims to make a profit** from the hospitality and catering services it provides.

The non-commercial catering services sector, where an organisation (e.g. a staff canteen in a shop, construction site or hospital) provides catering services, but **does not necessarily aim to make a profit** from them.

COMMERCIAL SECTOR

Residential

Examples of establishments where hospitality and catering is carried out

For business, leisure & tourism:

- Hotels
- Guest houses
- Bed & breakfast
- Inns & pubs
- Farmhouses
- Family holiday camps & parks
- Glamping (a type of luxury camping where accommodation and facilities are provided)
- Cruise ships
- Long-distance trains
- Airlines
- Motorway services
- Youth hostels

Client groups

Individuals/groups for business/conferences & meetings

Individuals/groups/families for leisure/holidays

Guests attending a wedding/birthday party/anniversary/funeral/religious celebration/office party, etc.

Overseas visitors/tourists

Individuals/groups taking part in a leisure/tourism/sport/health activity

Students on field trips

Travellers breaking a journey

Passengers on a journey

Hospitality and catering services provided

Accommodation/housekeeping/turn-down service (preparing a guest room for the evening/night, e.g. turning down the bedding, closing the curtains, emptying the rubbish bin)

Food & beverages in dining rooms or restaurants/room service/bar/cafeteria/takeaway packed lunch service

Banqueting and formal meals for special occasions

Business/study/training facilities, e.g. conference facilities/meeting rooms/Internet access

Transport catering service – before, during & after a journey

Hospitality and catering job roles required (depending on the type and size of the establishment)

Management	Front of house	Food & beverage	Housekeeping
• Managers	• Receptionists	• Kitchen brigade	• Housekeeper
• Administrators	• Porters	• Restaurant manager	• Room attendant
	• Security staff	• Waiters/waitresses	• Maintenance staff
		• Barista/bartender	• Conference staff

Key terms

- Client – a person/business/organisation using hospitality and catering services

- Commercial sector – the part of the Hospitality and Catering industry that aims to make a profit

- Non-commercial sector – the part of the Hospitality and Catering industry that does not aim to make a profit

- Non-residential – a place that provides catering and hospitality services but not accommodation for people to stay in

- Residential – a place that provides accommodation for people to stay in, as well as catering and hospitality services

COMMERCIAL SECTOR

Non-residential

Examples of establishments where hospitality and catering is carried out

For business, leisure & tourism:

- Restaurants, bistros & dining rooms
- Cafes, tearooms & coffee shops
- Takeaway & fast food outlets
- Pubs & bars
- Clubs & casinos
- Street food
- Pop-up restaurants
- Mobile/road-side food vans
- Visitor & tourist attractions, e.g. theme parks, museums, National Trust properties, spas
- Sport stadiums
- Concert/gig venues

Client groups

Individuals

Families

Groups – different age groups

Tourists and visitors

Workers on regular hours & shift workers

Hospitality and catering services provided

Food & beverages – eat in or takeaway

Private rooms for business/celebrations/training facilities, e.g. conference facilities/meeting rooms/Internet access

Hospitality and catering job roles required (depending on the type and size of the establishment)

Management
- Managers
- Administrators

Front of house
- Receptionists
- Dining room manager
- Head waiter
- Waiters/waitresses
- Barista/bartender

Food & beverage
- Kitchen brigade

NON-COMMERCIAL SECTOR

Residential

Examples of establishments where hospitality and catering is carried out

Public sector catering:
(non-profit making – costs are kept down by efficiency measures)

a) Health & welfare:
- National Health Service (NHS) hospitals
- NHS nursing & care homes
- Emergency services

- Prisons

b) Education:
- Colleges/universities

c) Armed forces:
- Army/Navy/Air Force

Other:
- Hostels & shelters

- Private nursing & care homes

- Boarding schools

Client groups

- Staff – all departments
- Patients – long & short term with different dietary needs
- Elderly people
- Disabled people
- People with mental health issues
- Visitors

- Prisoners
- Visitors

- Students
- Visitors
- Staff

- Armed forces personnel – all ranks
- Special events

- Homeless people
- People with personal problems
- Staff

- Elderly people
- Disabled people
- People with mental health issues
- Staff

- School-aged children & teenagers
- Staff

Hospitality and catering services provided

Accommodation

Food & beverages throughout the day (and night, where shift work takes place)

Hospitality and catering job roles required (depending on the type and size of the establishment)

Management
- Managers
- Administrators

Front of house
- Receptionists
- Porters
- Security staff
- Staff serving food at counter

Food & beverage
- Kitchen brigade
- Dining room manager
- Volunteers

NON-COMMERCIAL SECTOR

Non-residential

Examples of establishments where hospitality and catering is carried out	Client groups	Hospitality and catering services provided

Food & beverages

a) Workforce catering:
- Canteens/dining rooms for staff in factories, construction sites, shops, etc. → Staff from all departments in a business

b) Voluntary sector/Health & welfare:
- Senior citizen luncheon clubs
- Charity food vans, e.g. soup kitchens
- Day-care centres

→ Elderly people
→ Disabled people
→ Homeless people
→ People with mental health issues

c) Education:
- Childcare day nurseries
- School holiday clubs

→ Babies & pre-school-age children
→ School-age children & teenagers

Public sector catering:
- Schools

→ School-age children & teenagers
→ Staff

Hospitality and catering job roles required (depending on the type and size of the establishment)

Management
- Managers
- Administrators

Front of house
- Receptionists
- Porters
- Security staff
- Staff serving food at counter

Food & beverage
- Kitchen brigade
- Dining room manager
- Volunteers

Job roles in the Hospitality and Catering industry

For a business to run efficiently and be successful, it needs to have an employee structure, with different people performing different jobs (see p21 for a summary of the employee structure in a hotel). This is obviously important in large hospitality and catering businesses, such as hotels, hospitals or restaurants with many employees, but it is also important in small businesses where fewer employees have to perform multiple jobs.

The chart on the next page shows the job roles and responsibilities of different employees in the Hospitality and Catering industry:

Managers

What do they do?

- Responsible for the smooth running of a business
- Responsible for the finances and security
- Employment (and dismissal) of staff
- Staff training, development and promotion
- Responsible for making sure customers are satisfied with the service they receive
- Plan and develop the business for the future
- Responsible for the health, safety and welfare of customers and staff
- Responsible for the cleaning, maintenance of the buildings and infrastructure (water, gas, electricity, etc.)
- Responsible for making sure the laws on health, safety and employment are followed correctly
- Deal with problems and complaints

Examples in a large hotel

- General Manager
- Finance Manager
- Sales/Reservations Manager
- Front Office Manager
- Head Receptionist
- Human Resources (staff) Manager
- Restaurant Manager
- Conference Manager
- Food and Beverage Manager
- Executive Chef
- Logistics Manager (purchase of supplies, cleaning, maintenance, security, ICT)
- Head Housekeeper

Administrators

What do they do?

- Help the business to run smoothly
- Sort out and deal with correspondence (letters, emails and phone calls)
- Typing, filing and organisation of paperwork, e.g. staff details, customer bookings, tax forms
- Order supplies for the business
- Manage events
- Organise ITC support
- Organise the manager's diary and appointments

Examples in a large hotel

- Secretaries
- Assistant/Deputy Managers
- Accountant
- Cashier

Front of house staff

What do they do?

- Represent the business
- Help to promote the reputation of the business (and therefore its level of success)
- Work in direct contact with customers
- Act as a vital link between the customers and the back of house staff
- Take bookings
- Check customers in and out of the establishment
- Deal with customers' questions and problems
- Help customers to their rooms
- Set up rooms for meetings

Examples in a large hotel

- Receptionists
- Valets and drivers
- Waiters and waitresses
- Bartenders
- Cashier
- Concierge (assists guests by booking tours, making theatre and restaurant reservations, etc.)

Back of house staff

What do they do?

- Buy and organise supplies
- Prepare and cook food
- Store and organise drinks
- Clean all areas of the hotel
- Make sure that guest rooms, communal areas, dining rooms, conference facilities, bathrooms and other facilities are clean, tidy, safe, pleasant and comfortable
- Maintain all areas (inside and outside) of the hotel building and grounds (e.g. replace light bulbs, mend broken appliances, cut the grass, etc.)
- Maintain security

Examples in a large hotel

- Stockroom Manager
- Kitchen brigade (see p16)
- Maintenance team
- Gardeners/Groundskeeper
- Security guards
- Cleaners
- Guest room attendants

Kitchen brigade

The kitchen brigade is a system for setting out and explaining the job roles and responsibilities of those people who work in a kitchen.

The chart below shows what a full kitchen brigade looks like. You would only find a large brigade like this in a very big and busy kitchen, such as those in big hotels and restaurants.

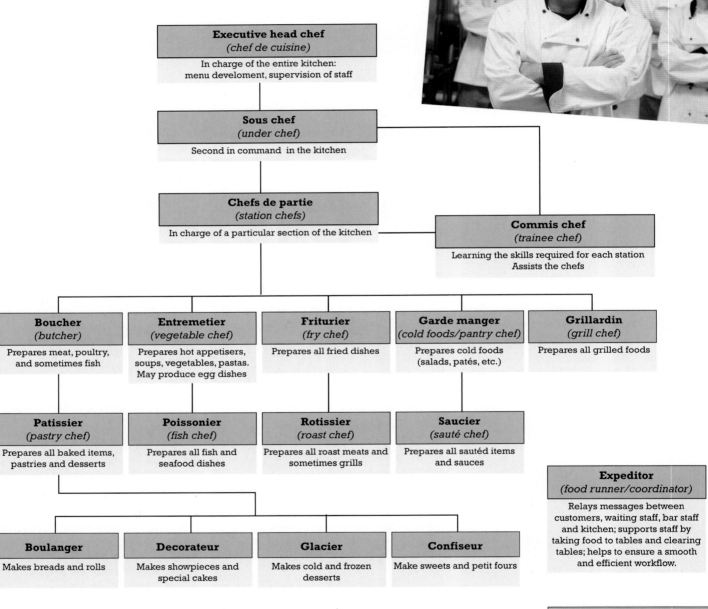

Executive head chef
(chef de cuisine)
In charge of the entire kitchen: menu develoment, supervision of staff

Sous chef
(under chef)
Second in command in the kitchen

Chefs de partie
(station chefs)
In charge of a particular section of the kitchen

Commis chef
(trainee chef)
Learning the skills required for each station
Assists the chefs

Boucher
(butcher)
Prepares meat, poultry, and sometimes fish

Entremetier
(vegetable chef)
Prepares hot appetisers, soups, vegetables, pastas. May produce egg dishes

Friturier
(fry chef)
Prepares all fried dishes

Garde manger
(cold foods/pantry chef)
Prepares cold foods (salads, patés, etc.)

Grillardin
(grill chef)
Prepares all grilled foods

Patissier
(pastry chef)
Prepares all baked items, pastries and desserts

Poissonier
(fish chef)
Prepares all fish and seafood dishes

Rotissier
(roast chef)
Prepares all roast meats and sometimes grills

Saucier
(sauté chef)
Prepares all sautéd items and sauces

Boulanger
Makes breads and rolls

Decorateur
Makes showpieces and special cakes

Glacier
Makes cold and frozen desserts

Confiseur
Make sweets and petit fours

Expeditor
(food runner/coordinator)
Relays messages between customers, waiting staff, bar staff and kitchen; supports staff by taking food to tables and clearing tables; helps to ensure a smooth and efficient workflow.

Kitchen porters/plongeur
Washing up and other duties

Did you know?

You will notice that the titles of each job role are in French. The French have a long history of writing systems and rules for cooking and passing them on to others, so French words and terms in cooking have been adopted and are in use in many countries. In the late 19th century, a famous French chef, Georges Auguste Escoffier, created the kitchen brigade system to simplify the job roles and work in a busy kitchen, so that everyone knows where they fit within it.

Here are some French terms used in cooking. You might see them in recipes. See if you can find out what they mean:

Bain-marie

Canapé

Coulis

Jus lie

Ragoût

Roux

Sauté

Vol-au-vent

Case study

'A day in the life of . . . '

Interview someone who works in a kitchen in a restaurant, cafe, or other food service business, and find out the following information.

1. When do they start and finish work?

2. What do they do in their job throughout a typical day?

3. What they like about their job.

4. What they dislike about their job.

Now write a short report about a typical day in their life in the Hospitality and Catering industry.

Front of house

The staff who work front of house are the first people that customers meet when they arrive at an establishment. They have a variety of important roles:

Head Receptionist and assistants	Porters	Night porters	Concierge
Take bookings Check customers in and out of the establishment Deal with customers' questions and problems	Help customers to their rooms Set up rooms for meetings	Work on reception at night Help late arrivals	Advises and helps customers with tourist trips Arranges taxis for customers Parks customers' cars

Housekeeping

Housekeeping staff work 'behind the scenes' to make sure that rooms, communal areas, dining rooms, conference facilities, bathrooms and other facilities are clean, tidy, safe, pleasant, comfortable and well maintained (e.g. replace light bulbs, mend broken appliances etc.).

Head Housekeeper and assistants	Room attendants	Maintenance Manager and assistants	General cleaning staff

Hospitality and catering standards and ratings

Hotels, restaurants, guest houses, etc., are often advertised as having one, two, three, four or five star status. If an establishment achieves a high star rating, it is likely to be very popular with customers, many of whom will pay more to be assured a high standard of service.

There are various categories in the Hospitality and Catering industry for which standards and ratings are used, including:

- Hotel and guest house rating
- Restaurant rating
- Food hygiene rating
- Environmental rating.

The following table describes how such ratings are awarded:

Hotel and guest house standards

What is being inspected?	How are the ratings awarded?
<ul><li>Open all year round?</li><li>Number of guest rooms (with/without en suite facilities)</li><li>Number and type of rooms available for socialising, e.g. lounges, bars</li><li>Environment – noisy/quiet?; plant/flower displays?/friendly and relaxing?</li><li>Reception facilities</li><li>Level of customer care</li><li>Access to facilities – all day/night or restricted?</li><li>Disabled access</li><li>Number of staff available over 24 hours</li><li>Meal facilities, availability, choice and standard</li><li>Licensed to sell alcohol?</li><li>Public liability insurance cover?</li><li>Meets all health and safety requirements?</li><li>Standard and maintenance of facilities, e.g. décor, furnishings, bedding, lighting, bathrooms, lifts, car parking</li><li>Extra facilities, e.g. gym, swimming pool, ballroom, spa?</li><li>Telephone, TV and Wi-Fi availability</li><li>Luxury apartment suite available?</li><li>Clean and tidy?</li></ul>	Star ratings: ★ ★★ ★★★ ★★★★ ★★★★★ **Who inspects?** <ul><li>Organisations such as the AA, Visit Britain, Tourist Boards, etc., visit hotels and guest houses and can award stars as well as advise proprietors about how they can improve their services.</li></ul>Increasingly, social media reviews are being used to help people judge hotels and guest houses, e.g.: <ul><li>Social media, e.g. Facebook, Twitter</li><li>Online review sites, e.g. Trip Advisor, Expedia, Booking.com, Google</li></ul>

Restaurant standards

What is being inspected?	How are the ratings awarded?	Who inspects?
<ul><li>Type/range of food being offered</li><li>Quality of food and ingredients used</li><li>Provenance of food (where the food comes from)</li><li>Consistency of the cooking, flavour, appearance and quality of the food</li><li>The level of culinary skill, creativity and excellence of the chef(s)</li></ul>	The Michelin Guide awards one, two or three stars: A very good restaurant in its category Excellent cooking, worth a detour  Exceptional cooking, worth a special journey The AA awards rosettes (one to five):  The Good Food Guide scores restaurants between 1 and 10	Organisations such as the AA, The Good Food Guide and the Michelin Guide, send people (often anonymously) to different restaurants to eat the food and then write a review about it.

The Food Hygiene Ratings Scheme

What is being inspected?	How are the ratings awarded?	Who inspects?
The Environmental Health Officer inspecting a business checks how well the business is meeting the law on food hygiene by looking at: <ul><li>How hygienically the food is handled – including preparation, cooking, re-heating, cooling and storage</li><li>The cleanliness and condition of facilities and building (including having appropriate layout, ventilation, hand washing facilities and pest control) to enable good food hygiene</li><li>How food safety within the business is managed, including a system or checks in place to ensure that food sold or served is safe to eat, evidence that staff know about food safety, and the Environmental Health Officer has confidence that standards will be maintained in future</li><li>The Environmental Health Officer will explain to the person who owns or manages the business if there are any improvements needed, what they are and how they can achieve a higher rating</li></ul>	 	<ul><li>The Food Standards Agency (FSA) runs the scheme in partnership with local authorities in England, Wales and Northern Ireland.</li><li>A similar voluntary scheme – The Food Hygiene Information Scheme, is run in Scotland.</li><li>When you eat out or shop for food, look out for a sticker in the window or on the door. If the food outlet is not displaying a sticker, you can ask the staff about the business's rating. You can also look up food hygiene ratings online at food.gov.uk/ratings.</li></ul>

Environmental standards

What is being inspected?

How well a restaurant or food service meets a set of ten standards aimed at promoting sustainability and reducing the impact of food production on the environment:

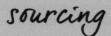

Celebrate Local & Seasonal   Serve More Veg & Better Meat   Source Fish Responsibly   Support Global Farmers

1. Use more locally grown food to cut down on food transport
2. Serve more vegetable-based meals and meat and dairy foods that have been produced with high animal welfare
3. Serve sustainably caught fish
4. Support farmers in other countries by buying fairly traded food products

Treat People Fairly   Support the Community   Feed People Well

5. Treat employees equally and fairly and give them opportunities to develop their skills
6. Get involved with the local community

Value Natural Resources   Reduce Reuse Recycle   Waste No Food

7. Produce healthy, balanced meals
8. Use energy-efficient equipment and avoid water wastage
9. Reduce food wastage
10. Recycle materials where possible

How are the ratings awarded?

Restaurants are assessed and a percentage (%) score is given to them for how much they are meeting the ten standards:

More than 50% = 1 star rating

60-69% = 2 star rating

More than 70% = 3 star rating

Who inspects?

The Sustainable Restaurant Association (UK)

Practice questions

1. Name three types of counter food service systems. *(3 marks)*
2. List four types of manager who work in a large hotel. *(4 marks)*
3. List four activities in the running of a hotel that a general manager has overall responsibility for. *(4 marks)*
4. List three types of front of house staff in a large hotel. *(3 marks)*
5. List four activities in the running of a hotel that back of house staff have responsibility for. *(4 marks)*
6. In the kitchen brigade in a large restaurant, what do the following people do? *(1 mark each)*

   a) Sous chef

   b) Boucher

   c) Patissier

   d) Plongeur

Hotel jobs structure

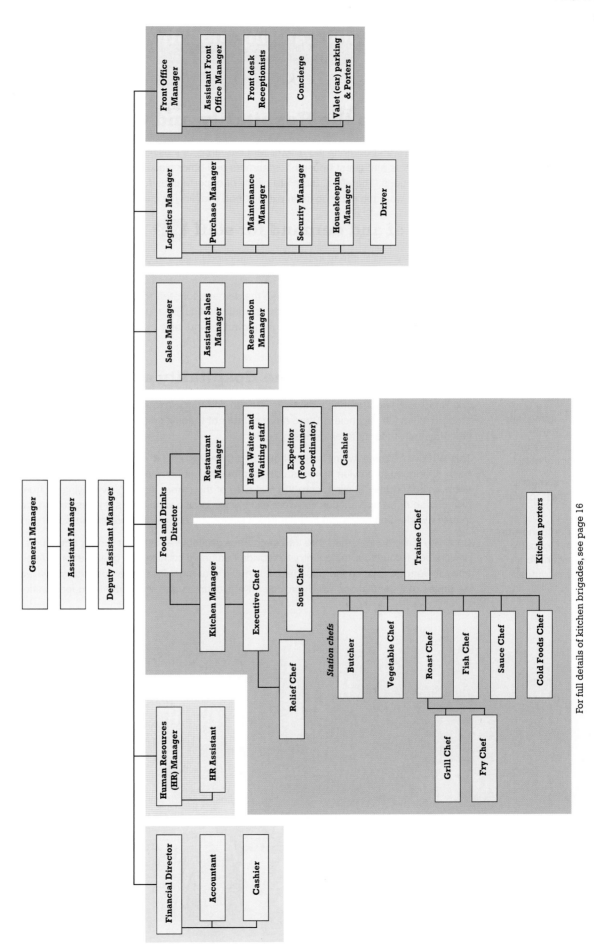

General Manager

Assistant Manager

Deputy Assistant Manager

Front Office Manager
- Assistant Front Office Manager
- Front desk Receptionists
- Concierge
- Valet (car) parking & Porters

Logistics Manager
- Purchase Manager
- Maintenance Manager
- Security Manager
- Housekeeping Manager
- Driver

Sales Manager
- Assistant Sales Manager
- Reservation Manager

Food and Drinks Director

Restaurant Manager
- Head Waiter and Waiting staff
- Expeditor (Food runner/co-ordinator)
- Cashier

Kitchen Manager
- Executive Chef
  - Sous Chef
    - Trainee Chef
  - Relief Chef
  - Station chefs
    - Butcher
    - Vegetable Chef
    - Roast Chef
      - Grill Chef
      - Fry Chef
    - Fish Chef
    - Sauce Chef
    - Cold Foods Chef
  - Kitchen porters

Human Resources (HR) Manager
- HR Assistant

Financial Director
- Accountant
- Cashier

For full details of kitchen brigades, see page 16

21

What will I learn?

In Chapter 1 you learned that there are many job roles available in the Hospitality and Catering industry. In this chapter, you will learn about job requirements and the working conditions in the industry.

Key terms

- **Employee** – someone who works in the industry and has an employment contract
- **Employer** – someone who hires staff to work for them
- **Worker** – someone who works in the industry but does not have an employment contract

Working in the Hospitality and Catering industry

The Hospitality and Catering industry provides a range of jobs, especially in busy locations where there are many hotels and guest houses, restaurants and other places to eat out, busy shopping areas, and tourist attractions. Therefore, there are plenty of opportunities for those people who are ambitious and are willing to work their way up in an exciting and challenging career.

Supply of and demand for staff (AC1.2)

The Hospitality and Catering industry has continued to grow in the past few years and the demand for employees and workers has grown with it.

There are certain times of the year when the demand for staff for different job roles in the Hospitality and Catering industry increases, e.g. the summer holiday season, Christmas, and other celebrations, such as the New Year. People who are employed to work only at these busy times are known as **seasonal workers**.

Training to work in the Hospitality and Catering industry (AC1.2)

The Hospitality and Catering industry is keen to employ people who have a good range of skills, in order to fill its job vacancies. There are a number of training courses available at different levels to gain these skills for different industry sectors.

This WJEC Vocational Award in Hospitality and Catering Level 1 and 2 course that you are studying has been developed to provide school students with relevant knowledge, skills and training in order to give them an opportunity to climb onto the first step of the career 'ladder', by moving on from school to a new course or an apprenticeship. Work experience is also valuable as it gives you an idea of how the industry works and helps you find out which sector you are most interested in working in.

Once you leave school, there are lots of courses available at different further education colleges and universities throughout the country to provide additional training and qualifications. Apprenticeships and/or work experience may also be available in your area. The table opposite shows you four examples of organisations which provide advice, courses and other training opportunities:

City and Guilds

A global leader in skills development that offers courses and training across 26 industries, including hospitality and catering. These are delivered through further education colleges and training providers.

Examples of courses and other training opportunities provided

There are many courses available, such as;

- Introduction to the Hospitality Industry
- Cooking and Service for the Hospitality Industry
- Culinary Skills
- Food and Beverage Service

Springboard UK

A business partner of the Springboard Charity that promotes careers in the Hospitality and Catering industry and provides careers advice.

This is Ruth Hansom (22), who reached the runner-up stage of FutureChef's National Final, and won the Craft Guild of Chefs National Chef of the Year 2017. Ruth now works as Head Chef in a luxury 5-star spa hotel.

Examples of courses and other training opportunities provided

- Springboard FutureChef work in schools
- FutureChef competitions and awards
- Mentoring, industry visits, visiting speakers etc.

Universities and Colleges Admissions Service (UCAS)

The organisation that provides information on higher education courses and the application process for applying to go to university.

There are a number of Hospitality and Catering courses available at various universities, such as:

Higher National Certificates and Diplomas (HNC and HND) and degrees (e.g. Bachelor of Arts) in:

- Hospitality Management
- Professional Cookery
- Culinary Industry Management
- Food and Culinary Arts

Chartered Institute of Environmental Health (CIEH)

A training and awarding organisation for qualifications in food safety and hygiene.

Examples of courses:

- Level 1 Introductory Certificate in Food Safety
- Level 2 Foundation Certificate in Food Safety

Personal attributes for working in the Hospitality and Catering industry AC1.2

A personal attribute is a quality or personality trait that someone has in their character.

In order for someone to be successful in a particular job role in the Hospitality and Catering industry, there are specific personal attributes that an employer looks for and would expect employees and workers to have. Some examples of specific personal attributes are given below:

Which personal attributes do you need in the Hospitality and Catering industry?

- Flexible/adaptable to different situations
- Hard working
- Punctual and reliable
- Willing to learn and develop skills
- Enthusiastic
- Ability to take the initiative in a situation
- Good communicator and listener
- Helpful/approachable
- Good commitment to completing a task
- A sense of humour
- Calm and composed
- Good team member
- Ability to take criticism and act on it

Study tip

REMEMBER: When exam questions ask you to write about the **qualities** a person needs to work successfully in a job role, these attributes are what you should include in your answer; NOT a description of what they actually do in the job; e.g.:

To be a successful member of the waiting staff in a restaurant, a person needs to be calm and composed, helpful and approachable, hardworking and enthusiastic, a good communicator and listener and have the ability to take the initiative in a situation.

This means they will be able to take customer orders accurately, answer customer questions, serve their food carefully and correctly, deal with any difficulties that arise, and prepare tables ready for new customers.

These are the qualities (personal attributes) a waiter/waitress needs

This is a description of what they actually do in the job.

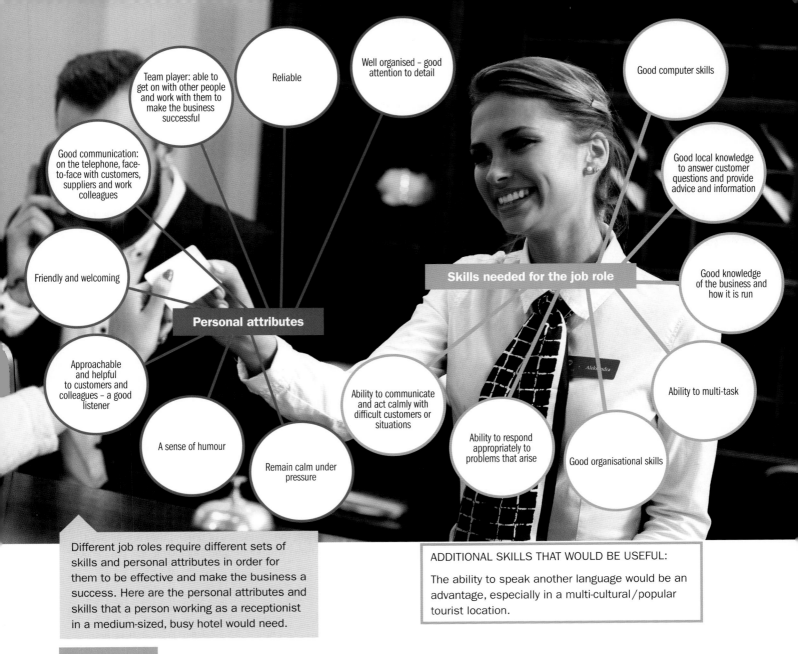

Team player: able to get on with other people and work with them to make the business successful

Reliable

Well organised – good attention to detail

Good computer skills

Good communication: on the telephone, face-to-face with customers, suppliers and work colleagues

Good local knowledge to answer customer questions and provide advice and information

Skills needed for the job role

Good knowledge of the business and how it is run

Friendly and welcoming

Personal attributes

Approachable and helpful to customers and colleagues – a good listener

Ability to communicate and act calmly with difficult customers or situations

Ability to multi-task

A sense of humour

Remain calm under pressure

Ability to respond appropriately to problems that arise

Good organisational skills

Different job roles require different sets of skills and personal attributes in order for them to be effective and make the business a success. Here are the personal attributes and skills that a person working as a receptionist in a medium-sized, busy hotel would need.

ADDITIONAL SKILLS THAT WOULD BE USEFUL:

The ability to speak another language would be an advantage, especially in a multi-cultural/popular tourist location.

Activity 2.1

Which personal attributes and skills do you think a head chef in a busy kitchen needs? Make a chart like the one below and write the attributes and skills in the two columns.

Then do the same for some other job roles, such as: fast food restaurant worker; waiter/waitress; bartender; commis chef, restaurant manager, kitchen porter.

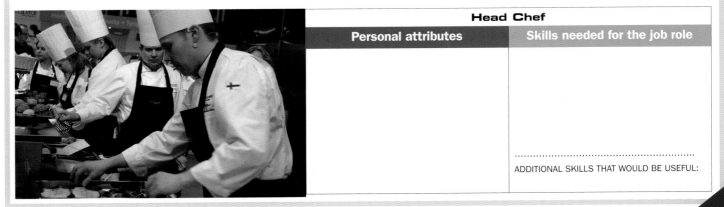

Head Chef	
Personal attributes	**Skills needed for the job role**
	....
	ADDITIONAL SKILLS THAT WOULD BE USEFUL:

Case study

Joe and Drew are both waiting staff in a busy city restaurant.

Here are their personal attributes:

Joe is punctual and well organised, has a cheerful personality, is always smiling, and talks to the customers in a polite and welcoming way, giving them clear information about the food on the menu and willingly answering any questions they may have.

Drew is frequently late for the start of the work shift and takes a while to get organised before starting work. Drew rarely smiles and often has a rather bored facial expression, speaking very briefly to customers and only giving them a little information about the menu, which is usually spoken in a mumble. Drew tries to avoid answering customer questions.

Comment on how Joe's and Drew's personal attributes would affect:

1. Customers coming to the restaurant for a meal

2. The success of the restaurant

3. Their own career prospects

4. Their work colleagues and the management of the restaurant

Employment rights and contracts (AC1.3)

Both employees and workers in the Hospitality and Catering industry have employment rights, which cover a range of issues, e.g. how long they work on a shift, the frequency of breaks they are allowed and protection against discrimination. Employees also have additional rights, including sick pay, flexible working and protection against unfair dismissal.

There are different types of employment contracts:

Full-time; permanent contract – hours of work and start/end times are specified. Any shift work is specified. The employee qualifies for sick pay and holiday pay.

Part-time; permanent contract – days of the week and hours of work and start/end times are specified. The employee qualifies for reduced sick pay and reduced holiday pay.

Casual work – seasonal or available through an agency, e.g. to cover someone who is away from work due to illness. The worker does not qualify for sick pay or holiday pay.

Zero hours contract – this type of contract is between an employer and a worker, where the worker may sign an agreement to be available to work when they are needed by the employer, but no specific number of hours or times to start and end work are given. The employer is not required to offer the person any work and the worker is not required to accept any work that may be offered. The employee does not qualify for sick pay or holiday pay.

Working hours and rates of pay AC1.2 AC1.3

In the UK, the **Working Time Directive** says that people cannot work for more than an average of 48 hours a week, which is calculated over a 17-week period. People can choose to opt out of this and work more hours if they want to.

People under 18 years of age cannot work more than 8 hours a day or 40 hours a week.

People are entitled to have one day off work each week and, if they work for 6 or more hours a day, they must be given a rest break of at least 20 minutes.

In the UK, workers and employees have the right, by law, to receive the **National Minimum Wage**. This is the **minimum hourly pay**, which most workers over school leaving age will earn.

There is also the **National Living Wage**, which is for all working people aged 25 years and over.

The hourly rates of pay for these are reviewed every year by the government, and employers can be taken to court if they do not pay their workforce the correct amount.

Remuneration AC1.3

Remuneration is a term used for the reward that people receive from working somewhere. It includes their basic pay, plus extra money to top up their income in the form of:

- **Tips and gratuities** – money given to someone by a customer as a way of saying 'thank you' for good service
- **Service charges** – a percentage added to a customer's bill to reward the employees who have provided the customer with a service
- **Bonus payments and rewards** – given by some employers as a way of rewarding their hard work throughout the year and helping to make the business successful

It is quite common for all the tips, gratuities and service charges to be divided equally amongst all the workers in, e.g. a restaurant. This is known as a **tronc** arrangement, and the person who works out and distributes the extra money to staff is called the 'troncmaster'.

Holiday entitlement AC1.3

Paid employees are entitled to paid leave (holiday) each year. This is for a set number of working days (not weekends) and can include some or all of the public and bank holidays that are available in England and Wales. It is important that people take time off from work for the sake of their physical and mental health, and employers need to be aware of the importance of making sure that their employees maintain a good work–life balance (making time for yourself, your family, leisure and personal activities, as well as the demands of your job).

Practice questions

1. a) List three personal attributes that a person would need to work as a trainee chef in a busy restaurant kitchen. *(3 marks)*

    b) Give a reason for each of your answers in a). *(3 marks)*

2. List three employment rights that employees and workers in the Hospitality and Catering industry have. *(3 marks)*

3. What is meant by a 'work–life balance' and why is it important? *(2 marks)*

Chapter 3

Factors affecting the success of hospitality and catering providers

What will I learn?

The employment of suitable people is one factor that is crucial to the success of hospitality and catering providers. In Chapter 2, you learned about the skills, training and personal attributes that are needed by people who work in the industry in different job roles, and the working conditions that influence how much people earn, their working hours and contracts. In this chapter you will learn about other factors that also influence the success of hospitality and catering providers.

Factors that affect success in the Hospitality and Catering industry AC1.4

There are various factors that are used to measure the success of a business, such as:

1. Profit:
- Is the business making or losing money?
- Can it pay all its bills and costs and still make a profit?

2. Customer satisfaction:
- Are the customers happy with the service provided?
  How does the business measure customer satisfaction?
- Do customers come back again?
- How many new customers use the business?

3. Employees:
- Are employees happy and working hard to make the business a success?
- Are there enough suitably trained employees?
- Does the business measure the performance of employees?

4. Competition:
- Are other similar businesses in the area more or less successful?
  Why might this be?
- Is the business keeping up with the competition?

5. Development:
- Is the business keeping up with developments in hospitality and catering and in society, e.g. new trends in eating; social media; leisure and lifestyle trends?
- Is the business conducting market research to find out what customers want and need?

To be a successful business, there are a variety of factors that need to be carefully managed, as described below.

Costs

There are many costs that a hospitality and catering business will have, all of which must be accounted for when working out how much to charge customers for all the services provided:

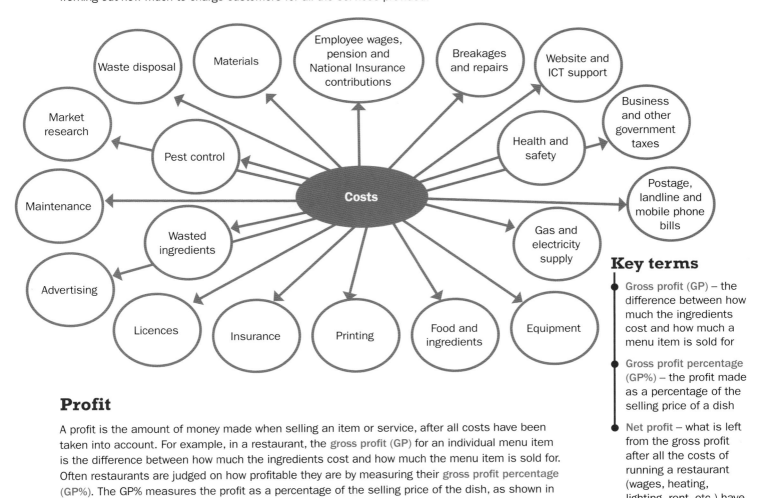

Key terms

- **Gross profit (GP)** – the difference between how much the ingredients cost and how much a menu item is sold for

- **Gross profit percentage (GP%)** – the profit made as a percentage of the selling price of a dish

- **Net profit** – what is left from the gross profit after all the costs of running a restaurant (wages, heating, lighting, rent, etc.) have been paid

Profit

A profit is the amount of money made when selling an item or service, after all costs have been taken into account. For example, in a restaurant, the gross profit (GP) for an individual menu item is the difference between how much the ingredients cost and how much the menu item is sold for. Often restaurants are judged on how profitable they are by measuring their gross profit percentage (GP%). The GP% measures the profit as a percentage of the selling price of the dish, as shown in the following examples:

Chocolate tart dessert
Ingredients cost: £2.00
Selling price: £5.50
GP = £3.50 (£5.50 – £2.00)
GP% = £3.50 ÷ £5.50 x 100 = 63.6%

Chilli sea bass starter
Ingredients cost: £5.00
Selling price: £9.50
GP = £4.50 (£9.50 – £5.00)
GP% = £4.50 ÷ £9.50 x 100 = 47%

Lamb main course
Ingredients cost: £7.00
Selling price: £16.99
GP = £9.99 (£16.99 – £7.00)
GP% = £9.99 ÷ £16.99 x 100 = 58.8%

Pasta lunch dish
Ingredients cost: £1.20
Selling price: £6.00
GP = £4.80 (£6.00 – £1.20)
GP% = £4.80 ÷ £6.00 x 100 = 80%

Activity 3.1

Work out the gross profit and gross profit percentage for each of the following menu items:

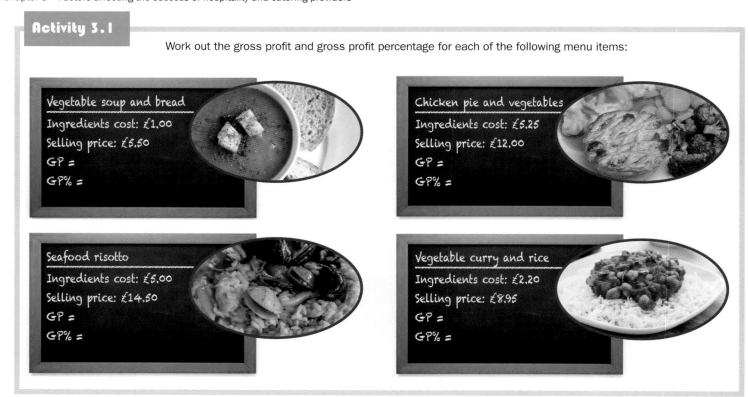

Vegetable soup and bread
Ingredients cost: £1.00
Selling price: £5.50
GP =
GP% =

Chicken pie and vegetables
Ingredients cost: £5.25
Selling price: £12.00
GP =
GP% =

Seafood risotto
Ingredients cost: £5.00
Selling price: £14.50
GP =
GP% =

Vegetable curry and rice
Ingredients cost: £2.20
Selling price: £8.95
GP =
GP% =

The profit made on each menu dish sold in the restaurant needs to cover the other costs of running the kitchen and restaurant, e.g. staff wages, cleaning costs, electricity and gas, etc., and still make a final **net profit** (what is left from the gross profit after all the costs of running the restaurant have been paid). Food businesses average about 4% net profit. Ideally, a profitable restaurant will have a GP% of about 65–70%, with ingredients costs kept down to around 30%.

Stretch and challenge

A restaurant is situated in a small rural town, ten miles inland from the sea. The town is surrounded by countryside where there are several farms producing fruit, vegetables, meat and poultry. The restaurant has a large garden at the back of the property.

In order to help increase its net profit, suggest some ways in which the restaurant can save on costs and get the best value for money when buying and using ingredients for the dishes they make. Give reasons for your answers. *(5 marks)*

The amount of profit made by a business is affected by:

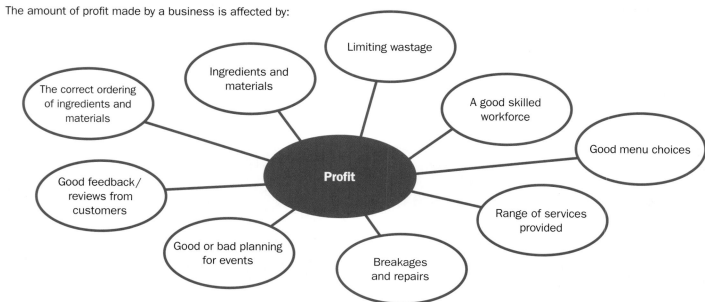

Limiting wastage

Ingredients and materials

The correct ordering of ingredients and materials

A good skilled workforce

Good menu choices

Good feedback/reviews from customers

Profit

Range of services provided

Good feedback/reviews from customers

Good or bad planning for events

Breakages and repairs

Economy

The Hospitality and Catering industry contributes a lot of money to the UK's economy in the form of taxes, e.g. Value Added Tax (VAT), which it has to charge customers for the services it provides, and income tax that is paid by its many employees. It also attracts and is used by millions of national and international tourists and visitors, who contribute to the economy by spending money.

The economy is affected by a number of issues that can influence how successful (and profitable) a business is, e.g.:

- The value of the pound (£) against other currencies in the world. This affects how many pounds people in other countries can exchange their own money for when they come to visit the UK. If people can get a good rate of exchange (i.e. a lot of pounds), they may be more willing to come to the UK and spend money here.

- If the economy is struggling, e.g. during a recession, people's wages may not increase for a long time or might even be cut. This means they have less money to spend, so they may decide to cut down on their spending on things such as going out for a meal or going on holiday.

- If the economy is in difficulties, e.g. during a recession, the price of goods such as foods, drinks and materials may increase, e.g. because more tax is charged for them.

- If the price of the oil and fuels the UK imports from other parts of the world goes up, heating, power and materials/food production costs will rise.

- If food production in other countries is affected due to poor weather conditions, disease or transport problems, the price of ingredients will rise.

Environmental factors

Environmentally friendly practices, e.g. using renewable energy such as solar power, and saving water, are becoming a normal part of business activities and are a factor which is taken into account when measuring their success. Many hospitality and catering establishments are installing technology such as solar panels, automatic switches to control lighting and air conditioning, and water-saving laundering and dishwashing equipment. Sustainable sourcing is also increasingly practised, whereby materials and ingredients that the business needs are traced back to find out where they come from and what their environmental impact is during production and distribution, before a purchase is made.

Waste

Every year in the UK, around 3.5 million tonnes of waste is produced by hotels, restaurants, pubs, coffee bars, fast food restaurants and other hospitality and catering businesses. This waste consists of food, paper, card, glass, plastics and other rubbish. There has been a lot of media coverage about the problems of waste and what happens to it, and much discussion about the problems of pollution that are caused by it, e.g.:

- A lot of plastic ends up in the oceans where it badly affects the health of wildlife.

- A lot of waste ends up in landfill sites, where it takes up space and produces a lot of gases that damage the environment.

- A lot of food packaging and takeaway food and drink containers are dropped in the streets and cause litter problems, which attract rats and other pests.

It costs businesses a lot of money to have waste products removed from their premises and disposed of properly. Businesses also spend a lot of money on disposable items, which they have to constantly replace, e.g. plastic cutlery, paper hand towels.

Business are encouraged to **Reduce, Reuse and Recycle** the waste they create. Apart from the benefits this brings to the environment, it can also help them to save money, save space, give them a good reputation with their customers and reduce their impact on the environment. There are various ways this can be achieved as described below.

Reduce

- The amount of **packaging** used in the kitchen and in the hospitality sector of a business by buying from manufacturers who use the minimum amount of packaging.

    Some plastics are **biodegradable**. This means that over a period of time they will break down by the action of micro-organisms, usually bacteria. Some of these are used for food packaging.

- The amount of **food waste** by:
    - Reducing portion sizes
    - Providing containers for customers to take left-over food home to eat later
    - Passing on good quality left-over foods to food charities to make into meals for poor people
    - If possible, turning the food waste into compost which can be used to grow, e.g. vegetables and herbs
    - Making stock from vegetable peelings and off-cuts and poultry and meat bones
    - Storing food correctly so that it doesn't get wasted.

- The amount of **plastic** and **paper** used by **not** using disposable cutlery, plates, dishes, serviettes, table cloths, drinking straws, hot drinks cups, individually wrapped portions of sugar, salt, sauces, milk, etc.

- The amount of **energy** used, by installing solar panels, low energy light bulbs, sensors that switch on lights when a person enters a room (and off when they leave), energy-efficient boilers, energy-efficient electrical appliances, e.g. showers, washing machines, dishwashers, refrigerators, freezers, ovens, etc.

- The amount of **water** used, by installing water-saving taps, and showers instead of baths in guest rooms; maintaining taps to ensure they do not drip; by only running dishwashers when they are full; by politely encouraging guests **not** to ask for their sheets and towels to be washed every day, etc.

Re-use

- **Left-over foods** to make new dishes, e.g. left-over vegetables can be turned into soups; left-over cooked meat can be turned into cottage pies and pasties.
- **Packaging and containers** – some are re-usable. Some empty containers can be used to store other ingredients or cleaning liquids – label them clearly.
- Discourage guests from requesting fresh towels and bedding each day.
- Discourage the use of disposable cutlery, plates, cups, etc.

Recycle

- Left-over used **cooking oil** can be recycled and turned into a bio-fuel that can be used by machines and vehicles.
- Some plastics, glass, aluminium foil, drinks cans, fabrics, paper and card can be recycled, and the local council will give advice on what to recycle.
- Special recycle bins can be used to help sort the materials into different types when they are thrown away.
- Products made from **recycled materials** can be bought and used, e.g. paper hand towels and toilet rolls from recycled paper; plastic chairs and containers from recycled plastics; bottles and glasses from recycled glass.

What can be recycled?

Plastic bottles

Cardboard

Glass bottles and jars

Food and drink cans

Aluminium foil

Some electrical items

Printer cartridges

Sustainable food production and diets

Research shows that the production of food and packaging materials (especially plastics), refrigeration and food transport (food miles) all have a major impact on climate change. When food and food products are processed and manufactured, large amounts of non-renewable energy from fossil fuels (coal, oil) are used.

As fossil fuels are burnt to release the energy they contain, large quantities of carbon dioxide (CO_2) gas are produced. CO_2 is a greenhouse gas.

Greenhouse gases (e.g. carbon dioxide, methane, nitrous oxide) are released into the atmosphere and form an insulating layer around the earth's atmosphere, which traps heat and raises the earth's temperature. Some of the heat is prevented from escaping into space, and the earth heats up too much (**global warming**). This is called the '**greenhouse effect**', which results in climate change that can affect life on earth, the climate and food production.

The production of meat and poultry, dairy foods and eggs produces approximately 18% of all greenhouse gases in the world. The number of people throughout the world who eat a lot of meat, poultry, dairy foods and eggs is continuing to increase. The production of vegetables, fruits, nuts, beans and cereals has a much lower impact on the environment.

There are several health and environmental campaigns that are trying to encourage people to eat a more sustainable diet by eating more plant foods and less meat and dairy foods.

The number of hospitality and catering businesses that offer vegetarian and vegan menus is increasing in response to the increasing number of people who want to follow a plant-based diet.

Key terms

- **Climate change** – changes in the earth's temperature that can lead to unusual and extreme weather conditions

- **Fossil fuels** – fuels such as coal, oil and gas that were created over millions of years by fossilised plants and animals

- **Greenhouse gases** – these form an insulating layer around the earth's atmosphere, which traps heat and raises the earth's temperature

- **Non-renewable energy** – energy produced from fossil fuels that cannot be renewed once they are used up

- **Sustainable diet** – a diet consisting mostly of plant foods, which has a minimal impact on the environment during its production

100%
VEGAN

Rating the environmental status of a hospitality and catering business

In Chapter 1, you learned that hospitality and catering businesses can be rated according to how well they meet a set of standards aimed at promoting sustainability and reducing the impact of food production on the environment. There is also another programme, called the Green Key Rating Programme, which rewards hospitality and catering businesses that are committed to improving their environmental standards in a range of activities:

| Staff involvement | Environmental management | Guest information | Water | Energy | Washing & Cleaning | Food & Beverage | Waste | Administration | Indoor Environment | Green Areas | Green Activities | Corporate Social Responsibility |

Technology

Technology affects many aspects of business and it is important to be aware of technological developments and incorporate them into a business where it is appropriate to do so, for example developments in:

- Information and Communication Technology (ICT) – may mean the need to perform an upgrade or replacement of existing computer systems in a business
- Social media – may be used for customers to provide feedback and suggestions for developing a business, and for advertising and promotion of the business
- Kitchen technology – e.g. equipment, food storage and packaging, food service, hygiene and food safety
- Food technology – e.g. preservation techniques, flavouring, ingredients and ready-made foods, food deliveries by drone.

Emerging and innovative cooking techniques

As with all industries, innovative (new, original) production techniques and technology are continually emerging and being taken up by hospitality and catering businesses. This is especially true in the kitchen, where successful chefs will keep up with new developments and bring some of them into their menus. Some recent examples of these emerging techniques are:

- **Food pairing** – putting different ingredients together in a recipe in unusual combinations, based on how closely their aromas (the natural chemicals that give foods a particular smell) match up; see www.foodpairing.com

Food pairing calculation for strawberries

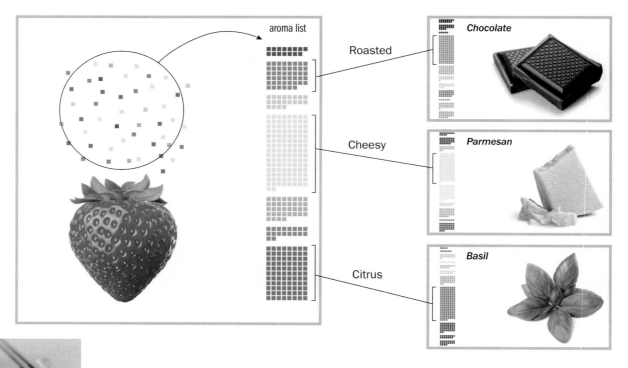

- **Fermented foods** – using foods such as fermented vegetables (sauerkraut, olives, kimchi, etc.), fermented soybeans (e.g. miso, tempeh) and dairy products (live probiotic yogurt, kefir and buttermilk) to produce meals that help the gut to work well
- **Insect foods** – cooking edible insects such as crickets, grasshoppers and larvae as an alternative to meat, poultry and fish, and using them in creative recipes
- **Infra-red technology** – uses rapid cooking times and to reduce energy consumption.

Customer demographics and lifestyle and expectations

The word **demographics** means a collection of data (information) about the number of people who live in a particular area, e.g. their age groups, how much money they earn, what they buy with their money, etc. The word **lifestyle** means how someone lives and what they like to do. The Hospitality and Catering industry uses demographic data and lifestyle information to help it plan and provide the services that people want so that they keep up to date with trends, which will help them to be successful.

There are different groups of people who use the services that the industry provides, including couples, families, business travellers, backpackers, solo travellers and leisure travellers. Each group will have different needs and requirements, and a successful business will aim to provide these in order to attract customers. For example, families with young children may want inexpensive restaurants that have a children's menu, business travellers may require technology-enabled meeting places and Internet access throughout a hotel, and a large leisure travelling group may require a space in a hotel where they can meet and eat together separated from other customers. A hotel may offer special 'packages' at times in the year when they have fewer guests, e.g. 'out of [holiday] season' in the winter. Such a package may offer reduced-price accommodation and include one or two evening meals as well as breakfast. This will attract couples and small groups of people who want a short leisure visit for two or three days.

One group of customers that is having an increasing influence on the industry is the **millennials**. These are people who were born around 1980 to 2000. Surveys show that millennials have the following lifestyles and requirements when they use the Hospitality and Catering industry:

Customer service and service provision

Customer service skills are an essential part of a hospitality and catering establishment's image, and they should be of a consistently high standard in all of the services provided. Customer satisfaction is vital for making a business successful, because if customer service in, e.g. a restaurant, is good, customers will be happy and are likely to tell other people about it and recommend that they have a meal there. They are also likely to return to the restaurant themselves and become loyal customers.

There are a variety of features and actions that make good customer service, including:

Friendly, polite and prompt service

Staff who pay attention to detail, e.g. write down a meal order correctly

Providing all services efficiently and effectively

Staff who are willing to learn new skills

Meeting (and maybe exceeding) customer expectations

Staff who listen to and answer customer questions

Staff who are well trained and knowledgeable

Staff who understand and anticipate what customers need

Staff who communicate clearly with customers

Staff who aim to solve customer complaints promptly and politely

Paying attention and responding to reviews and feedback from customers

Staff who make eye contact with customers, smile and are cheerful

Competition

The Hospitality and Catering industry is very large and there is a lot of competition between businesses to attract and retain customers.

To be successful, it is important for a business to use a variety of competitive strategies:

Hospitality and catering business aim for success

To offer a range of products and services to attract different types of customer and compete with other similar local businesses

Examples of products and services that could be offered to achieve the aim

- Wedding venue
- Birthday and celebration parties (e.g. Bar mitzvahs, wedding anniversaries, company dinner and dance)
- School and college proms
- University graduation ceremonies
- Conferences and training courses
- Quiz nights and other competitions
- Special food events, e.g. curry nights, Christmas meals, food, beer and wine festivals
- Craft fairs and other community events
- Special sports events viewing and celebrations, e.g. national and international rugby games, world athletic events, etc.
- Venue decoration services

Competitive strategies to help achieve the aim

Competitive strategies that *should* be used:
- Reply to customer enquiries and provide a proposal and price quote within 24 hours
- Make sure the business has an extensive, reliable, user-friendly and regularly updated website
- Carry out market research to find out the number and types of businesses that will be in competition with your business, and their competitive strategies
- Research the demographics in the local area:
  - How many people?
  - What are their age groups?
  - What are their lifestyles?
  - What are their needs and wants?

Competitive strategies that *could* be used:
- Advertise in different ways and places, using good quality images and clear explanations of the services on offer and the prices
- Offer competitive prices, group discounts, customer loyalty schemes (e.g. collect tokens to earn a free meal)
- Offer meal deals, e.g. discounts for pensioners, free bottle of wine with a meal, buy two meals, get third one free
- Offer competitive/discounted accommodation for party/celebration guests

Trends

A **trend** means the direction in which something is developing or changing. A business should be aware of and keep up with trends which will directly affect their success. An example of a continually developing trend which has been influencing businesses in all industries (including Hospitality and Catering) for many years, and continues to do so, is the use of information and communications technology (ICT), which has grown very rapidly with the development and use of social media, smartphones and other communication devices.

For the Hospitality and Catering industry, there are some important trends in ICT that are designed to attract customers and improve their experience:

- **Satellite technology and beacons** – these are already used to show people on their mobile phones their location or the directions to another location. They are also now being used by businesses to seek and locate potential customers and let them know that they are near to a restaurant, hotel, bar or other establishment that they might like to try. They can also give them links to the services provided so that they can choose what to eat or drink.

- **Customer Relationship Management systems (CRMs)** – these are used to enable hospitality and catering establishments to send information about their services to customers and enable the customers to make online bookings, order food and drinks, etc., directly to the establishment, e.g. a restaurant, so that it knows how many customers are expected and can manage their food provision and customer needs more efficiently.

- **Social media** – this has enabled businesses to receive feedback (good and bad!) from customers who write reviews and send photographs of their experiences to other people. This has now moved on to sending live videos of customer experiences in different establishments, which helps businesses to see directly how well they are doing and what their customers think about their services.

- **Smart devices linked to smartphones** – devices such as smart watches linked to smartphones use apps to monitor things and allow people to send requests or instructions to other devices. Hospitality and catering companies will be able to use this technology to enable customers to do things such as place orders for food, etc., when they are elsewhere, and check in to hotels without having to queue up at a desk, open their hotel room door with a smart watch or similar device, control their TV or room blinds, etc.

ICT technology has also improved the services and efficiency of the Hospitality and Catering industry in a variety of ways:

- It is easier and less space is needed for businesses to store customer/guest details, booking information, etc. Businesses have to comply with the laws on **Data Protection**, i.e. storing the personal details of customers securely so that they cannot be accessed by other people.

- Customers, suppliers, employees, etc., can be emailed and payments can be made using online bank transfers, which cuts down on paperwork and has reduced the need to use and securely store and handle cash.

Political factors

Policies, laws and regulations are made by politicians and many have a direct effect on the running of and success of hospitality and catering businesses.

Licensing laws

- The requirement for a business to have a licence to sell alcohol
- The trading hours during which businesses are allowed to sell alcohol
- The minimum age that a person has to be to buy or sell alcohol.

Employment laws

These cover a wide range of issues, including:

- Health and Safety regulations
- Pension and National Insurance contributions
- Working hours and holiday entitlement
- Gender, age, religious, disability and racial anti-discrimination laws
- Income tax and insurance
- Child care
- Sick pay
- Redundancy and dismissal
- Employment contract
- Trade unions
- Employment of overseas workers.

Customer (and employee) health and safety

- Fire escape regulations – to avoid fires starting and to ensure people's safety in the event of a fire starting, e.g. unblocked fire escapes
- Building regulations – to ensure appliances, electrical switches and equipment are safe to use
- Use and storage of chemicals, e.g. for cleaning and maintenance
- Tobacco and e-cigarette smoking regulations
- Food Safety Act and other regulations to protect customers and businesses and ensure that food is safe to eat
- Public liability insurance cover in the event of an accident.

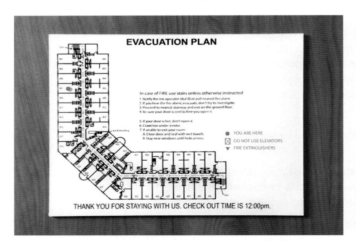

Tax collection

- Value Added Tax (VAT) – collected by businesses from customer purchases on behalf of the government
- Income Tax – from employees

Businesses need to be aware of all the regulations and laws that will affect them, and make sure that they have the appropriate checks carried out and up-to-date certificates to prove that they have complied with the law.

If a business does not comply with one or more laws or regulations and it can be proven that they did so knowingly, they could be prosecuted and made to pay a large fine or have an aspect of their licence to trade taken away. This will affect their reputation and profits.

Political factors also affect the planning and building of premises, such as a new hotel, in a particular area and the change of use of existing buildings from, e.g., a home into a restaurant.

Media

- There is much competition in the Hospitality and Catering industry.

- It is important for businesses to advertise and promote their products and services.

- The media has a big influence on the success of hospitality and catering businesses.

- The tourist industry uses social media, television and films, magazines and other printed media to promote tourism throughout the world, and this has greatly benefitted the Hospitality and Catering industry, which has developed alongside it.

- Food tourism has also become popular as people explore food cultures in different countries.

- Although advertising is expensive, the returns in the form of increased numbers of customers paying for services may be worth the effort and investment.

- In particular, online searching and booking for services has become very popular and it is important to invest in this form of media.

© EAT WELL, TRAVEL BETTER

Practice questions

1. Why are the following important for the success of a hospitality and catering business? (Give two reasons for each):

a) Social media. *(2 marks)*

b) Market research when planning to open a new restaurant. *(2 marks)*

c) Customer service. *(2 marks)*

d) Keeping up with trends. *(2 marks)*

2. a) Give two reasons why hospitality and catering businesses are being encouraged to become more concerned about environmental issues. *(2 marks)*

b) Suggest three ways in which a hospitality and catering business can become more environmentally friendly. *(3 marks)*

Stretch and challenge

1. There is an increasing requirement for businesses to explain how they address issues around environmental sustainability.

   a) Suggest different ways in which the various sectors of the Hospitality and Catering industry can address the requirements and targets to 'reduce, re-use and recycle'. *(8 marks)*

   b) Explain how addressing environmental sustainability issues will help a business to be more successful. *(6 marks)*

2. Explain, giving reasons and examples, how the use of Information and Computer Technology (ICT) in the Hospitality and Catering industry is beneficial to:

   a) Businesses

   b) Suppliers

   c) Customers

   d) Employees. *(12 marks)*

LO2 Understand how hospitality and catering provision operates

What will I learn?

In this chapter you will learn why good organisation of a kitchen is essential for making sure that high-quality and safe food is produced in good time for customers, and that the use of ingredients, equipment and employees is as efficient as possible.

Key terms

- **Covers** – customer food orders that are sent to the kitchen

- **FIFO** – first in, first out – using food stocks in rotation

- **Workflow** – the way food passes through the kitchen from delivery to the dining room

Operational activities in a kitchen AC2.1

There are four main operational activities that are carried out in a catering kitchen:

1. Receiving and storing kitchen deliveries – ingredients, materials, equipment and cleaning chemicals
2. Organising and preparing food ready for cooking
3. Cooking, presenting and plating food for service to customers
4. Cleaning and maintaining kitchen equipment and premises

Depending on their size, catering kitchens are usually divided into separate areas in which these different operational activities take place:

1. Storage area

For storing different ingredients and materials in suitable conditions of temperature, humidity and ventilation

Dry area: For storing dried, canned and packaged foods that do not need to be refrigerated

Cool dry area: For housing freezers and refrigerators, so that they work efficiently and are not affected by heat from cookers, grills, etc.

2. Preparation and cooking areas

Wet area: For preparing fish, vegetables, meat, cold dishes

Hot dry area: Where grilling, roasting, frying, baking and microwaving are carried out

Hot wet area: Where steaming, poaching and boiling are carried out

3. Serving area (servery)

Where food is presented and plated ready for service to customers

4. Dirty area

Where rubbish, waste food, pot washing and dish/cutlery washing is carried out and cleaning equipment and materials are stored

5. Staff area – away from main kitchen

Where employees can change into their work clothing, store their personal belongings, use the toilet and wash their hands

Workflow and layout of a kitchen AC2.1

Catering kitchens are busy places, usually with several people working at the same time in different operational activities to produce a range of different menu items for customers. For the kitchen to work efficiently and effectively, it needs to have a logical layout, so that a good workflow can be established. Workflow means the way in which food passes through the kitchen from delivery at the kitchen door (as separate foods and ingredients) to service (as a complete meal) in the dining area, with as little obstruction as possible and minimal risk of cross-contamination by microbes (see page 76):

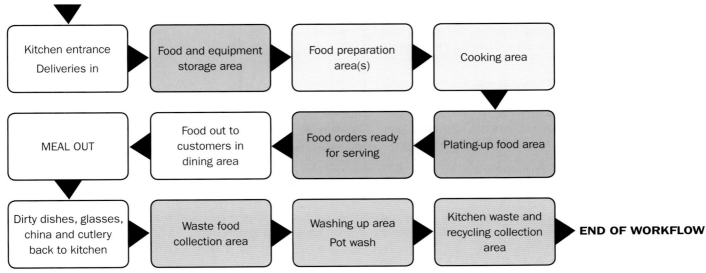

START OF WORKFLOW

| Kitchen entrance / Deliveries in | ▶ | Food and equipment storage area | ▶ | Food preparation area(s) | ▶ | Cooking area |

| MEAL OUT | ◀ | Food out to customers in dining area | ◀ | Food orders ready for serving | ◀ | Plating-up food area |

| Dirty dishes, glasses, china and cutlery back to kitchen | ▶ | Waste food collection area | ▶ | Washing up area / Pot wash | ▶ | Kitchen waste and recycling collection area | ▶ **END OF WORKFLOW** |

The design of the kitchen layout will depend on:

- The size and shape of the space available
- The type(s) and quantities of food that will be made
- How much of the food is prepared from raw ingredients and how much is bought in ready prepared by contract food service caterers (see page 8)
- How many customers are expected to be served in a given period of time (in the industry customers' food orders that are sent to the kitchen are called covers).

There are some general rules that need to be considered when designing a kitchen layout:

Design rule	Reason
Foods should be stored correctly.	To prevent wastage of ingredients due to poor storage, which would result in the loss of profits.
Raw and cooked foods should be kept separate.	To prevent cross-contamination (see page 76) and make sure foods are safe to eat.
Areas where there are sources of contamination, e.g. vegetable preparation (soil), food waste and washing up areas should be sited away from food preparation areas.	To prevent cross-contamination.
Equipment, ingredients, cooking areas and water supply should be within easy reach for different food preparation processes.	To prevent employees from having to walk unnecessary distances around the kitchen, which would result in them wasting time and becoming tired.
There should be enough working space for each employee.	To enable them to work efficiently and avoid accidents.
Employee changing, hand-washing and toilet facilities should be provided away from the main working area of the kitchen.	To enable employees to meet the requirements of food hygiene and safety regulations.

The kitchen should be well lit and ventilated with fresh air.	To enable employees to work in comfortable conditions.
There should be extractor fans and hoods over equipment to remove fumes, steam and heat.	To prevent accidents and avoid illness due to heat exhaustion and lack of air.
	Humidity (moisture in the air) should be no more than 60%. Steam can make surfaces, such as floors, a slip hazard.
	Steam can also encourage the growth of moulds if it is not removed.
The kitchen should have some form of air conditioning to control the temperature.	The air temperature should be no higher than 26°C in cooking areas and between 16 and 18°C in food preparation areas.
The kitchen should be designed to reduce noise levels where possible, e.g. by using materials that absorb sound, and by locating noisy machinery where it will have limited impact on noise levels.	Noise levels need to be monitored to make sure employees' hearing is not affected by noisy machinery or other noise in a busy kitchen.
The floor surface should be made from a non-slip material.	To prevent slips and falls.
The kitchen should be easy to maintain and clean. Ideally, the floor and walls should not have lots of joints in them where dirt can collect.	To prevent the build-up of dirt, which would increase the risk of cross-contamination. To prevent pests, e.g. mice, flies, etc., from infesting the kitchen.
Cleaning materials and equipment should be stored away from food storage and preparation areas.	To prevent cross-contamination and risk of food poisoning.

How many employees work in each section of a kitchen will depend on the number of people expected to be catered for, and good planning ahead will help workers to know when and where they are required to work.

Here is an example of a layout for the kitchen of a medium-sized hotel. The kitchen prepares a variety of menu items to suit the different requirements of the hotel guests, who are mainly tourists who visit the nearby historic town and walk in the surrounding countryside. The workflow has been highlighted.

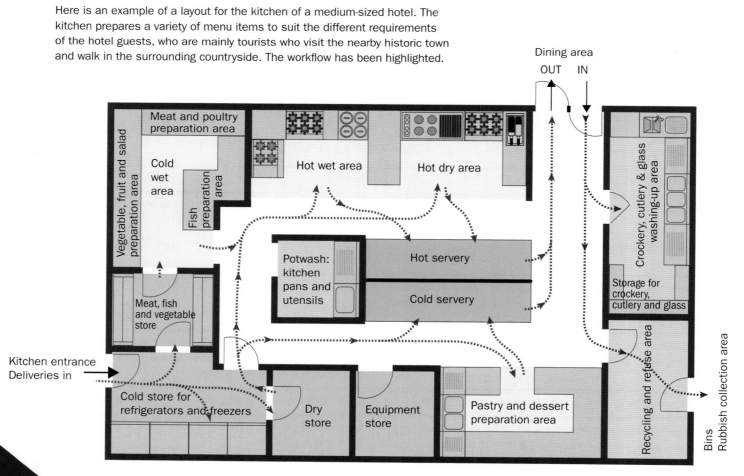

Scenario

Using the plan on page 41 as a guide, copy and complete the empty plan below to show what the workflow for the sandwich production company described on the right would look like. Fill in as many of the boxes as you need.

A contract catering business that specialises in making sandwiches is setting up business in a new industrial estate on the edge of a large town. They will operate from a medium-sized warehouse building.

They will make a range of sandwich fillings and ingredients, including:

- Cooked chicken, ham, beef and prawn (bought in already cooked)
- Cheese, hard-boiled egg (eggs to be cooked on premises)
- Bacon, roasted vegetables (to be cooked on premises)
- Salad vegetables
- Hummus (bought in ready-made)
- Mayonnaise, pickles, mustard (bought in ready-made)
- Sliced bread (bought in ready-made) – wholemeal, white and brown

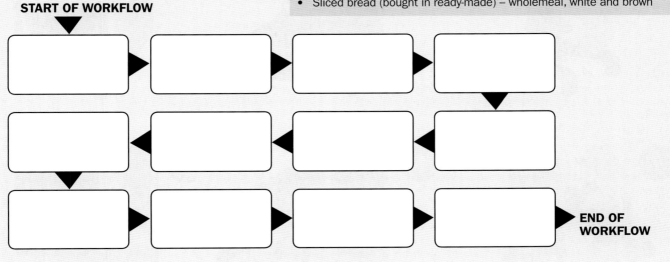

START OF WORKFLOW

END OF WORKFLOW

Kitchen equipment AC2.1

Good quality kitchen equipment is expensive but is essential for the efficient and safe production of food. A lot of large equipment and machines are made from stainless steel, which is strong, easy to keep clean and does not rust or react with foods.

Equipment is divided into four groups:

Large equipment

E.g. ovens, cooking ranges, walk-in freezers and refrigerators, steamers, grills, floor-standing mixers and processors, deep fat fryers, blast chiller

Mechanical equipment

E.g. mincer, food processor, mixer, vegetable peeler, dough mixer, dishwasher

Small hand-held utensils and equipment

E.g. bowls, jugs, pans, whisks, spatulas, knives, chopping boards, sieves, food temperature probes, etc.

First aid and safety equipment

E.g. first aid kit, safety and emergency exit signs, fire extinguishers, smoke, gas and carbon monoxide alarms, safety and emergency lighting

Activity 4.1

The chart below shows a number of pieces of large equipment used in catering kitchens.

Find out and write down what each is (answers online), what it is used for and the health and safety rules that would apply when using each piece of equipment.

When choosing equipment for the kitchen, a number of things need to be taken into consideration before buying it:

The size of the equipment (will it fit in the kitchen?)

How is it drained of water/oil?

Is it well made, with safety features, e.g. insulated handles?

Can it be used for multiple jobs?

How easy is it to use/carry/maintain?

How long is the manufacturer's warranty?

The weight of the equipment

How noisy is it when operating?

Does it need a water supply?

How easy is it to clean?

What is its energy efficiency rating?

Is it possible to buy spare parts if they are needed?

How long does it take to heat up/cool down food?

What fuel does it use?

Food safety equipment in the kitchen

Food safety is a top priority in the operation of a catering kitchen. The management of the business and its workers must all act responsibly to make sure that customers do not become ill after eating food prepared and sold by the business.

Later in the book you will learn about food safety laws and how food is kept safe throughout its storage, preparation, cooking and serving. To help food handlers ensure that food is prepared safely in the operation of the kitchen, some items of catering equipment are coloured coded, including:

Chopping boards

To prevent cross contamination of bacteria from one food to another, different types of food are prepared on specific coloured chopping boards, as shown in the image, which tells you which board is used for which food.

N.B. Bakery items are also often prepared on white chopping boards.

Other colour coded equipment to avoid cross-contamination is available, such as tongs and knives:

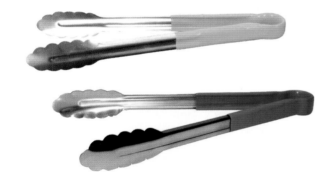

Colour coded 'day of the week' food labels are used so that left over food or food samples can be dated and labelled, to be stored in the refrigerator for later use, or for the purposes of a food safety inspection.

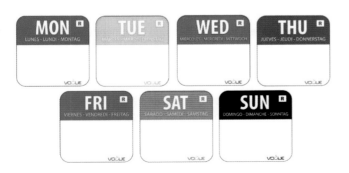

Materials AC2.1

Besides equipment (and ingredients), kitchens need a continuous supply of materials so that they can operate effectively.

Cleaning materials:

- Detergents for cleaning dishes, glasses, pans, cutlery
- Detergents for washing fabrics (drying-up cloths, dishcloths, aprons, oven gloves, etc.)
- Scourers, washing-up cloths, floor cloths, mops, dustpans and brushes, brooms, buckets
- Floor, wall and equipment cleaning chemicals.

Materials for food preparation:

- Kitchen papers and foils for baking, roasting, steaming, etc.
- Food labels for food storage
- Food storage bags and boxes
- Dishcloths, drying-up cloths, oven gloves, disposable gloves.

Waste disposal materials:

- Waste bags and bins
- Recycling bags and bins.

Employee welfare:

- First aid materials
- Hand-washing cleansers
- Paper towels or hand driers
- Toilet paper
- Feminine hygiene disposal bags
- Fire extinguishers and smoke/gas alarms.

Maintenance:

- Replacement filters for extractors
- Oil for greasing machines
- Replacement light bulbs and batteries.

Stock control AC2.1

All the materials, ingredients and equipment that are in use in a catering kitchen are collectively known as 'stock'.

In order to make sure that the business stays in profit, it is necessary for good stock control to take place. Depending on the size of the business, there should be one or more employees who look after the stock and keep accurate records of what is purchased, what is used and what needs to be re-ordered.

Stock control has been made much easier and more efficient by computer technology, which has enabled accurate stock databases to be created and regularly updated. It is now possible, for example, for the stock controller(s) to receive an accurate computer-generated list from a chef for all the ingredients and quantities required for a menu for a specified number of people for a particular date. The stock controller will need to work alongside the kitchen, cleaning, maintenance and housekeeping departments, front of house and bar in a hospitality and catering business to ensure that all their stock needs are met.

What does a stock controller do?

Stock controller's duties	Reason
Order ingredients, materials and equipment as required by the business at the best prices and value for money; e.g. when food is in season or when sale or bulk order prices are offered by suppliers.	To make the business as profitable as possible.
Keep lists of current prices for all stock.	So each department knows how much it will need to spend from its budget when it makes an order.
Store all foods correctly.	To make sure they remain safe to eat. To make sure foods are used in rotation. This is called FIFO. It means that the stock is rotated so that the oldest ingredients (first in) are the first to be used (first out) and do not go out of date.
Keep all stock tidy, clean and well organised in the storage facilities provided. Put pest control procedures in place, e.g. traps, fly exterminators, etc.	To make it easy to find items for each department in the business. To prevent damage or contamination by dirt or pests.
Know what is held in stock by keeping a detailed list – this is called a **stock ledger** (sometimes called a stock book or inventory).	To avoid over- or under-ordering stock. To be prepared when an order comes in from a department.
Use **bin cards** for individual stock items. Bin cards are attached to stock items and show how much of each has been received (and when), how much has been used (when and by which department) and how much is left in stock. The information for all items is then put all together into the stock ledger.	To help the stock controller account for and organise the ordering of stock items. Computer technology using bar codes has made this process much more efficient.
Check all orders and deliveries from suppliers and keep all invoices, receipts, delivery notes, emails and supplier statements in a well-organised filing system.	To make sure the correct items have been delivered and at the correct cost. To make sure that it is possible to track and account for all goods supplied to a business.
Make sure there is always enough stock available.	So that no department in the business runs out of stock for its specific operations Use ICT when ordering ingredients and equipment to make sure that the kitchen is not over-stocked.
Prepare and send out orders for stock from each department on time.	To prevent any interruption to the smooth running of a department's operations.

Documentation and administration for a catering kitchen and front of house AC2.1

It is important to have a well-organised and efficient administrator to help the smooth running of the kitchen and front of house by organising and filing all the **documentation** (paperwork and forms) that is needed.

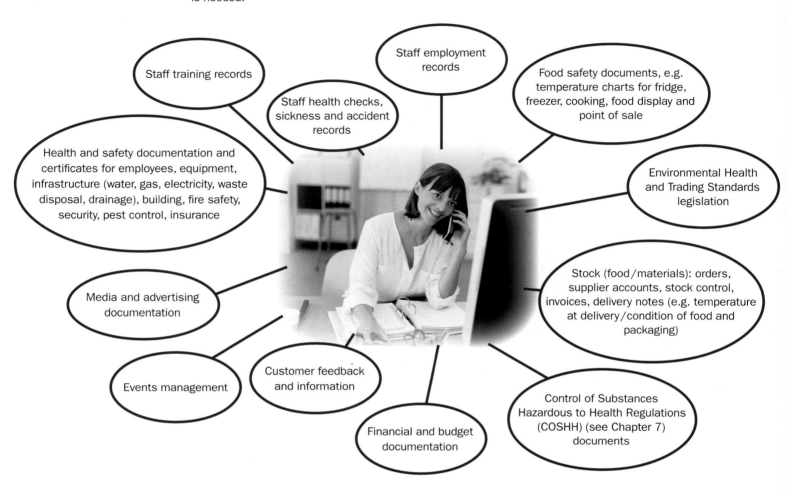

Keeping documents is important for the success of a business as it helps to maintain good organisation, the safety of workers and customers, and ensures that bills are paid on time.

It is good practice to organise and keep all documents tidy and in order in a filing cabinet, so that they can easily be found when they are needed.

Documents should be easy to read, completed accurately and signed and dated.

It is a legal requirement to keep certain documents, e.g. gas safety certificate, fire safety certificate, accident reports.

An example of a COSHH (see Chapter 7) document is on the page opposite:

COSHH Risk Assessment
A Local Restaurant

Location of activity/process:

Date:

Signed:

Description of activity/process:

- How often carried out
- How long for
- How much substance is used
- Which substance(s) is/are being used (give brand name, manufacturer and provide product safety sheet)

Who is at risk?

Employee ☐   Customer ☐   Contractor ☐   Supplier ☐

Category of danger

Flammable   Explosive   Toxic   Corrosive   Environmental hazard   Biohazard

☐   ☐   ☐   ☐   ☐   ☐

Type of hazard

Gas ☐   Fumes ☐   Vapour ☐   Mist ☐   Dust ☐   Solid ☐   Liquid ☐   Other? ☐

Exposure to which part of the body?

Lungs ☐   Eyes ☐   Skin ☐   Digestive system ☐   Other? ☐

Risks to health

Dfress code in the kitchen

Dress code in the kitchen

The cook's/chef's dress code is a uniform that is worn in kitchens all over the world and is a recognised symbol of the catering industry. It has been in use for over a hundred years.

Wearing the uniform indicates to customers that an employee:

- Represents the business.
- Is professional, clean, neat and tidy.

The traditional uniform consists of:

- A white hat – called a toque.
- A necktie.
- An optional name tag.
- A long-sleeved, double-cuffed, double-breasted, white cotton buttoned jacket.
- A dish cloth or 'torchon' – worn tucked over the ties of an apron at the waist.
- A knee-length cotton apron.
- Patterned or plain cotton trousers.
- Sturdy, well-fitting, slip-resistant shoes, with toe protectors and low heels.

White was traditionally used to represent cleanliness, but many modern chef's uniforms are multi-coloured and patterned.

The uniform is designed to:

- Protect the body (especially the chest and arms) from burn injuries caused by splashes and spills from boiling hot liquids or heat rays from grills and ovens – the jacket has four layers of cotton over the chest area.
- Fit the body well and be comfortable to wear while working in a hot and steamy kitchen.
- Absorb perspiration (sweat) while working in a hot kitchen.
- Be easy to wash and iron, look clean, fresh and smart.
- Be a hygienic barrier between the food handler and the food.
- Portray a professional image.

The hat is designed to:

- Protect hair from smoke and oil.
- Allow air to circulate at the top of the head.
- Stop loose hairs from falling onto the food.
- Absorb perspiration from the forehead.

The apron is designed to:

- Protect the lower body from burns and spills.
- Be tied around the waist at the front so it can be easily removed.

Rules for wearing a chef's uniform

- Food hygiene rules say that cooks and chefs should change into their uniform at their place of work.
- They must not wear their uniform in public areas like buses and trains because the uniform may become contaminated by microbes.
- Their jacket, apron and necktie should be changed at least once a day, and their hat and trousers as soon as they become dirty.
- The uniform should be washed and ironed before wearing again.
- Jewellery must not be worn in the kitchen as it can collect food residues and become a food safety hazard.

Did you know?

Traditionally, chefs wore tall hats and less experienced chefs wore shorter hats, more like a cap.

The folded pleats that you see in a tall chef's hat, are said to have represented the number of ways in which a chef could cook an egg.

- Heavy make-up, false nails and nail polish must not be worn in a kitchen, as they can become a food safety hazard, e.g. a false eyelash or false nail may fall into or come off in the food.
- Strong scents should not be worn as they can taint the food (make it taste or smell of the perfume).
- A hairnet should be worn if their hair is longer than their collar line.

Safety and security in the kitchen

Employees need to be aware of potential safety and security issues in a kitchen.

Potential safety issues:

- Risk of fire or electrocution
- Risk of trips, slips and falls
- Risk of injury from machinery, e.g. electric food slicer, steamer
- Risk of cuts, burns and scalds
- Risk of heavy stored items falling from shelves or cupboards.

Potential security issues:

- Theft of personal items from staff area
- Theft of equipment, e.g. knives, small electrical items and utensils
- Theft of stored ingredients, alcohol and materials
- Vandalism of premises
- Arson (deliberately setting fire to a place)
- Problems with alcohol and drug misuse. The Hospitality and Catering industry has one of the highest rates of alcohol and drugs misuse amongst employees in the UK.

Correct procedures and training should be put in place by the management to make sure that employees and customers know what to do in the event of a problem (see Chapter 8).

Practice questions

1. List three operational activities that are carried out in a kitchen. *(3 marks)*

2. What does the term 'workflow' mean? *(1 mark)*

3. Why should extractor fans be installed in a catering kitchen? *(3 marks)*

4. Give three reasons why stainless steel is used to make a lot of kitchen equipment. *(3 marks)*

5. a) List three different pieces of a chef's uniform. *(3 marks)*

   b) Explain the purpose of each of these pieces of uniform. *(6 marks)*

Stretch and challenge

For each of the following aspects of the operation of a kitchen, explain and give three detailed reasons why they are essential for the success of a hospitality and catering business:

1. The work of the stock controller. *(3 marks)*

2. Regular cleaning of the kitchen and its equipment. *(3 marks)*

3. A logical kitchen layout and workflow. *(3 marks)*

4. The dress code. *(3 marks)*

LO2 Understand how hospitality and catering provision operates

What will I learn?

'Front of house' means all the areas in a restaurant where customers are located (e.g. the bar, dining area, waiting area, cloakrooms and toilets) and in which they are welcomed and served. In a hotel, the front of house also refers to the reception area where guests are checked in and out. In this chapter you will learn why good organisation of the front of house in a restaurant or hotel is essential for making sure that customers are processed efficiently and to a high standard so that they feel they have been welcomed, treated and served well. If they are satisfied with the service they receive, they are more likely to recommend the business to other people and to come back themselves, which is important for the success of the business.

Operational activities of the front of house in a restaurant AC2.2

A range of front of house operational activities take place in different locations within a restaurant:

Purpose and operational activities		Importance to the success of the business
	**Entrance/reception** To greet customers and guide them to a table.	Critical – first impressions really matter, both outside and inside the restaurant: is the environment of the restaurant tidy, appealing, welcoming, informative, e.g. are menus displayed in the window? Are customers greeted with a smile and a friendly welcome? Do disabled customers have suitable access?
	**Waiting area** To hold and entertain customers at busy times whilst they wait for a table to become free.	Critical – customers may be irritated at having to wait, so the waiting area should be comfortable and welcoming to encourage them to stay; drinks should be offered, and menus made available to help customers choose their meal while they are waiting.
	**Bar area** For customers to have a drink and socialise before their meal.	Important – the bar area should be welcoming and provide some seating so that customers feel relaxed as they have a social drink before they go to their table.
	**Dining area** To serve customers with their meal and enable them to socialise around a table in comfortable surroundings. The dining area is usually divided into stations, and each station is served and managed by one or more waiters who deal with the customers at a specific number of tables. This means that those customers' needs will be attended to and they will be served as soon as possible, with minimal delays, because the waiter(s) are concentrating on just their needs and not the whole restaurant.	Critical – the dining area should provide customers with an enjoyable experience that they would like to repeat. It should: • Be a comfortable temperature/no draughts of cold air/no strong smells and fumes drifting in from the kitchen • Provide enough space for each customer and for waiting staff to move around freely • Have comfortable chairs • Have a menu that suits different needs • Be a pleasant environment to be in, e.g. nice decorations, plant displays, ornaments, flowers, background music, artwork, sculptures, etc.; good acoustics so that it is not too noisy • Welcome disabled customers and their guide dog/assistance dog.
	**Cloakrooms/toilets** For customers to use to make their stay more comfortable.	Important – these should be of a high standard of cleanliness and have disabled access.

Front of house workflow

Restaurants can have very busy periods during the day and evening, with many customers moving through the different areas at any one time. For a restaurant to work efficiently and effectively, it needs to have a logical layout so that, like a kitchen, a good workflow can be established.

Front of house workflow means the way in which food passes from the kitchen as completed meal items to customer service at the tables in the dining area, with as little obstruction and minimal time delay as possible. This also applies to drinks service from the bar to the customers.

Here is an example of the front of house workflow in a restaurant:

CUSTOMERS ENTER RESTAURANT

| Seat customers at a table Give them a meal menu | ▶ | Take customer orders for drinks from the bar and serve them | ▶ | Take customer orders for food and send to the kitchen | ▶ | Serve meal to customers |

| Take orders for desserts and send to kitchen | ◀ | Give customers the dessert menu | ◀ | Clear table and take used plates and cutlery to the kitchen | ◀ | Check customers are happy during their meal |

| Serve desserts | ▶ | Clear table and take used dishes and cutlery to the kitchen | ▶ | Take orders for coffee and other drinks | ▶ | Provide customers with the bill for the meal |

| **END OF WORKFLOW** | ◀ | Reset table ready for next customers | ◀ | Customers leave the restaurant | ◀ | Take payment for the meal |

There are some general rules that need to be considered when designing a restaurant's front of house layout:

There should be adequate space for waiters and customers to move around safely. Cramming too many tables into a limited space will not be comfortable, appropriate or efficient.

There should not be any electrical leads, unmarked steps, low ceilings and arches or other obstacles that might cause people to slip, trip, fall or receive a head injury.

Reason

To prevent possible risks to people's welfare in the event of, e.g., a fire.

There should be sufficient fire exits that are clearly signposted in case of an emergency.

Fire exits must not be locked or blocked.

FIRE EXIT KEEP CLEAR NO ACCESS

Reason

To be able to manage an emergency evacuation of the restaurant rapidly and safely.

Lit candles must be carefully positioned and managed so that they do not fall over or set light to some material and cause a fire.

Reason

To prevent a fire from starting.

Lighting should contribute to the atmosphere of the restaurant, and should not be too dim or too bright.

Reason

To enable employees and customers to see comfortably and properly to move around the restaurant, choose from the menu and see what they are eating.

There must be emergency lighting available in the event of a power failure.

Reason

To enable people to vacate the premises safely in the event of a power failure or other emergency.

There should be plenty of storage space for items that are needed in the restaurant, e.g. cutlery, etc., can be stored in a 'dumbwaiter' unit.

Reason

To enable the waiting staff to quickly clear and set up a table for the next customers.

Employee changing, hand washing and toilet facilities should be provided away from the main working area of the restaurant.

Reason

To enable employees to meet the requirements of food hygiene and safety regulations.

The design of the restaurant layout will depend on:

- The size and shape of the space available and where facilities such as toilets can be sited
- The expected customer target group, e.g. mixed age group, young families, business customers, couples, etc.
- How many customers are expected to be served in a given period of time.

Here is an example of a restaurant layout:

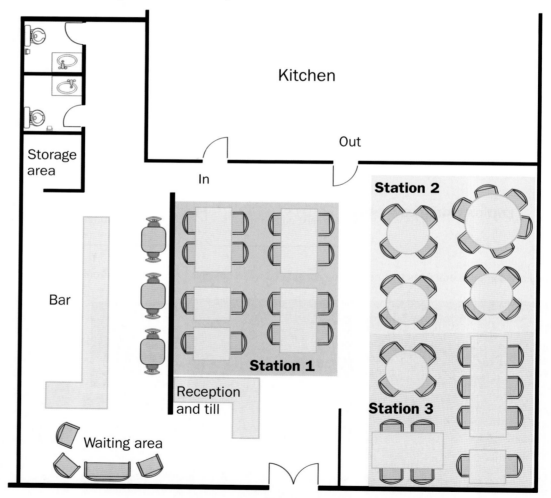

How many employees work in the bar area, reception and as waiting staff will depend on the numbers of people expected to be eating in the restaurant at any one time, and good planning ahead will help workers to know when and where they are required to work.

Front of house equipment AC2.2

Good quality front of house equipment is essential for the presentation, serving and eating of food in a restaurant. The equipment that is needed is divided into seven groups, as shown below.

Table top

Napkins/serviettes (made of fabric or paper), table cloths, menu holders, condiment sets (sauces, vinegars, seasonings), cruet sets (salt and pepper mills and shakers), sauce boats and jugs, butter dishes, sugar bowls, candle holders, flower vases, table signs and numbers, place mats, coasters (small mats for drinks glasses), bread baskets, toast racks, finger bowls, cutlery, glasses, side plates, table top food warmers, water jugs or bottles

Food service

China and ceramic plates, dishes, bowls, glass dishes, cups, saucers, wooden platters, sizzle platters (can be heated up to serve, e.g. a steak), slate platters, stainless steel bowls and plates, ramekin dishes, individual oven-to-table dishes, e.g. pie dish, melamine ware (plastic), stainless steel individual chip baskets, miniature cast iron casserole dishes

Waiting at table

Trays, tray stands, serving spoons and tongs, fabric serviettes, bottle openers, ice buckets, wine carafes (open-topped glass flasks that are used for serving wine or water in a restaurant), customer order notepads, pens, computer-generated customer ordering and payment equipment, candle lighter, plate covers, dumbwaiter storage unit

Customer seating

Chairs, stools, high chairs for babies, booster seats for children, arm chairs and sofas in waiting areas, garden seats and sun shade parasols for outside areas

Organisation

Rope barriers for queueing, direction signs, menu posters, blackboards and holders, cutlery storage trays, wine racks, glass holders, cupboard/shelf system for storing tabletop and waiting equipment

First aid and safety

First aid kit, safety and emergency exit signs, fire extinguishers, smoke and gas alarms, safety lighting

Bar area

Drinks measures, refrigeration, ice buckets and tongs, bottle openers, food blender/juicer (to make fresh smoothies and juices), coffee machine, glasses, washing-up equipment, till, menus, blackboard and chalks

When choosing equipment for the front of house, a number of things need to be taken into consideration before buying it:

How easy is it to clean? e.g. table cloths, serviettes, coffee machine

Breakable or unbreakable?

How heavy? e.g. plates and serving dishes (especially when full of food)

Can it be cleaned in a dishwasher?

Easy to stack and store?

Safety features, e.g. for highchairs, candle holders, coffee machines

Materials AC2.2

Besides equipment (and ingredients), the front of house needs a continuous supply of materials so that it can operate effectively.

Cleaning materials:

- Detergents for cleaning glasses, etc., at the bar
- Washing-up cloths, floor cloths, mops, dustpans and brushes, brooms, buckets, etc., to clean the tables, bar area, floor, toilets and waiting area

Materials for food service:

- Disposable serviettes, napkins
- Individual sachets and pots, or environmentally friendly refillable containers of sauces, condiments, seasonings, sugar, milk, cream, jams, marmalade, butter, vegetable fat spread, etc.
- Candles and table decorations, e.g. fresh flowers

Waste disposal materials:

- Waste bags and bins
- Recycling bags and bins

Employee welfare:

- First aid materials
- Hand-washing cleansers
- Paper towels or hand driers
- Toilet paper
- Feminine hygiene disposal bags

Maintenance:

- Replacement filters for extractors
- Replacement light bulbs and batteries
- Replacement of broken equipment, e.g. glasses, china plates, etc.

Stock control AC2.2

All the materials and equipment that are in use in the front of house areas are collectively known as 'stock'.

As with the kitchen, in order to make sure that the business stays in profit, it is necessary for good stock control to take place, especially as the front of house is dealing with expensive commodities such as wines and spirits. Depending on the size of the business, there should be one or more employees who look after the stock and keep accurate records of what is purchased, what is used and what needs to be reordered.

Stock control has been made much easier and more efficient by computer technology, which has enabled accurate stock databases to be created and regularly updated. The stock controller will need to work alongside the kitchen, cleaning, maintenance and housekeeping departments, front of house and bar to ensure that all their stock needs are met.

Dress code in the front of house AC2.2

Unlike the chef's/cook's dress code, which is a uniform that is worn all over the world, the dress code for front of house employees is more varied.

In some cases it may be as simple as requiring all the employees to wear a particular colour, e.g. black. In many cases, though, front of house employees are required to wear a uniform, such as those shown in the images.

The dress code is important because:

- It creates an important first impression – smart-looking employees give a positive and professional impression of the business
- A uniform sets a standard and avoids employees working in inappropriate clothing
- It makes the employees feel part of a team and as important a part of the business as the kitchen employees
- It gives employees pride in their work and makes them more productive when they feel good about how they look
- It makes the employees stand out from the customers and easy to identify when a customer needs some attention or has a problem that needs to be solved.

Rules for wearing a front of house uniform:

- Food hygiene rules also apply to front of house staff, so they should change into their uniform at their place of work and should not wear their uniform in public areas like buses and trains because it may become contaminated by microbes.
- Their uniform should be changed daily.
- Their uniform should be washed and ironed before wearing it again.
- Jewellery must not be worn as it can collect food residues and become a food safety hazard.
- Heavy make-up, false nails and nail polish should not be worn, as they can become a food safety hazard, e.g. a false eyelash or false nail may fall into or come off in the food.
- Strong scents should not be worn as they can **taint** the food (make it taste or smell of the perfume).

Safety and security in the front of house area

Employees need to be aware of potential safety and security issues in the front of house area.

Potential safety issues:

- Risk of fire
- Risk of trips, slips and falls
- Risk of injury from, e.g. coffee machine, blender, hot food
- Risk of cuts, burns and scalds
- Risk of heavy stored items falling from shelves or cupboards.

Potential security issues:

- Theft of personal items from staff area
- Theft of equipment, e.g. cutlery, glasses, etc.
- Theft of stored ingredients, alcohol and materials
- Vandalism of premises
- Arson (deliberately setting fire to a place)
- Problems with inebriated (drunk) or aggressive customers.

Correct procedures and training should be put in place by the management to make sure that employees and customers know what to do in the event of a problem (see Chapter 8).

Activity 5.1

Food safety is an important priority in the operation of a kitchen. Food safety should also be a priority in front of house operations.

Look at the images below, which show ingredients/materials, equipment and activities that are all used or occur in front of house operations.

For each one, list all the food safety points you can think of that front of house staff need to be aware of and regularly check to ensure that they meet the requirements of food safety regulations (see Chapter 11) and customer care:

Sachets of sauces, condiments (e.g. salt, pepper, sugar)

Individual jars of jams and marmalade

Individual packs or pots of butter or vegetable fat spread

Fresh condiments and sauces served at a buffet in a hotel restaurant

Hot food self-service area in a restaurant

Cold dessert self service area in a restaurant

Serving food to customers

Cleaning glasses at the bar

Using a coffee machine

Making milkshakes and smoothies in a café

Crockery, glassware and cutlery used in food service

Practice questions

1. Give two reasons why good front of house service is important for the success of a hospitality and catering business. *(2 marks)*

2. List three features of the dining space in a restaurant that are important for customer satisfaction. *(3 marks)*

3. Why is good workflow important in a restaurant business? *(3 marks)*

4. Give three reasons why the front of house dress code is important to the success of a hospitality and catering business. *(3 marks)*

Stretch and challenge

For each of the following design and layout features, explain and give three detailed reasons why they are important for the success of a restaurant business:

1. Lighting. *(3 marks)*

2. Tables and chairs. *(3 marks)*

3. Organisation and storage. *(3 marks)*

4. Waiting area. *(3 marks)*

What will I learn?

In Chapter 3 you learned about the factors that influence the success of hospitality and catering providers, and in Chapters 4 and 5 you learned why efficiency and good organisation are crucial for the smooth operation of a kitchen and front of house, and for customer satisfaction. In this chapter, you will learn about the importance of knowing and providing for customers' needs and requirements and why this is also important for the success of hospitality and catering businesses.

Customer needs, requirements and expectations AC2.3

A **customer need** forms the start of a relationship between the customer and the hospitality and catering provider; e.g. a customer is away from home and needs a meal, so chooses to visit a restaurant to buy and eat a meal.

Customer requirements and expectations are the factors that decide whether or not the customer is satisfied with the service they receive from the hospitality and catering provider; e.g. at the restaurant the customer chooses, how welcoming, friendly and helpful the customer service is; the standard of cleanliness and comfort; whether the meal meets their expectations of a good range of menu choices, value for money and how well it is cooked.

There are three levels of customer requirements and expectations:

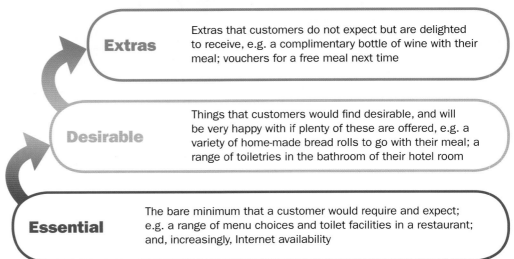

Extras
Extras that customers do not expect but are delighted to receive, e.g. a complimentary bottle of wine with their meal; vouchers for a free meal next time

Desirable
Things that customers would find desirable, and will be very happy with if plenty of these are offered, e.g. a variety of home-made bread rolls to go with their meal; a range of toiletries in the bathroom of their hotel room

Essential
The bare minimum that a customer would require and expect; e.g. a range of menu choices and toilet facilities in a restaurant; and, increasingly, Internet availability

Key terms

- **Customer need** – starts the relationship between a customer and a business

- **Customer requirements and expectations** – factors that decide whether or not a customer is satisfied with the service they receive

- **Market research** – ways of finding out what customers' needs, requirements and expectations are, e.g. surveys, feedback

Customer requirements are decided by customers. A hospitality and catering provider needs to find out what those requirements are by carrying out some **market research**, e.g.:

- Conducting a survey with potential customers about what they think are the essential and desirable features of a restaurant.
- Talking to customers and getting verbal feedback from them.
- Asking customers and checking online for feedback after they have eaten at the restaurant – this can be done in the form of an online survey or review.
- Conducting a survey to find out what other restaurants in the area offer to their customers.
- Keeping up to date with customer requirement trends by reading industry journals and publications.

It is important to provide quality requirements for customers. Quality gives something a value that is more than its basic function and features. In a hospitality and catering business, the quality requirements include those shown on the next page.

The benefits of good customer service

Meeting customer requirements and providing good customer service has many benefits:

- Customer satisfaction, loyalty and repeat business
- Increase in customer numbers and business opportunities as the reputation of the business becomes well known
- Greater employee confidence and self-esteem
- Greater job satisfaction
- Lower turnover of employees
- Fewer complaints from customers.

Customer trends AC2.3

Customers are consumers of goods and services. Over recent years there have been many changes (trends) in the variety and ways in which customers choose and use goods and services. It is important that hospitality and catering businesses keep up with these trends, the majority of which are influenced by computer technology and include:

- The use of **online services** has changed how efficient people expect businesses to be – people want services to be instantaneous/fast/user-friendly/up to date with communications technology.
- **Messaging** is now the main method for people to communicate with each other in various forms, e.g. texts, emails, Twitter, Facebook, WhatsApp, etc. – businesses need to make use of these forms of communication in order to attract and maintain their customers.
- The increasing use of **social media** has made customers more empowered, e.g. they can find out about and comment on/review hospitality and catering businesses; they use **online comparison sites** to choose goods and services; they are less tolerant of poor service.
- Businesses are expected to be available all the time; e.g. customers expect to be able to order takeaway food online for delivery at any time of the day or night.
- There are more goods and services to choose from than ever before, so businesses have a lot of competition and need to stay up to date in order to attract and maintain consumers' attention and custom.

- Customers expect a **personalised service**, e.g. being able to find the type of restaurant they like on their mobile phone, close to their location when they are out.
- Customers are increasingly choosing to buy goods and services that are **environmentally and ethically conscious** – businesses need to be aware of this in their customer service provision and interactions.
- Many customers prefer to use **self-service** rather than deal face to face with a person.

Dietary requirements

Customer dietary requirements include:

- **Nutritional information** about the dishes they choose – available on menus and/or online.
- **Food allergy and intolerance information** clearly stated alongside menu choices.
- Suitability of menu choices for particular **dietary needs**, e.g. vegetarian, vegan, dairy free, low salt, etc.

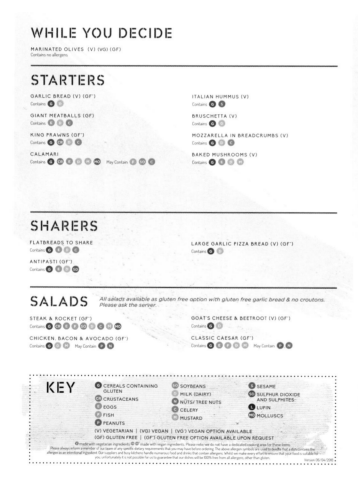

Hospitality and catering businesses need to ensure that their employees are fully trained to understand dietary requirements and are able to answer customer questions about them. They also need to ensure that their food operation activities avoid potentially dangerous issues such as:

- Contamination of food by known allergens, e.g. chopped or powdered nuts
- Inclusion of small amounts of ingredients in a dish that can cause intolerance, such as wheat flour to thicken a sauce or coat a food before frying, and forgetting to state this on the menu.

More information about this can be found in Chapters 10 and 16.

Customer rights and equality AC2.3

Customers are recognised by law and have certain legal rights to protect them when they buy products or services. There are several laws and regulations that protect customers, including:

Trade Descriptions Act 1968

- Makes it illegal to mislead customers by incorrectly describing or making false statements about products, services, facilities or accommodation.

The Consumer Protection Act 1987

- Prohibits the manufacture and supply of unsafe products
- Manufacturers must put certain information on products, e.g. health and safety messages
- Prohibits misleading prices being put on products and services.

► Do not use with a voltage converter.

Hazards

⚠ **Danger! Electric shock due to damage to appliance**

► Do not operate the appliance with a broken cord or plug, or if the appliance malfunctions, or is dropped or damaged in anyway.

► If the supply cord is damaged, it must be replaced by the manufacturer or its service agent or a similarly qualified person in order to avoid a hazard.

► Do not let the cord hang over the edge of the work surface or let it touch any hot surfaces.

► The use of attachments that are not supplied by the manufacturer may cause fire, electric shock or injury and damage to the appliance.

🚫 **WARNING**: Do not use this appliance near bathtubs, showers, basins or other vessels containing water.

See Chapter 11 for information about food safety laws.

Equality Act 2010

- Combines many previous pieces of legislation
- Protects the rights of individuals
- Promotes equal opportunity for all people regardless of age, race, religion, disability, sexual orientation, gender
- Promotes a fair and more equal society
- Protects people from unfair treatment.

Consumer Rights Act 2015

Products that have been bought have to:

- Be of satisfactory quality
- Be fit for purpose (work as they are supposed to)
- Match the description that has been given for them
- Be installed correctly.

Services that have been paid for must be:

- Carried out with reasonable care and skill
- Completed for a reasonable price
- Completed within a reasonable time and according to what was agreed between the provider and the customer.

Leisure requirements AC2.3

Leisure includes activities such as:

- Sports activities
- Holidays – for families, groups, individuals
- Tourism – visiting places
- Outdoor pursuits, e.g. walking, water activities.

The Hospitality and Catering industry is a major part of the leisure industry as it provides food, drink and accommodation, which are three essential customer requirements and expectations. To meet these requirements and expectations, businesses and their employees need to:

- Have detailed and reliable knowledge of their products and services so that they can advise and answer customer questions about choices, prices and availability, suitable alternatives, special requirements (e.g. for disabled customers), health, safety and security.

- Have a professional, positive, helpful, polite, customer-centred approach so that customers feel that their needs are being met and that they are valued and being listened to.

Business/corporate requirements AC2.3

'Corporate' is short for 'corporation', which is a large business that is run by a group of people. A business is smaller and is usually owned and run by one person or a small number of people.

Businesses and corporations use the Hospitality and Catering industry for events such as:

- Conferences
- Meetings
- Exhibitions
- Trade shows
- Award ceremonies
- Staff training
- Team building events.

The Hospitality and Catering industry meets their requirements by providing:

- Meeting and conference rooms – including suitable IT and other equipment, refreshments and meals provided
- Temporary restaurants and cafes for trade shows and exhibitions
- VIP (very important people) lounges with refreshments and meals at conferences and shows
- Drinks and buffets for informal gatherings during and after a meeting or conference
- Special events and activities, e.g. wine tasting, cooking demonstrations, team-building activities involving food.

Local residents (AC2.3)

Hospitality and catering businesses are often located in or near residential areas in cities, towns and villages. Many will employ local people and therefore contribute to the local economy. Businesses need to make sure that they build and maintain good relationships with local residents, by:

- Preventing noise levels from customers, music and cars from becoming a nuisance, especially late in the evening.
- Providing parking for customers to prevent traffic congestion in local streets.
- Employing security officers and installing closed circuit cameras to maintain order and monitor the local area.
- Offering reasonable prices for hosting local events such as fetes, school proms and festivals.

Scenario

A secondary school has contacted a local hotel to arrange a school prom for their Year 11 pupils at the end of their GCSE exams in July. There will be at least 200 teenagers attending the prom.

a) List the customer needs and requirements for the prom under these headings:

Facilities

Food and drinks

Entertainment

Health, welfare and safety

b) Explain how the hotel can take steps to ensure that local residents and other hotel guests are unaffected by the prom.

c) List the various hotel employees who will be needed at work during the day and on the evening of the prom and the jobs they will be required to do.

Practice questions

1. Explain what is meant by 'customer requirements and expectations' and give three examples. *(4 marks)*

2. Give three ways of conducting market research to find out about customer requirements. *(3 marks)*

3. List four benefits of good customer service. *(4 marks)*

4. Give three ways in which developments in communication technology are changing customer behaviour and requirements. *(3 marks)*

Stretch and challenge

Write a report on why and how businesses and corporates are important customers for the Hospitality and Catering industry.

Explain how the industry can best meet the requirements of these customers and why good customer service is particularly important. *(12 marks)*

What will I learn?

In this chapter you will learn about the responsibilities of hospitality and catering employers and employees for personal safety in the workplace, to help prevent accidents and injuries.

Introduction

Every year in the UK, many work-related injuries are reported to the Health and Safety Executive (HSE), which is a government department that regulates and enforces health and safety in the workplace. The information below from the HSE shows how many people were affected by work-related injuries and the main causes of these in 2016–2017. You can see from the statistics that workplace injuries are common, and all businesses must ensure that they minimise health and safety risks for their workers and customers.

Source: *HSE Health and safety at work: Summary statistics for Great Britain 2017*

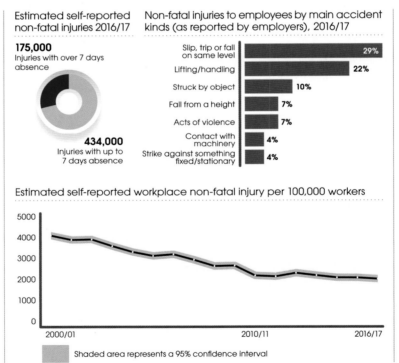

Key facts | Ill health | Injury | Costs to Britain | Industries | European comparisons | Enforcement | Sources | Definitions

Health and safety at work
Summary statistics for Great Britain 2017

➕ Workplace injury

137
Workers killed at work in 2016/17

609,000
Estimated non-fatal injuries to workers according to self-reports from the Labour Force Survey in 2016/17

70,116
Employee non-fatal injuries reported by employers under RIDDOR in 2016/17

5.5 million
Estimated working days lost due to non-fatal workplace injuries according to self-reports from the Labour Force Survey in 2016/17

Estimated self-reported non-fatal injuries 2016/17

175,000
Injuries with over 7 days absence

434,000
Injuries with up to 7 days absence

Non-fatal injuries to employees by main accident kinds (as reported by employers), 2016/17

Slip, trip or fall on same level	29%
Lifting/handling	22%
Struck by object	10%
Fall from a height	7%
Acts of violence	7%
Contact with machinery	4%
Strike against something fixed/stationary	4%

Estimated self-reported workplace non-fatal injury per 100,000 workers

Shaded area represents a 95% confidence interval

- There has been a long term downward trend in the rate of fatal injury, with indications of levelling off in recent years.

- The rate of self-reported non-fatal injury to workers showed a downward trend up to 2010/11; since then the rate has been broadly flat.

- The rate of non-fatal injury to employees reported by employers also shows a long-term downward trend, which has continued in more recent years. Reporting is known to be incomplete and may be distorting the trend.

To find out the story behind the key figures, visit **www.hse.gov.uk/ statistics/causinj/index**

page 7 of 13

Laws about personal safety that you need to be familiar with

Health and Safety at Work Act (HASAWA)

What an employer must do by law	What you as an employee must do
• Protect the health, safety and welfare of their employees and other people (e.g. customers, people making deliveries) • Assess and control the risks that could cause injury or health problems in the workplace • Give information to employees about risks in the workplace • Train employees to deal with risks • Tell employees how they are protected against these risks	• Take reasonable care of the health and safety of yourself and of other people who might be affected by what you do or do not do • Work in co-operation with your employer on health and safety issues • Follow instructions from your employer • Attend health and safety training sessions • Do not misuse equipment that is provided for the safety of you and other people • Report any safety or health hazards and problems with equipment, etc., to your employer

Reporting of Injuries, Diseases and Dangerous Occurrences Regulations (RIDDOR)

What an employer must do by law	What you as an employee must do
• The employer or whoever is in charge of work premises must report serious workplace accidents, diseases and certain dangerous incidents (near misses) to the HSE or other health and safety organisation • Employers must keep a record of any injury (particularly one that lasts more than 3 days) disease or dangerous incident	• If you see or are concerned about a health and safety issue, first tell the person in charge, your employer or your union representative • If nothing is done about it, you can report your concerns to the HSE • If you are injured at work, there should be an accident book in which to record your injury

Control of Substances Hazardous to Health Regulations (COSHH)

What an employer must do by law	What you as an employee must do

• Prevent or reduce employees' exposure to things and substances that are hazardous (unsafe/harmful) to their health
 	
• These things and substances include:
  – Cleaning chemicals
  – Fumes, e.g. from machinery, cooking processes or vehicles
  – Dusts and powders, e.g. icing sugar, flour, ground nuts
  – Vapours, e.g. from cleaning chemicals, machinery, pest control chemicals
  – Gases, e.g. from cookers
  – Biological agents, e.g. pests and their waste products, moulds, bacteria
 	
• Some of these substances can cause short- or long-term illness such as cancer, asthma, skin problems, liver damage
	• Attend training sessions
	
	• Carefully follow instructions for using substances
	
	• Make sure you learn the international symbols that are used to identify different types of substances and how they can harm people:

	*Carcinogenicity means that a substance can cause cancer to develop in the body

Manual Handling Operations Regulations (MHOR)

What an employer must do by law

- Avoid risky manual handling operations if at all possible

- Assess any handling operations that cannot be avoided

- Reduce the risk of injury as far as possible, e.g. by using mechanical handling equipment such as forklift trucks, wheeled furniture transporters, trolleys

- Store heavy equipment, e.g. food mixer, so that it is easily accessible; e.g. on a worktop or on a low shelf in a cupboard or storeroom

> **Manual handling** means transporting or supporting a load by lifting, putting down, pushing, carrying or moving it by hand or with the force of the body

What you as an employee must do

- Attend training sessions on how to lift and handle loads

- Be aware of your own strengths and weaknesses

- 'Think before you lift'

- Do not take unnecessary risks

- Ask for help if you need it

- Assess the load before you attempt to lift or move it – is it hot, cold, sharp, hard to grip, heavy, likely to be become unbalanced if moved?

- Assess the area in which you are working – is there enough room to lift something properly?/Is the flooring uneven, slippery, unstable?/Are there steps or obstructions?

- Follow the advice on lifting heavy and large objects:
  - Squat down with your feet either side of the load to begin picking it up

correct   incorrect

  - Keep your back straight as you move to a standing position
  - Keep the load close to your body when you walk with it
  - Make sure you can see where you are going
  - Be very careful when lifting down heavy objects from high shelves. Use a purpose-built, sturdy set of step ladders or a step stool to stand on so that you can reach the object properly.

Personal Protective Equipment (PPE) at Work Regulations (PPER)

What an employer must do by law

- PPE protects different areas of the body, including:

  - **Masks** to prevent breathing in contaminated air into the lungs

  - **Hard hats and reinforced shoes** to protect head and feet from falling objects

  - **Goggles/eye shields** to prevent the eyes being splashed with chemicals or injured by particles in the air

  - **Thick/protective clothing** to prevent skin contact with heat, extreme cold or corrosive chemicals

Eye protection must be worn in this area

- Provide employees with appropriate PPE where it is needed

- Train employees so they understand the importance of PPE

Foot protection must be worn

- Put up signs to remind employees to wear PPE

- Ensure that employees wear the PPE at all times when they are working in an area with health and safety risks

High visibility clothing must be worn in this area

- Make sure PPE is good quality and is maintained properly

What you as an employee must do

- Attend training sessions on the importance of and how to wear PPE

- Wear PPE as instructed by your employer, e.g.:

  - Chef/cook uniform to protect the body/arms from heat

  - Gloves and protective clothing when working in a freezer or handling frozen/chilled foods

  - Mask to protect the lungs when working with, e.g. flour, icing sugar, powdered nuts

  - Protective footwear, mask and gloves when using cleaning chemicals

  - Chain mail (metal) gauntlets (gloves with extensions that cover the arm up to the elbow) when using large sharp knives in butchery, e.g. boning and jointing a meat carcase

  - Reinforced and closed kitchen clogs or shoes to protect the feet from being injured by falling heavy objects or hot liquid spillage

Practice questions

1. List the two main causes of injury in the workplace. *(2 marks)*

2. Give two responsibilities that an employer has under the Health and Safety at Work Act. *(2 marks)*

3. Give two responsibilities that an employee has under the Health and Safety at Work Act. *(2 marks)*

4. Name three substances that are listed as hazardous under the COSHH regulations. *(3 marks)*

5. Explain what each of the following COSHH symbols means: *(3 marks)*

a)   b)   c)

Chapter 8

Risks and control measures for personal safety in hospitality and catering

LO3 Understand how hospitality and catering provision meets health and safety requirements

What will I learn?

In Chapter 7, you learned about the regulations and responsibilities of employers and employees for personal health and safety in the workplace. In this chapter you will learn about the types of risk that employees, employers, customers and suppliers may be exposed to in the Hospitality and Catering industry and how these can be controlled in order to reduce the risk of harm to health or injury.

Key terms

- **Control measure** – a way of reducing the risk of a hazard causing harm
- **Hazard** – something that causes harm
- **Risk** – how likely it is that someone will be harmed by a hazard
- **Risk assessment** – a way of identifying risks in activities (e.g. carrying a heavy saucepan), situations (e.g. how easy it is to escape from a building in an emergency) or when using objects (e.g. a piece of kitchen equipment)

Risks and control measures

- A **hazard** is something that could cause harm to someone's health or physically injure them.

- A **risk** is how likely it is that someone may be harmed or injured by a hazard. If something is **high risk** it is more likely to cause harm or injury than something that is **low risk**.

- A **risk assessment** is a process that is used to identify and evaluate the level of risk involved in an activity (e.g. carrying a heavy pan containing hot food), a situation (e.g. evacuating a building in an emergency) or the use of an object (e.g. using a large slicing machine in the kitchen).

- A **control measure** is an activity or action that is put in place to prevent or reduce the risk of a hazard causing harm or injury.

The following table lists the potential hazards and risks to the personal health and safety of employees, employers, customers and suppliers in the Hospitality and Catering industry, and the control measures that are used:

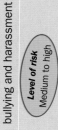

Front of house employees
Reception staff; Security staff / door staff; Waiting staff; Bartenders

What are the potential hazards and risks to personal health, safety and security? AC3.2

Health hazards and risks:

- Muscle strain and back problems from lifting and carrying heavy items, moving tables and chairs, etc.

  Level of risk Medium to high

- Long working hours leading to fatigue (tiredness) and an increased risk of injury

  Level of risk Medium to high

- Stress leading to high blood pressure, headaches, poor eating habits, days off sick from work, etc. – often caused by workload and problems between employees, e.g. bullying and harassment

  Level of risk Medium to high

What are the control measures? AC3.3

Employers should:

- Train employees how to lift and carry heavy objects correctly

- Provide equipment, e.g. trolleys, to assist moving equipment and materials

- Design customer service areas, e.g. bars, so that they limit the amount of twisting, reaching up, bending down and carrying that employees have to do

- Limit the amount of repetitive work and standing for long periods of time that employees have to do – arrange the staff rota so that they change job roles several times during their work shift – provide them with sit–stand stools and anti-fatigue mats to stand on

- Encourage a positive culture in the workplace

- Encourage employees to report problems with work demand, shift patterns and rotas, and implement changes where they are needed

- Have policies and procedures in place to deal with workplace bullying and harassment

- Encourage employees to report workplace stress problems and incidents and use counselling and support services where they are available

Front of house employees

Reception staff; Security staff / door staff; Waiting staff; Bartenders

What are the potential hazards and risks to personal health, safety and security? AC3.2

Safety risks:

- Slips, trip, falls
- Burns and scalds from coffee machines, etc.
- Electric shocks

Level of risk
Medium to high

Caution
Risk of fire
Highly flammable material

What are the control measures? AC3.3

Employers should:

- Make sure all work areas are well lit, free from obstructions and that floors are in good condition
- Provide equipment, e.g. ladders, to enable employees to access equipment safely
- Train employees to use all equipment correctly
- Ensure that all electrical wiring and equipment is in good working order and regularly safety tested by a qualified electrician
- Install electrical safety switches and sufficient electrical sockets to avoid overloading electrical circuits
- Avoid having electrical equipment near water sources and wet areas
- Put up appropriate warning and safety signs
- Ensure that all emergency exits are working properly and clear of any obstructions that would stop people being able to get out in an emergency

Employees should:

- Wear non-slip shoes
- Wipe up any spills when they happen
- Make sure items are put away and drawers and doors are closed
- Avoid obstructing passageways

Security risks:

- Physically and verbally aggressive customers
- Potential intruders into the hospitality and catering establishment
- Theft of personal belongings

Level of risk
Low to medium

(depending on location and type of establishment)

Employers should:

- Employ security staff and enable other staff to contact them quickly from any part of the building
- Install closed circuit television cameras (CCTV)
- Install security lighting outside the building, especially in quiet areas, e.g. where bins are located near the back entrance to the kitchen
- Provide staff with security passes to enter the building and secure places to store their personal belongings when they are working

Employees should:

- Make sure they lock up their personal belongings in a secure place when working
- Report potential intruders to security staff

Back of house employees

Chefs and cooks; Stock controller; Kitchen hands; Pot wash; Cleaners

What are the potential hazards and risks to personal health, safety and security? AC3.2

Health risks:

- Exposure to particles in the air, e.g. flour, icing sugar, aerosols
- Exposure to cleaning chemicals
- Exposure to extremes of heat and cold
- Exposure to diseases from pests
- Repetitive strain conditions, e.g. in the wrists and hands from repeated chopping, kneading and mixing
- Muscle strain and back problems from lifting, carrying and storing heavy items
- Muscle and back strains from bending awkwardly, e.g. cleaning and scrubbing the insides of large pots, cleaning inside ovens, reaching into a chest freezer, lifting heavy equipment or containers of ingredients, standing for long periods of time

Level of risk
Medium to high

What are the control measures? AC3.3

Employers should:

- Provide protective equipment, e.g. rubber gloves, eye protection and masks
- Train employees to store and use chemicals safely and follow COSHH guidelines
- Make sure the kitchen is well ventilated and has air conditioning
- Make sure employees have constant access to cold drinking water to keep them hydrated
- Design the kitchen layout so work stations are as far away from sources of heat as possible
- Make sure employees take plenty of rest breaks in a cool place
- Provide insulated gloves and clothing to work in cold and hot areas
- Train employees how to lift and carry heavy objects correctly
- Provide equipment, e.g. trolleys, plate dispensers, conveyors, etc., to assist moving equipment and materials
- Provide equipment, e.g. mixing, kneading, cutting, slicing, peeling machines if appropriate, to reduce repetitive manual actions
- Install foot rails so that workers can move their body weight and reduce the stress to their lower back and legs
- Where possible, install workbenches that have different heights in areas where chopping and food preparation is done, to avoid straining the back when bending or reaching

Employees should:

- Follow COSHH guidelines for using and storing chemicals
- Wear personal protective equipment and clothing
- Follow training guidelines for lifting and carrying loads
- Use equipment as instructed with safety guards and personal protective clothing and equipment in place where appropriate
- Stay hydrated – have regular drinks of water throughout the work shift
- Report any problems, potential hazards and risks, and faulty equipment to their employer

Back of house employees

Chefs and cooks; Stock controller; Kitchen hands; Potwash; Cleaners

What are the potential hazards and risks to personal health, safety and security? `AC3.2`

What are the control measures? `AC3.3`

Safety risks:

- Slips, trips and falls
- Cuts and abrasions
- Burns and scalds
- Electric shocks

Level of risk
Medium to high

Employers should:

- Make sure all work areas are well lit, free from obstructions and that floors are in good condition
- Provide equipment, e.g. ladders, to enable employees to access equipment safely
- Ensure all machinery has the correct safety guards fitted
- Fit splatter guards around deep fat fryers to stop hot oil burns
- Fit guards around hot surfaces
- If possible, arrange the plumbing so that hot liquids can be drained from large pans rather than being tipped out manually
- Have gas ovens, grills and hobs regularly tested for gas leaks, correct ignition and correct burning of the gas (if it does not burn correctly, poisonous carbon monoxide gas can be given off)
- Ensure that all electrical wiring and equipment is in good working order and regularly safety tested by a qualified electrician
- Install electrical safety switches and sufficient electrical sockets to avoid overloading electrical circuits
- Avoid having electrical equipment near water sources and wet areas
- Provide employees with personal protective equipment/clothing
- Put up appropriate warning and safety signs
- Train employees to use all equipment correctly
- Train employees in first aid in case of an injury
- Ensure that all emergency exits are working properly and clear of any obstructions that would stop people being able to get out in an emergency

Employees should:

- Wear non-slip shoes
- Wear personal protective equipment and clothing
- Wipe up any spills when they happen
- Pick up any food that has fallen on the floor
- Make sure items of equipment are put away correctly and drawers and doors are kept closed
- Avoid obstructing passageways where people have to walk through
- Carry and use knives safely
- Handle electrical equipment with dry hands
- Use insulated oven cloths to handle hot baking trays and pan handles
- Report any actual or potential safety problems to their manager/employer

Customers

What are the potential hazards and risks to personal health, safety and security? `AC3.2`

What are the control measures? `AC3.3`

Health risks:

- Food poisoning
- Illness due to food allergies and intolerances

Level of risk
Low to medium

- Hazard Analysis of Critical Control Points (HACCP) – see Chapter 11
- Provide detailed information about ingredients in dishes on menus, so customers with food allergies can make appropriate choices

Safety risks:

- Trips, slips, falls
- Fire or other emergency

Level of risk
Low to medium

Management should:

- Make sure all customer areas are well lit, free from obstructions, floors are in good condition and steps / stairs are clearly marked and have handrails
- Ensure that all emergency exits are clearly signposted, working properly and clear of any obstructions that would stop people being able to get out in an emergency

Security risks:

- Credit card fraud
- Theft of personal belongings
- Accessing customers' personal details and data, e.g. date of birth, address, bank cards and account information, passport information, etc.

Level of risk
Low to medium

Management should:

- Make sure that customer payment transactions are carried out in front of the customer
- Provide customers with secure places to leave their belongings, e.g. secure cloakroom, digital safe in hotel bedrooms

Suppliers

What are the potential hazards and risks to personal health, safety and security? AC3.2

What are the control measures? AC3.3

Health risks:

- Muscle strain and back problems from lifting, carrying and storing heavy items

Level of risk
High to medium

Management should:

- Train employees how to lift and carry heavy objects correctly so they can assist suppliers and delivery personnel

Safety risks:

- Trips, slips, falls
- Fire or other emergency

Level of risk
Medium

Management should:

- Provide equipment, e.g. trolleys, to assist moving equipment and materials
- Make sure all areas are well lit, free from obstructions, floors are in good condition and steps/stairs are clearly marked and have handrails
- Ensure that all emergency exits are working properly and clear of any obstructions that would stop people being able to get out in an emergency

Security risks:

- Possible attempted theft of property

Level of risk
Low

Management should:

- Check the identity of callers to the kitchen, e.g. suppliers
- Lock away their personal belongings in a secure place

Practice questions

1. List two potential health risks and two control measures for them for front of house employees. *(4 marks)*

2. List two potential safety risks and two control measures for them for back of house employees *(4 mark)*

3. List two potential health risks and two control measures for them for customers in a restaurant. *(4 marks)*

Chapter 9

Food-related causes of ill health

What will I learn?

In this chapter you will learn what causes food to become unsafe and make people ill, and how this can be prevented. Each year, many thousands of people become ill because of something they have eaten. Most people recover after a few days, but some become extremely ill and can die as a result.

People who work in the Hospitality and Catering industry (and all other food handlers) must be trained to understand how to keep food safe when they are handling, preparing, cooking, storing and serving food, so that it does not make people ill.

In Chapter 10 you will learn how some people can become ill after eating food, even though it has been handled safely, because they react badly to something it contains.

In Chapters 11 and 12, you will learn how consumers are protected from food-related ill health by food safety laws, and the responsibilities of food handlers to make sure that food is safe to eat.

Key terms

- **Bacteria** – microscopic, single-celled living organisms, some of which cause food poisoning

- **Contaminate** – making a food unsafe to eat by allowing it to come into contact with microbes that will grow and multiply in it

- **Cross-contamination** – how microbes are spread from one place onto some food

- **Food spoilage** – when something happens which makes food unfit and unsafe to eat

- **Micro-organism** – tiny plants and animals that are only clearly visible under a microscope (also called **microbes**)

- **Moulds** – tiny organisms, related to mushrooms

- **Pathogenic** – something that is capable of causing illness in people

- **Toxins** – another name for poisons; if something is toxic, it is poisonous

- **Yeasts** – microscopic, single-celled fungi that ferment foods containing sugar

Causes of food-related ill health (AC4.1) (AC4.4) (AC4.5)

There are three main causes of food-related ill health:

1. Microbes: bacteria, moulds and yeasts – some of these cause food spoilage and contaminate (infect) food by growing in it, which makes the food unfit and unsafe to eat.

2. Chemicals, metals and poisonous plants – these poison food by either mistakenly being added to it (chemicals); reacting with certain foods (metals) or by producing toxins (plants).

3. Food allergies and intolerances (see Chapter 10) – these happen in a minority of people, who unfortunately react to something natural in a food (not a microbe or poison) and become ill as a result.

This chapter will cover causes 1 and 2, and Chapter 10 will cover food allergies and intolerances.

Microbes

The word 'microbe' is short for micro-organism, which means a tiny living plant or animal that you can only see clearly under a microscope. As they are so small, microbes can get onto food and start growing (if the conditions are right) and multiplying in it, without being seen.

There are many different types of microbes. Microbes that are harmful to humans and cause food poisoning are called pathogenic microbes.

Some microbes are **not** harmful to people and are used to produce different foods, e.g.:

- Some types of bacteria are used to make cheese and yogurt
- Some types of yeast are used to make bread and alcohol
- Some types of mould are used to make cheeses such as Brie and blue Stilton.

Cross-contamination

Microbes from one place can easily be transferred onto some food, where they will contaminate it. This is called cross-contamination. Here are some examples:

- Handling raw chicken then handling some cooked meat, without washing your hands in between.
- Sneezing into your hand, then handling some food without washing your hands in between.
- Using a knife to fillet some raw fish, then cutting some bread rolls with the same knife that has only been quickly wiped with a dirty dishcloth.
- Storing some muddy leeks next to an uncovered plate of left-over cooked chicken in the refrigerator.

Put it into practice

When you are preparing food, which coloured chopping board (and why) should you use for each of the following foods?

- Raw fish
- Root vegetables
- Cooked meat, fish and poultry
- Bakery and dairy foods
- Salads, leaves and fruits
- Raw meat and poultry

Food poisoning

What is food poisoning?	*The symptoms of food poisoning*		
	Non-visible symptoms	*Visible symptoms*	
- Food poisoning is a common and unpleasant illness that can lead to serious health problems - Pathogenic (harmful) bacteria cause the most cases of food poisoning - Food poisoning is particularly dangerous for young children, pregnant women, elderly people and those people who have been ill or have a weak immune system	- Headache - Weakness - Feeling cold and shivery - Bad stomach ache - Feeling sick (nausea) - Loss of appetite - Aching muscles	- Diarrhoea - A high body temperature - Being sick (vomiting) - Dizziness	- A person with food poisoning is not likely to have all these symptoms - Different types of bacteria cause different symptoms - A person can start to feel ill from a few hours to several days after they have eaten contaminated food - They may feel ill for several days

The bacteria, moulds and yeasts that cause food spoilage and food poisoning all have some things in common with each other:

The conditions they need to grow and reproduce

	Conditions needed by microbes	Reason	How can food handlers control the growth and multiplication of microbes?
1	A suitable temperature	• Most microbes grow and multiply the fastest in a warm temperature: 37°C is their **optimum** [best] temperature • If the temperature is too hot, microbes will be destroyed • If the temperature is too cold, microbes will grow and reproduce very slowly, until they become **dormant** ('asleep'), which means they are still alive, but not active	• Cook food thoroughly and for long enough at high enough temperatures to destroy micro-organisms • Do not leave food out in a warm room for a long period of time • Cool down left-over cooked food quickly (within 1½ hours) and refrigerate it between 0°C and 5°C, or freeze it at minus 18°C or below
2	A supply of moisture	• Micro-organisms need water for all their biological processes • If there is not enough moisture, they cannot grow or multiply	• Preserve food by drying it, e.g. dried milk, dried soups, dried fruit • Preserve food with high concentrations of either sugar (e.g. jam making) or salt (e.g. salted fish), which removes water from the microbes by a process called osmosis
3	A supply of food	• Microbes need a supply of nutrients and energy from food to enable them to grow and multiply	• Prevent microbes from coming into contact with food and contaminating it by: ▪ Keeping food covered ▪ Keeping food away from places where there are microbes, e.g. raw food, dirt, dust, animals, flies
4	Enough time	• It takes time for microbes to grow and multiply, and the more suitable the conditions, the quicker they will do so	• Store, cook, and cool foods quickly, thoroughly and correctly in order to avoid giving microbes the time to grow and multiply • Use food by its use-by date
5	The right pH (acidity or alkalinity)	• If conditions are too acidic or too alkaline, this will affect how microbes grow and multiply	• Preserve the food in acid (e.g. vinegar in pickles and chutneys) to prevent micro-organisms from growing and multiplying

How they make food unsafe

• By putting their waste products into the food

• By producing and putting toxins (poisons) into the food

• By irritating the digestive system and/or causing damage to organs in the body, e.g. the kidneys.

Bacteria

Bacteria can multiply every 15 minutes in the right conditions. Large numbers can grow in food in a short space of time.

The chart below shows the names of the most common bacteria that cause food poisoning, the foods they are found in and the symptoms of the illness they cause.

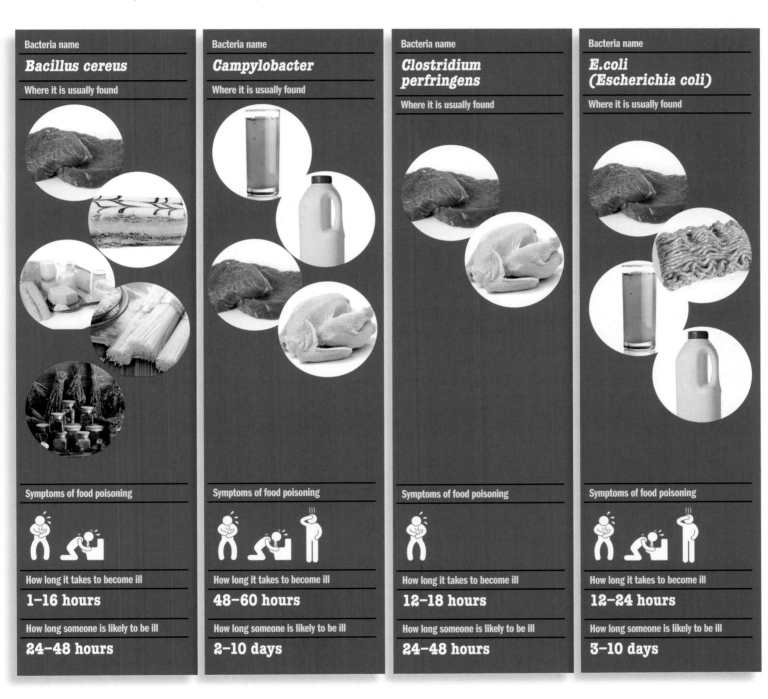

Bacteria name

Bacillus cereus

Where it is usually found

Symptoms of food poisoning

How long it takes to become ill

1–16 hours

How long someone is likely to be ill

24–48 hours

Bacteria name

Campylobacter

Where it is usually found

Symptoms of food poisoning

How long it takes to become ill

48–60 hours

How long someone is likely to be ill

2–10 days

Bacteria name

Clostridium perfringens

Where it is usually found

Symptoms of food poisoning

How long it takes to become ill

12–18 hours

How long someone is likely to be ill

24–48 hours

Bacteria name

E.coli (Escherichia coli)

Where it is usually found

Symptoms of food poisoning

How long it takes to become ill

12–24 hours

How long someone is likely to be ill

3–10 days

Bacteria name

Listeria

Where it is usually found

Symptoms of food poisoning

Feels like having influenza ('flu)

Can cause miscarriage of unborn baby

How long it takes to become ill

1–70 days

How long someone is likely to be ill

A few days to several weeks

Bacteria name

Salmonella

Where it is usually found

Symptoms of food poisoning

How long it takes to become ill

12–36 hours

How long someone is likely to be ill

4–7 days

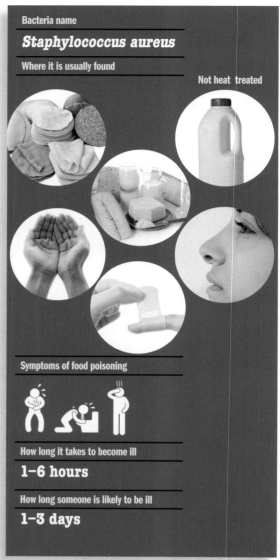

Bacteria name

Staphylococcus aureus

Where it is usually found

Not heat treated

Symptoms of food poisoning

How long it takes to become ill

1–6 hours

How long someone is likely to be ill

1–3 days

Activity 9.1

Foods are grouped according to whether they have a **low risk** or **high risk** of allowing the growth and multiplication of food-poisoning bacteria. Look at these pictures of different foods and say which you think are low risk and which are high risk. Give reasons for your answers:

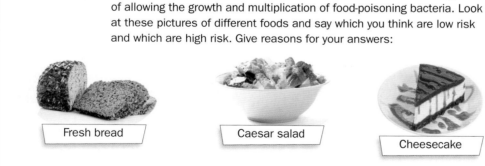

Fresh bread

Caesar salad

Cheesecake

Chicken pie

Pasta dish

Uncooked dry pasta

Biscuits

Cooked breakfast

Moulds

Moulds are tiny fungi. They are related to mushrooms and there are lots of different types. The chart below explains how moulds grow and multiply and can spoil food and make it unfit and unsafe to eat.

What makes moulds grow and multiply?	The right conditions: • Warm temperatures, moisture, food, right amount of acidity, time • Moulds will grow slowly in cold conditions (refrigerators) • Moulds will grow where there is a lot of moisture, e.g. inside an air tight plastic food box or a poorly ventilated cupboard (no fresh air)	
How do moulds make food unsafe and unfit to eat?	• Moulds send out tiny spores which land on the surface of food • If conditions are right, the spores germinate and send down roots into the food 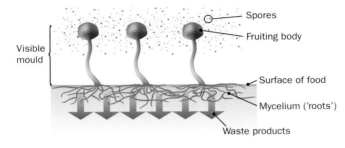 Visible mould · Spores · Fruiting body · Surface of food · Mycelium ('roots') · Waste products • You can see moulds growing on the surface of food • They make food taste and smell very unpleasant • The waste products produced by the mould go into the food • The waste products contain poisons (toxins) that can make people ill • The waste products can stay in the food even if the mould you can see is cut off.	  

Yeasts

Yeasts are tiny single-celled fungi. They are found in the air and will settle on sweet foods, e.g. fruit (fresh and dried). Wild yeasts are used to make sourdough bread.

The chart below explains how yeasts grow and multiply and can spoil food and make it unfit and unsafe to eat.

What makes yeasts grow and multiply?	• Sugars in food • Warm temperature – ideally 37°C • Moisture • Time Yeasts multiply by 'budding'	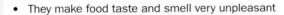 Bud · Yeast cell · Two yeast cells produced
What do yeasts do to food to make it unsafe and unfit to eat?	• They ferment (break down) sugars into CO_2 gas and alcohol • Lots of pale brown spots will appear on the surface of the food • Fermentation by yeasts can happen in processed foods such as fruit yogurts, dried fruits and fruit juices	

Key terms

Fermentation – the process in which yeast turns carbohydrate into alcohol and CO_2

Germinate – when a seed or spore starts to grow and develop

Spores – the name for the 'seeds' which moulds send out so they can spread to other foods

Chemicals, metals and poisonous plants

Some chemicals and metals are very poisonous and will cause symptoms such as severe abdominal pain, vomiting, headache and dizziness within a very short time after being taken into the body. There are other chemicals that gradually build up in the body, and over a period of time have the potential to start to damage tissues and organs and may cause illnesses such as cancer and liver or kidney failure.

It is very difficult to know if a food contains harmful chemicals, metals or poisonous plants, but food handlers need to be aware of how to avoid accidentally contaminating food in this way.

Chemicals

Chemicals that are harmful to humans, in either small or large amounts, can sometimes get into foods. Here are some examples of the different ways in which this can happen.

Situations that food handlers can take direct action to avoid:

- Accidentally adding too much of a food additive, such as food colouring or a preservative, to a food product during its manufacture

- Using too much chemical cleaning product to clean equipment in a food factory or catering kitchen, some of which may get left behind and contaminate the next batch of food that is made with the equipment

- Storing a chemical, e.g. bleach, in an unlabelled container, so that it may be added by mistake to a food.

Situations that are out of the control of food handlers in catering and hospitality, but which they should be aware of:

- Spraying or applying too much of a chemical pesticide or fertiliser onto a vegetable crop, which leaves a residue on the fruits or vegetables that are being grown

- Environmental pollution, from leaks, spills or disposal of waste chemicals that are used in industrial processes, which then get into streams, rivers and the sea or into the soil, and are taken up by plants and animals that humans then eat

- The spread of chemicals from food packaging (e.g. plastics) into food.

Metals

There are several metals that are poisonous if they are taken into the body. This can either cause severe symptoms very quickly, or a gradual build up in the body, which may cause problems after a period of time.

Many metals react with acids that are in foods such as citrus fruits, tomatoes, rhubarb and wine, and the resulting chemical reaction may allow the metal to enter the food and risk poisoning the body. The chart below shows how metals are used in some kitchen equipment:

Metal	Types of equipment containing the metal	
Aluminium	Old aluminium pans and baking equipment	
Antimony	Enamel coated kitchen equipment – especially if it is chipped	
Copper	Pans and bowls	

Lead	Lead in earthenware and lead crystal glass  
Tin/iron	Food cans – these are often lined with plastic to prevent reactions between the food and the metal from happening 
Zinc	Galvanised (coated) equipment 

Poisons in plants

Some plants contain natural substances that are poisonous to humans. Some examples are given in the chart below:

Plant	What it contains
Red kidney beans	Raw red kidney beans contain a toxin called **haemagglutinin** (also known as lectin), which causes nausea, vomiting, abdominal pain and diarrhoea. It is destroyed by boiling the beans for at least 15 minutes. Canned beans have already been cooked and are safe to eat. 
Nuts and cereals	If nuts and cereal grains are stored incorrectly in a place where they become damp, they may develop a mould which produces **aflatoxin**. This toxin can cause illness that may affect the liver and cause tumours. 
Rhubarb leaves	Rhubarb leaves contain **oxalic** acid, which can cause illness and affect the kidneys. The stems are safe to eat. 
Poisonous wild mushrooms	Many wild mushrooms are poisonous. The picture shows the 'death cap' mushroom, which is one the most poisonous fungi known to exist. If eaten, it quickly causes liver and other organ failure, and has caused many deaths. 
Poisonous berries on wild plants	You should never try eating the leaves, seeds or berries from wild or garden plants if you do not know what they are and whether or not they are safe to eat, as they may contain natural poisons and make you very ill. A few examples of very poisonous wild and garden plants are: deadly nightshade berries, yew tree berries and laburnum tree seeds.   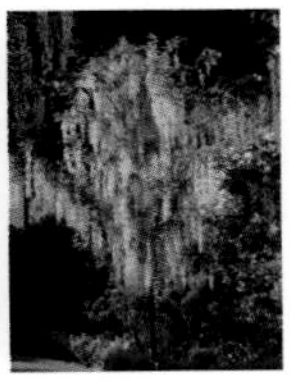

Case study

A restaurant in a small rural town specialises in producing menu dishes that are made from locally grown foods and foods that have been gathered from the wild in the surrounding countryside, e.g. wild mushrooms and herbs.

Two of their specialities are chilli con carne and wild mushroom risotto.

For each of these dishes, list the food safety precautions that the restaurant needs to follow to ensure that none of the ingredients used becomes a potential food safety risk to their customers.

Use the headings below to help you:

- Buying and sourcing the ingredients
- Storing the ingredients
- Cooking the ingredients
- Keeping the cooked ingredients hot before serving
- Serving the ingredients

Main ingredients used:

Chilli con carne

Organically produced minced beef, onions, fresh chillies, garlic and tomatoes

Dried spices

Dried red kidney beans

Wholegrain rice

Wild mushroom risotto

Organically produced onions, garlic and cream

Locally produced white wine

Wild mushrooms, collected locally

Fresh herbs – grown and collected locally

Arborio rice

Scenario: Street food

List some different ways in which street food vendors, who only have a limited amount of space and limited access to water and electricity, can keep their food safe to eat, especially on warm days.

Practice questions

1. What does cross-contamination mean? *(1 mark)*

2. What is a pathogenic micro-organism? *(1 mark)*

3. Name two groups of people for whom food poisoning is particularly dangerous. *(2 marks)*

4. Name three conditions that microbes need to grow and reproduce. *(3 marks)*

5. List two ways in which a food handler can avoid harming someone with a chemical cleaning product that is used in the kitchen. *(2 marks)*

6. Why do raw red kidney beans have to be boiled for at least 15 minutes before they are eaten? *(1 mark)*

Stretch and challenge

Explain how the following pieces of equipment found in a catering kitchen enable food handlers to keep food safe and prevent food poisoning. *(2 marks each)*

1. Temperature probe

2. Blast chiller

3. Hand-washing station

4. Separate preparation areas for different foods

5. Foot-operated rubbish bin

Chapter 10

Food allergies and intolerances

LO4 Know how food can cause ill health

What will I learn?

You have learned that sometimes people can become ill after eating food that is unsafe and unfit to eat, because it has been contaminated with microbes, chemicals or toxins. For some people, certain foods can also make them ill because they are either allergic or intolerant to something the food contains. In this chapter, you will learn what a food allergy and a food intolerance is and how these affect people's health, and which foods cause food allergies and intolerances.

Key terms

- **Allergen** – something that causes an allergy

- **Anaphylaxis** – a severe and potentially life-threatening allergic reaction, which affects body systems such as breathing, the heart and circulation, the digestive system and the skin

- **Food allergy** – a condition where the body's immune system reacts unusually to specific foods and causes a range of mild to severe symptoms

- **Food intolerance** – a long-term condition where certain foods cause someone to feel unwell and have a range of symptoms; it is usually not life threatening

Introduction

Food handlers need to know and understand what causes people to have a food allergy or intolerance so that they can act responsibly and:

- Advise customers about the ingredients in the food they are selling or serving them

- Label foods correctly, showing all the ingredients it contains, so that customers avoid buying foods they know they cannot eat

- Avoid contaminating foods with known food allergens (ingredients that people are allergic to)

- Devise menus that contain advice about the ingredients used in dishes, so that customers are informed and feel confident about choosing and eating those dishes

- Recognise and know what to do if a customer suddenly becomes ill with the symptoms of a food allergy.

Food allergy

A food allergy is a serious and possibly life-threatening reaction to certain foods or ingredients in foods. People can also be allergic to other things such as insect bites and certain medicines. An allergic reaction can happen within a few seconds, minutes or hours after eating food. The severe and dangerous allergic reaction is called anaphylaxis (it is sometimes called anaphylactic shock). It is caused by the body's immune system reacting to something in the food (an allergen) and producing *histamine*, which results in any of the following symptoms:

Visible symptoms

(You can easily see or hear that the person is having an allergic reaction by changes in their appearance or how they sound)

- The skin becomes flushed and red

- A raised, red/pink itchy rash appears on the skin (called hives)

- The skin swells – often on the face

- They may have difficulty with breathing and will wheeze and cough

- The lips and eyelids swell

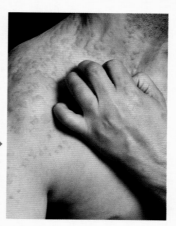

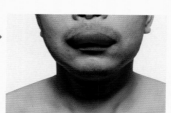

Invisible symptoms

(These happen inside the body, so you may not realise that the person is having an allergic reaction)

- The mouth, tongue and throat swell so the person cannot breathe, swallow or speak properly

- Pain in the abdomen, nausea and vomiting

- They may collapse and become unconscious – this can then lead to death

How to treat someone who is having an anaphylactic reaction

Stay calm and tell someone to telephone for an ambulance. Make the patient as comfortable as possible and calmly reassure them that help is coming. If they have an EpiPen, use it (see below).

People who have an allergy often have an **EpiPen** with them, which is a medical device for injecting a dose of adrenaline (epinephrine) into someone who is having an anaphylactic reaction. It helps to control their symptoms while they are being taken to hospital for specialist treatment for their allergy. People who work in the Hospitality and Catering industry should be trained how to use these.

Which foods cause allergies?

Common foods that cause allergic reactions include:

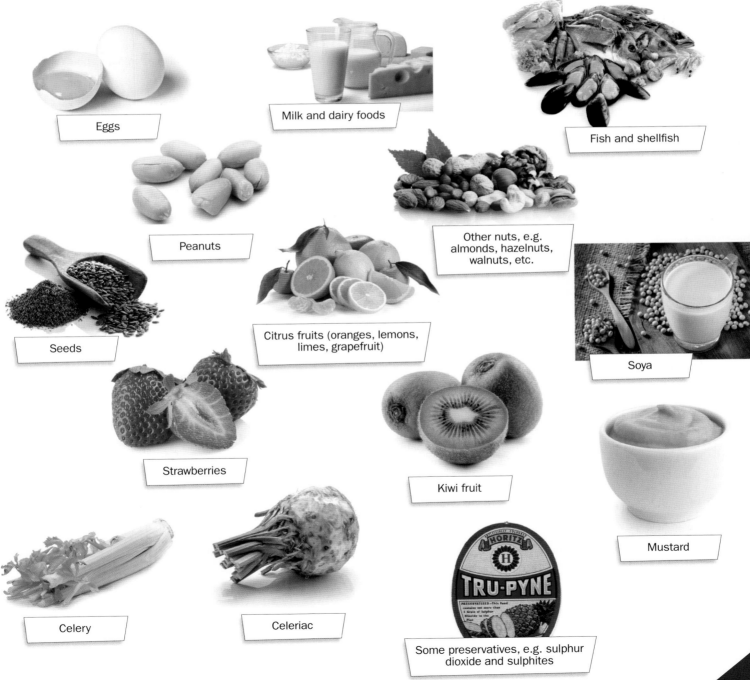

Eggs

Milk and dairy foods

Fish and shellfish

Peanuts

Other nuts, e.g. almonds, hazelnuts, walnuts, etc.

Seeds

Citrus fruits (oranges, lemons, limes, grapefruit)

Soya

Strawberries

Kiwi fruit

Mustard

Celery

Celeriac

Some preservatives, e.g. sulphur dioxide and sulphites

Ingredients: Water, Carrots, Onions, Red Lentils (45%), Potatoes, Cauliflower, Leeks, Peas, Cornflour, **Wheat**flour, Salt, **Cream**, Yeast Extract, Concentrated Tomato Paste, Garlic, Sugar, **Celery** Seed, Vegetable Oil (Sunflower), Herb and Spice, White Pepper, Parsley.

Someone who is allergic to one or more foods must avoid eating them and read food labels very carefully in case they appear in the ingredients list.

By law, any of 14 food allergens must be declared and emphasised within the ingredient list (e.g. in bold, underlined or a different colour) like this example from the Food Standards Agency.

Case study

This is a photograph of Sarah Reading, with her father, David. In October 1993, when she was 17 years old, Sarah ate some lemon meringue pie in a restaurant. Within a few hours she died as a result of anaphylaxis. Her father later discovered that the lemon meringue pie she had eaten had been topped with a small amount of crushed peanuts. The peanuts are what caused Sarah to have such a severe and devastating allergic reaction.

As a result of her tragic death, David Reading became a co-founder of the charity called Anaphylaxis Campaign (www.anaphylaxis.org.uk), whose aim is to raise awareness about severe allergies and campaign to create a safer environment for people at risk.

Today, approximately 2 million people in the UK suffer from food allergies.

1. What precautions would a restaurant now need to take to help avoid a death like Sarah Reading's?

2. Nuts of various types are frequently used in baked products such as cakes, biscuits, breads, buns and pies. If the nuts are crushed, some of the dust they create in this process can be carried in the air to other foods and surfaces in a bakery. Make a list of the precautions a bakery should take to help prevent the contamination of other products by nuts and the advice they should give to their customers.

Scenario

You are serving food in a restaurant when suddenly a customer, who is having a meal with three friends, becomes ill. The customer is unable to breathe properly and their lips are starting to swell. The customer's friends start to panic and indicate to you that they think the person is having an allergic reaction to something they have eaten.

Explain what you should do:

a) To help the customer

b) After the customer has been taken to hospital.

Food intolerance AC4.1 AC4.5

Food intolerance is hard for a doctor to diagnose, but it can cause people to feel unwell most of the time. The symptoms of food intolerance may include one or more of the following:

Lactose intolerance

Lactose intolerance is fairly common and can develop at any age. Lactose is the natural sugar that is found in milk and milk products.

People who have lactose intolerance cannot digest it normally, so the bacteria in the large intestine break it down instead. The bacteria produce a lot of gas and this causes bloating, flatulence, abdominal pain, diarrhoea and nausea. People with lactose intolerance can feel unwell most of the time.

Lactose intolerant people must control their condition by avoiding drinking milk and eating milk products such as yogurt, cheese, butter and cream. They must also look on food labels to see if any milk has been used as an ingredient in food products.

It is possible to buy lactose-reduced and lactose-free dairy products, e.g. milk and yogurt.

Dairy free 'milks' made from oats, rice and soya beans can also be used instead of cow's milk.

Coeliac disease

In the body, food is broken down during digestion and individual nutrients are released, ready to be absorbed in the small intestine.

The small intestine is lined with thousands of tiny projections – a bit like fingers – called villi. The villi give the small intestine a large surface area, so lots of nutrients can be absorbed and then sent into the bloodstream to go around the body.

Approximately one in one hundred people in the UK have coeliac disease. It is caused by their immune system reacting to gluten, which is found in wheat, barley, oats and rye and food products that contain them. The immune system 'thinks' that the gluten will damage the body, so it sends out antibodies to destroy it.

Unfortunately, the antibodies damage the villi lining the small intestine, which means they cannot absorb as many nutrients as they should, as shown in the diagram below:

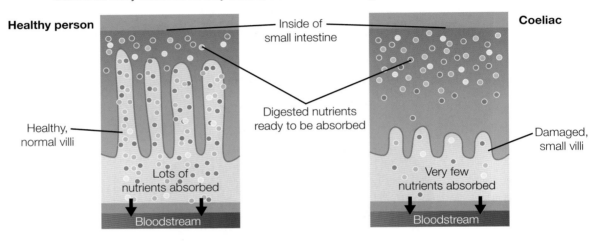

Healthy person — Inside of small intestine — **Coeliac**
Healthy, normal villi
Digested nutrients ready to be absorbed
Damaged, small villi
Lots of nutrients absorbed
Very few nutrients absorbed
Bloodstream — Bloodstream

The result of not enough nutrients being absorbed causes the coeliac to become malnourished and have these symptoms: anaemia, lack of energy, tiredness and weight loss. Children with coeliac disease do not grow properly.

What can coeliacs eat?

Coeliacs must avoid eating any food containing gluten. There are many gluten-free food products available in food shops.

Coeliacs can also eat these foods: agar, almonds, buckwheat, carrageenan, cassava (manioc/tapioca), chestnuts, corn (maize), linseeds, gram flour, millet, polenta, potato flour, peas, beans, lentils, quinoa, rice, sago, sorghum, soya flour, lentil flour.

Put it into practice

You have been asked to cater for a six-year-old child's birthday party and have been advised by the parents that two of the ten children coming to the party have coeliac disease. They do not want these children to feel different from the rest, so have asked you to provide a gluten-free menu for all the children.

Plan and make four savoury and two sweet party food items that will appeal to all the children.

Explain how you have ensured that these items are gluten-free.

Choosing foods if you are allergic or have a food intolerance

Food manufacturers use symbols on their food products to indicate whether or not they contain foods or ingredients that contain known allergens or may be unsuitable for people with a food intolerance. This makes it easier for people to choose the right foods and avoid any problems, e.g.:

Practice questions

1. Suggest two ways in which someone who works in the Hospitality and Catering industry can act responsibly about food allergies and intolerances in their job. *(2 marks)*

2. List three symptoms (visible/invisible) that may occur when someone has an allergic reaction to a food. *(3 marks)*

3. List four foods that commonly cause allergic reactions. *(4 marks)*

Stretch and challenge

Ready-made gluten-free food products can be quite expensive to buy.

Using the list of foods that coeliacs can eat (see above), research and plan a low budget three-course menu that uses some of these foods in an imaginative, appetising way for a special occasion for four adult coeliacs.

Explain how and why you have used these foods and work out the cost of the menu.

Chapter 11

Food safety legislation

What will I learn?

In Chapters 9 and 10, you learned how food can make people ill if it is not stored, handled or cooked properly, or if it contains something which makes certain people ill because they are allergic or intolerant to it. In this chapter, you will learn about how food safety legislation (law) protects consumers (people who buy food) from food-related ill health, by enforcing high standards of food safety in the food industry, including the hospitality and catering sector.

Food safety legislation AC4.3

Food poisoning can affect one person or a group of people. The exact number of people who are affected by food poisoning in the UK each year is difficult to find out, but it is thought that only a small number of consumers who become ill after eating some food visit their GP or get medical advice. Most cases of food poisoning are not reported, often because the illness is short-lived.

Whatever the numbers are, most causes of food poisoning are avoidable, and food safety legislation is there to make sure that food is safe to eat. People expect to eat food and not become ill afterwards, and the law expects food businesses to do everything they can to make food safe.

Food safety legislation protects both consumers and food businesses:

How does legislation protect food businesses?	How does legislation protect consumers?
• By making sure that all food handlers are trained to handle food safely and hygienically	• By helping to prevent them from becoming ill with food poisoning
• By making sure that working conditions are good so that food handlers can comply with all the requirements of food safety law	• By ensuring that the highest standards of food safety are in place in all food businesses
• By helping to prevent consumers from making false claims about being ill after eating food, which could give a business a bad reputation and make them lose a lot of money	• By providing a way to prosecute food businesses that break the law

All sectors of the food industry are covered by food safety legislation:

Food production:

Farmers, crop pickers, abattoirs, fishing boats, fish farms

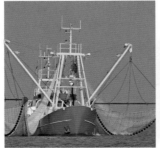   

Food processing and product manufacture:

Dairies, mills, vegetable washing and packing stations, bakeries, factories, wineries, small independent producers, food packaging manufacturers

Warehouse storage and food distribution:

Warehouses, delivery vans and lorries, takeaway delivery

Preparation and sale of food:

Supermarkets, restaurants, cafes, hotels, guest houses, markets, street food, independent shops, takeaway shops, pubs, independent caterers, hospitals, prisons, charity events, non-profit organisations, e.g. senior citizen luncheon clubs

All laws and regulations are complex and have many parts and much legal wording. You are not expected to know all of the detail for food safety legislation! However, you need to understand the basic rules and responsibilities that are set out in the following three sets of legislation and apply to all food businesses and the people who work for them:

- The Food Safety Act 1990
- Food Hygiene Regulations
- Food Labelling Regulations.

The Food Safety Act 1990 (AC4.3)

The Food Safety Act 1990 applies to all food businesses and also includes non-profit-making organisations such as charities.

The Act requires that all food businesses make sure that all the food they produce for sale (including food that is given as a prize or reward or given away, e.g. a free trial of a new product) is:

1. **Safe to eat**, i.e. the food has had nothing added to or taken away from it that would make it unsafe for people to eat.

2. **What people expect it to be**, i.e. the food or ingredients used in a food product must be suitable and intended for sale for human consumption; e.g. you must not sell products for people to eat that are meant to be used for pet food only.

3. **Not labelled, advertised or presented in a way that is false or misleading**, e.g. if you are selling a ready meal advertised as containing beef, it must be beef and not another meat; if you are selling a cake with a fresh cream filling, the filling must be made from dairy cream and not an artificial cream made from vegetable oils.

Food Hygiene Regulations (AC4.3)

Key terms

- Critical control points – stages in a food production operation where food safety could go wrong

- Due diligence – being able to prove that reasonable actions to avoid a health risk have been taken

- Hazard Analysis of Critical Control Points (HACCP) – a food safety management system to identify hazards to food safety

These regulations apply to all types of food and drink and their ingredients, at all stages of food production, except primary production, e.g. slaughter of livestock, harvesting crops, milking, catching fish, which have their own regulations.

There are separate regulations for England, Scotland and Wales, e.g. Food Hygiene (Wales) Regulations.

Under the regulations, anyone who owns, manages or works in a food business, whatever its size, must:

1. Make sure food is handled, supplied and sold in a hygienic way.

2. Identify potential food safety hazards in the operation and activities of the food business.

3. Know which stages in their food handling activities are critical for food safety: i.e. identify the stages at which things could go wrong – the critical control points.

4. Decide what controls can be put in place to prevent risks to food safety.

5. Ensure that safety controls are in place, are always followed and are regularly maintained and reviewed.

This can be achieved using the HACCP food safety management system.

HACCP

All food businesses have a legal duty to protect the health of their customers and must be able to show due diligence in their everyday activities (i.e. that they have carried out reasonable actions to avoid a risk to health). The emphasis of Food Hygiene (England/Scotland/Wales) Regulations is on identifying and controlling potential food hazards. Hazard Analysis of Critical Control Points (HACCP) is a **food safety management system** that is used to ensure that such hazards are identified.

Scenario

Copy the chart below and carry out a HACCP on the kitchen where you have your food lessons, or on a commercial kitchen that you know. An example of the type of information to include in a HACCP has been written for you.

Example: HACCP for a takeaway fish and chip restaurant

Operation stage	Potential hazards	Controls in place to prevent risk of food poisoning
Purchase of food	• Fish may not be very fresh and starting to break down because of bacterial growth and enzyme action • The temperature of the fish delivery van/lorry may be above 5°C for chilled fish or minus 22°C to minus 18°C for frozen fish	• Suppliers have been visited to check what HACCP controls they have in place • Temperature of chilled delivery van/lorry each delivery is checked before accepting fish • Delivery is not accepted if the van is above the correct delivery temperatures
Storage of food	• Cold storage may be above 5°C for eggs and chilled fish or minus 22°C to minus 18°C for frozen fish, which will put foods at risk of bacterial growth • Dry foods, e.g. flour, may become contaminated by pests • Potatoes may become green and develop a natural poison when stored in the light	• Refrigerator and freezer temperatures are regularly checked and recorded in a log book • Refrigerators and freezers are regularly checked and serviced • Flour is stored in a cool, well-ventilated cupboard in a covered, pest-proof container • Stored foods are regularly checked and older stocks used up first • Potatoes are stored in a dark room or inside a sack to prevent light getting in
Food preparation	• Fish must be prepared and cooked soon after preparation, to prevent bacterial growth	• Prepared fish is placed on covered trays in refrigerator until ready to cook • Raw fish is stored away from cooked fish
Cooking of food	• Fish may not be cooked all the way through	• Make sure the oil is hot enough before cooking by checking thermostat on fryer • Fish fryer equipment is regularly serviced and maintained to ensure it reaches the correct temperature • Timer is used to make sure the fish is cooked for long enough • A temperature probe is used to measure the core temperature of the cooked fish to make sure it has reached a minimum temperature of 70°C for 2 minutes

Serving of food	• Bacteria could spread from the food handlers to the cooked food • Cooked food may lose heat and allow bacterial growth • Food may be contaminated by takeaway containers and paper	• Food is served with metal tongs, not hands • Tongs for raw foods are kept separate from those for cooked foods • Cooked food is held at a minimum core temperature of 63°C in a special hot cabinet that is regularly checked • Takeaway containers and wrapping paper are stored in a clean, dry place and protected from the risk of contamination by pests
Washing up and cleaning	• Residues of food could remain on the mixing, cooking and serving equipment and allow bacterial growth • Cooking oil can deteriorate after it has been used for frying several times	• All equipment is washed at a minimum temperature of 82°C in a dishwasher • Cooking oil is regularly changed according to manufacturer's instructions and the deep fryer is cleaned before refilling with fresh oil
Disposal of waste	• Food scraps attract pests and are a source of bacteria	• Old frying oil is sent to the local recycling centre • Potato peelings are placed in green bins for composting • Fish waste is placed in secure bins and collected weekly
Care of the kitchen	• Dirt and food waste and splashes can collect in corners and on walls and become a source of contamination	• Kitchen and servery is cleaned at close of business each day • Kitchen and servery have a deep clean every month • Refrigerators are cleaned each week • Freezer is defrosted and deep cleaned every 6 months

Food premises

In order to meet the requirements of the Food Safety Regulations, there are some basic requirements for the premises (buildings/rooms) in which food businesses operate, and especially where food is prepared.

The premises must:

- Be clean and maintained in good repair
- Be designed and built in a way that allows good hygiene practices
- Have a sufficient supply of good quality drinking water
- Have suitable controls in place to protect against contamination by pests, e.g. rats and mice, flies, ants, cockroaches, birds
- Have adequate natural and/or artificial lighting
- Have sufficient natural and/or mechanical ventilation
- Provide clean staff toilets, which do not lead directly into food rooms
- Have proper and hygienic hand-washing facilities for staff
- Have enough drainage to get rid of dirty water
- Have surface finishes that are easy to clean and disinfect, i.e. walls, floors, ceilings, worktops, cupboards
- Have proper and sufficient facilities for washing food and equipment
- Have proper and sufficient facilities for storing and removing food waste
- Have proper and sufficient space and facilities to prepare, cook and serve food safely.

Responsibilities of food handlers

According to the Food Hygiene Regulations, in order to control the spread of bacteria, people who handle food must follow these basic hygiene rules:

1. Always wash your hands:
    - before handling food
    - after going to the toilet
    - after coming in from outside
    - after coughing, sneezing, or blowing your nose
    - after touching money
    - after handling rubbish or the rubbish bin
    - after touching animals and insects
    - after handling raw eggs, raw meat, raw fish and poultry.

2. Tell your employer at once if you have any skin, nose, throat or digestive/bowel illness. Make sure that any cuts and skin sores you have are covered with a food-grade waterproof dressing (blue in colour so it is easily found if it comes off).

3. Keep yourself clean and wear clean clothing. Do not allow loose hair to dangle or drop into food.

4. Do not smoke in a food room.

5. Never cough or sneeze over food.

6. Clear away and clean as you go – keep all equipment and surfaces clean.

7. Use very hot water and clean dishcloths/tea towels for washing/drying equipment and surfaces.

8. Prepare raw and cooked food in separate areas with separate equipment.

9. Keep food covered and either refrigerated (at 5°C) or piping hot (at least 70°C in the centre of the food).

10. Foods kept in storage cupboards should be properly sealed and used in rotation, following the food manufacturer's guide to the best-before date of each product.

11. Keep your hands off food as far as possible – use disposable gloves to handle foods where appropriate.

12. Make sure that waste food is disposed of properly – keep the lid on the dustbin (which should be located outside of the kitchen) and wash your hands after using it. Kitchen bins should be regularly cleaned and disinfected.

13. Tell your employer if you cannot follow the rules. Do not break the law.

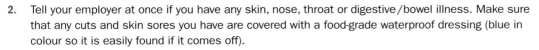

Did you know?

- Most people have 2–10 million bacteria on the skin between their fingertips and elbows.

- If your hands are damp, at least 1000 times more bacteria will be on them than when they are dry.

- Millions of bacteria become trapped under rings and watches, and can spread to food.

- Toilet paper does not protect the hands from bacteria – at least twice the number of bacteria will be on your hands after you have used the toilet.

Transport of food

- All vehicles, e.g. lorries, vans, tankers and containers in which food is transported and the containers that hold food, must be regularly cleaned and disinfected, and be fit to transport food safely and hygienically.

- Vehicles that carry chilled or frozen food must be regularly checked to make sure they keep the food cold enough.

- All vehicles and containers must be used for food only and clearly marked to avoid the risk of contamination.

Equipment

- Any item of equipment that comes into contact with food must be made of materials that can easily be cleaned and disinfected, e.g. stainless steel, to avoid contamination.

- Equipment needs to be designed so that there is little risk of food residues being trapped and difficult to remove when cleaning.

Food Labelling Regulations AC4.3

The purpose of food labels is to:

- Inform and educate consumers about food products they choose to buy.

- Protect the consumer, manufacturer and retailer by requiring certain information to be shown on the label by law (e.g. what the ingredients are, how to safely store the product and prepare it for eating, etc.).

Consumers, food manufacturers and retailers are all protected by Food Labelling Regulations.

In the UK, there are several laws and regulations that have to be followed, and food labels should be:

- Clear and easy to read

- Permanent – the information cannot be erased (rubbed off)

- Easy to understand

- Easily visible – the information must not be 'hidden' or the font (printed words) too small to read

- Not misleading (e.g. if a picture of the food product is shown, the product inside must look the same).

The UK government issues mandatory (required by law) **food labelling and packaging guidance and regulations** for food manufacturers, caterers and retailers. Certain information must be shown on a food label by law, as shown in the example at the top of the next page.

The UK Department of Health (DoH) has responsibility for nutritional labelling.

The UK Food Standards Agency (FSA) is responsible for overseeing and enforcing food labelling in relation to food safety.

1. Nutrition information
2. Ingredients that are known food allergens
3. List of ingredients (in descending order)
4. The quantity of certain ingredients
5. The name of the food product
6. A description of the food product if it is not obvious to the consumer from the name what the food product actually is
7. Indication of minimum durability (the shelf-life of the food product) by 'use-by' or 'best-before' date
8. The net weight/quantity of the food product
9. Place of origin (provenance) of the food product or a specific ingredient
10. Cooking or usage instructions
11. Storage conditions and instructions
12. Contact details of food product manufacturer, distributor or retailer

Practice questions

1. What is HACCP and why is it used in the catering industry? *(2 marks)*

2. Give four situations when a food handler should always wash their hands. *(4 marks)*

3. List four pieces of information that must appear on a food label by law. *(4 marks)*

Stretch and challenge

For each of the following aspects of the operation of a kitchen, explain and give three detailed reasons why they are essential for the success of a hospitality and catering business.

1. What are the benefits of good food hygiene and safety practices for:

   a) The management of a catering business? *(3 marks)*

   b) The workers in a catering business? *(3 marks)*

   c) The customers in a catering business? *(3 marks)*

2. What might be the consequences of poor food hygiene and safety practices for:

   a) The management of a catering business? *(2 marks)*

   b) The workers in a catering business? *(2 marks)*

   c) The customers in a catering business? *(2 marks)*

Chapter 12

The role and responsibilities of Environmental Health Officers

What will I learn?

In this chapter, you will learn about the role and responsibilities of Environmental Health Officers (sometimes called Food Safety Officers) in relation to food safety and hygiene, when they carry out inspections in the Hospitality and Catering industry.

Environmental Health Officers AC4.2

Environmental Health Officers (EHOs) are employed in the UK by local authorities and overseen by the Food Standards Agency to enforce food safety legislation. They do this by inspecting businesses where food is sold to the public. In the Hospitality and Catering industry they inspect restaurants, cafes, hotels, guest houses, pubs, etc.

The purpose of an inspection is to make sure that:

- Food is being stored, handled and cooked hygienically and safely
- Food is not being contaminated and is safe to eat
- Food handlers have been trained in food hygiene and safety
- Food handlers are aware of the importance of personal hygiene (washing hands, clean clothing, etc.)
- There are control measures in place to prevent pests from contaminating food
- The premises are in good condition and regularly cleaned.

The EHO will also:

- Check to make sure that food safety hazards and risks have been identified and are being controlled by using a food safety management system such as HACCP (see Chapter 11)
- Offer advice on training and improving food hygiene and safety in the business.

Environmental Health Officers are allowed by law to:

- Enter the premises of a food business, without an appointment, at reasonable hours when the business is operating
- Inspect the premises and the food being stored, prepared, cooked and sold there
- Take food samples away for testing in a laboratory for food poisoning bacteria
- Take photographs as evidence of what they find during an inspection
- Look at data and records that the business has kept, e.g. refrigerator and freezer temperatures, staff training records, etc.

If the EHO finds a problem, they are allowed by law to:

- Take food that they suspect is a food safety hazard away from the business, so it cannot be sold
- Tell the owners of the business to make hygiene improvements within a set time and come back to inspect that they have done so
- Close the premises and stop them selling food if there is a high risk of food poisoning – this is called an Emergency Hygiene Prohibition Notice
- Give evidence in a court of law if the owners of the business are prosecuted for breaking the law, which can result in a large fine (a sum of money that has to be paid to a court as punishment for breaking the law), a ban on the owner working in the food industry, a criminal record, or a prison sentence in very serious cases.

EHOs will also carry out an inspection if they receive a complaint from a member of the public about poor hygiene in a food business or if one or more people get food poisoning after eating some food from a business.

Food poisoning is a **notifiable illness**. If someone is ill after eating food and they think that it may have been caused by food from a particular food business, they should **notify** (tell) their doctor and describe their symptoms. If the doctor agrees that their illness is probably food poisoning, samples of faeces/ diarrhoea from the patient should be sent to a laboratory to identify the bacteria that has caused the illness and the local Environmental Health Department should be notified straight away so that an EHO can investigate the complaint.

What does the EHO do during an inspection? AC4.2

Checks the use-by and best-before dates on foods to make sure they have not expired.

Checks equipment used for food preparation, cooking and storing food to make sure it is clean, working properly, etc.

Checks for evidence of pests/pest control.

Checks the cleanliness of the kitchen and storerooms and takes samples and photographs.

Watches how food is prepared and cooked and the personal hygiene standards of the staff.

Inspects food waste system and bins.

Food & Catering Waste Only

Checks paperwork and records kept by the business.

Practice questions

1. Give three reasons why inspections are carried out in food premises by Environmental Health Officers (EHO). *(3 marks)*

2. List four things that an EHO does during an inspection. *(4 marks)*

3. List two things that an EHO is allowed to do by law if they find a food business has broken food safety law. *(2 marks)*

Stretch and challenge

1. Explain, giving reasons and examples, why and how the work of an EHO protects both food businesses and customers. *(8 marks)*

2. What can/should a food business do to provide evidence and protect their reputation in case a customer complains that they have been ill after eating food the business has produced? *(8 marks)*

3. A consumer contacts the local Environmental Health Department and tells them that they and their partner have both been very sick and unwell after eating a meal in a local restaurant.

   Explain what the Environmental Health Department will need to do to investigate this complaint:

   a) What questions should they ask the person who made the complaint? *(3 marks)*

   b) What questions should they ask the restaurant? *(3 marks)*

   c) What should they look for when they inspect the restaurant? *(3 marks)*

Chapter 13

Hospitality and catering provision for specific requirements

What will I learn?

In the previous chapters, you have learned about the structure, job requirements and factors that affect the success of the Hospitality and Catering industry; how the kitchen and front of house operate in hospitality and catering establishments; how customer requirements are met, and the need to understand the risks and controls for personal and food safety for both employees and customers.

In this chapter, you will learn how this information is used and applied when considering and preparing structured proposals for suitable options for hospitality and catering provision for specific needs, locations and situations, which would operate successfully, efficiently and within the law. You will be required to do this for one of your assessments in Unit 1 of the course.

Options for hospitality and catering (H&C) provision AC5.1

In Chapter 1 you learned that there are different types of hospitality and catering provision, all of which have advantages and disadvantages which need to be taken into account when considering a range of options for a specific requirement:

+ **Advantages**	− **Disadvantages**

Restaurants, bistros and dining rooms

+ Can attract a wide range of customers
+ Can be very successful if situated in a good location and prices are competitive

− A lot of competition
− A poor location/facilities will limit success, e.g. limited parking, noisy area, building in poor condition
− Rent and business tax for premises reduce profit

Cafes, tearooms and coffee shops

+ Can be very successful, especially in tourist or busy areas

− Competition and location may limit success
− Rent and business tax for premises reduce profit

Takeaway and fast food outlets

+ Fast turnover, so potentially can make a good profit

− A lot of competition
− Rent and business tax for premises reduce profit

Pubs and bars

+ Long opening hours mean potentially many customers
+ A good location, plenty of parking and attractive building will attract customers from a wide area

− Landlord may restrict what can be sold on the premises in terms of food
− Location and size of premises may limit the customer numbers
− Rent and business tax for premises reduce profit

Clubs and casinos

+ Customers are usually members, so regularly visit
+ Customers may stay for several hours, so potentially require regular food and drinks

− Membership fee may limit customer numbers
− Rent and business tax for premises reduce profit

Street food

+ Many potential customers if in a busy location
+ Lower rent and costs than if in a building
+ Fast turnover, so potentially can make a good profit

− Limited food preparation, power and cleaning facilities
− Need to physically remove equipment and ingredients and store them elsewhere each day
− Outside in all weathers

Pop-up restaurants

+ Many potential customers if in a busy location
+ A useful way to find out if customers like the food and if there would be enough customers to make a permanent restaurant worthwhile and successful

− Limited time allowed to run the business – time is needed to build up a regular customer base and judge how successful a business is

Mobile/roadside food vans

+ Many potential customers if in a busy location
+ Fast turnover, so potentially can make a good profit
+ Lower rent and costs than if in a building

− Need to physically remove equipment and ingredients and store them elsewhere each day
− Competition for roadside pitches
− Rent and business tax for use of the pitch reduce profit

Visitor and tourist attractions, e.g. theme parks, museums, National Trust properties, spas

+ Many potential customers if in a popular location

− Out of holiday season may significantly reduce customer numbers, or venue may close down for several weeks

Sport stadiums and concert/gig venues

• Many potential customers on a regular basis

− Limited space available to prepare and sell food and drinks
− Rent and business tax for premises reduce profit

Choosing an option for hospitality and catering provision (AC5.2)

In order to help choose a hospitality and catering provision option for a specific requirement, a range of information needs to be gathered to provide evidence and data to support and prepare a **structured proposal**.

A structured proposal will be required by an organisation, e.g. a bank, who may be approached to provide a loan of money to start the business.

The table below shows the types of information that are required in a structured proposal, and uses the scenario below as an example.

Scenario

The number of people choosing to eat a vegetarian diet is increasing each year in the UK, particularly the number who are choosing to follow a vegan diet (see page 137).

Two chefs want to open a vegetarian restaurant in a large town, and specialise in vegan food.

Section of structured proposal

Information that is needed

Examples of information that would need to be provided for the scenario of a vegetarian restaurant

1. Summary of proposal

- A brief explanation of what you want to do and why

To set up a restaurant that caters for a wide range of vegetarian and vegan customers throughout the day and in the evenings, in order to meet the growing consumer demand for vegetarian food.

2. Unique selling points (USPs)

- A brief explanation of how and why your proposed business would be different and better than your competitors – what features will make it stand out and attract customers?

The restaurant will provide breakfasts, lunches and evening meals, six days a week, in order to attract different target groups of customers, particularly families.

A takeaway food and drinks service will also be offered all day and in the evening.

Ingredients will be mainly sourced from local producers, and as many as possible will be organically grown.

Local producers will be able to sell some of their produce in the restaurant.

Afternoon, evening and school holiday vegetarian cookery classes and demonstrations for adults and children will be offered in a separate kitchen on the premises.

A link with a local food charity will be established to donate surplus food at the end of each business day.

A social media group will be set up to promote special events and offers to previous customers who subscribe to it.

3. Current trends in the H&C industry

- Information about current consumer eating trends and statistics to support this, in order to show that you have carefully researched the industry and are aware of what is likely to make it successful.

Statistics for:

- – The number of people changing to a plant-based diet each year in the UK.
- – The annual increase in the number of people eating a lacto/ovo vegetarian or vegan diet in the UK over a period of a few years to show trends.

Reasons why these numbers are changing, i.e. health concerns, environmental sustainability, media coverage and promotion.

Parental concerns about children's diets.

Availability of cookery classes in the area.

Demand for learning how to cook.

4. Potential customers

Results of local surveys and market research about the number of people following a vegetarian diet.

Survey of people's attitudes towards vegetarian food and how much they would be prepared to pay for it in a restaurant.

Survey of their attitude towards cooking classes and local foods.

Survey of tourism and seasonal effects on numbers of potential customers.

Survey of local businesses and potential lunchtime/evening customers.

- Information about target customers and their needs and expectations (e.g. from a local survey of eating habits and food preferences).

- Information about the demography (age groups) of the customers; their socio-economic groups (the differences in their income), and their attitudes, lifestyles and opinions.

- Information about tourism and seasonal effects on businesses.

- Information about local businesses and potential customers.

5. Competition

- Information about similar businesses in the area that are likely to compete for customers.

- Competitor strengths and weaknesses.

- How you plan to compete with them.

Results of a survey of all H&C businesses that offer vegetarian food in a wide area around the proposed restaurant location.

6. Promotion plan

- How you will attract customers by advertising, a website, promotional deals.

Advertising plan – local newspaper/postal drop of leaflets and takeaway menus/local radio/social media/posters in local amenities, e.g. library, town hall, bus shelters, etc., local tourist attractions.

Website featuring information about menus, online ordering a takeaway meal, local suppliers, special events, cooking classes and demonstrations, booking system for meals and classes, information about chefs.

Opening party with free samples of menu items to try and a tour of the restaurant and teaching kitchen.

Promotional deals – e.g. buy two meals for the price of one for a limited time/price reduction for children/discount for booking multiple cooking classes/discounts for, e.g., senior citizens, students/extra free menu item added to takeaway orders over a certain price.

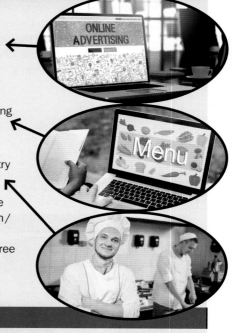

7. Operation of the business

- How many staff will be needed/job descriptions/opening times/shift patterns/staff training in food safety, etc./management structure/record keeping/maintenance of equipment and premises/setting up orders with suppliers, etc.

List of staff to be recruited in front and back of house plus teaching kitchen.

Details of who will manage the staff training/finances/maintenance/ordering of supplies/stock control.

List of menus.

Kitchen and front of house plans showing workflow.

HACCP documentation.

Health and Safety at Work documentation.

COSHH documentation.

Licensing and insurance documentation.

Certificates for fire, gas, electricity safety and water quality.

8. Financial plan

- How much the business will cost to set up and run.
- Expected profit margin.
- How much money should be set aside for unexpected costs, e.g. equipment failure and replacement.

Details of set up costs including:

- Building work / decoration of restaurant.
- Kitchen equipment and storage.
- Setting up teaching kitchen.
- Restaurant furniture, service bar, shelves for display of suppliers produce.
- Website and IT equipment.
- Menu and leaflet production and distribution.
- Opening party.
- Takeaway set up – containers, etc.
- Purchase of supplies.

Running costs, including:

- Staff wages and costs (e.g. pension, National Insurance).
- Ingredients and other supplies.
- Training.
- Utilities – gas, electricity, water, Internet and telephone.
- Insurance.
- Advertising.
- Cover for staff absence.
- Business Tax, Value Added Tax, etc.
- Replacement equipment, maintenance, cleaning.

Activity 13.1

Using the table above as a guide, decide what type of H&C provision you would choose, and prepare a structured proposal for the scenario below:

A charity that helps and supports low-income families and residents in a medium-sized town has approached the local council with a proposal to open a facility in the town centre, in which residents, especially elderly people, single adults, disabled people and parents with young children, who feel isolated and lonely, could meet other people socially and be able to buy inexpensive meals and drinks.

What will I learn?

This chapter has been designed to help you understand the terminology (words) that is used for the e-assessment in Unit 1. It includes information, advice and tips to help guide you to success in this online assessment.

In this chapter you will learn about several important aspects of the e-assessment:

- How the e-assessment is structured, including sample questions and completed examples with pointers to show how marks have been awarded.

- The different types and styles of questions that could appear in the exam.

- A breakdown of what you may be assessed on, including an outline of what you should revise.

- Useful hints and tips to help you through the e-assessment.

What is an e-assessment?

An e-assessment is an electronic online assessment that uses computer technology to manage and deliver the assessment. The e-assessment is completed in an online screen format. You will answer a series of questions on the computer and once completed these will be uploaded to the WJEC server for external assessment and grading.

An e-assessment is similar to a standard written exam; the main difference is that you will complete your answers online rather than on paper. It will be completed under exam conditions; you will have an allocated amount of time to complete the e-assessment, which usually takes place in June.

What will you be assessed on?

The e-assessment will be based on Learning Outcomes (LOs) for **Unit 1**.

You will be asked questions about the following LOs and Assessment Criteria in your e-assessment. Each LO is worth between 10 and 30 marks. You can see how many marks each LO is worth in the chart below.

Learning Outcome	Assessment Criteria	Marks
LO1 **Understand the environment in which hospitality and catering providers operate**	AC1.1 Describe the structure of the Hospitality and Catering industry AC1.2 Analyse job **requirements** within the Hospitality and Catering industry AC1.3 Describe **working conditions** of different job roles across the Hospitality and Catering industry AC1.4 Explain factors affecting the success of hospitality and catering providers	15–29
LO2 **Understand how hospitality and catering provisions operate**	AC2.1 Describe the **operation** of the kitchen AC2.2 Describe the **operation** of front of house AC2.3 Explain how hospitality and catering provision meet **customer requirements**	15–28
LO3 **Understand how hospitality and catering provision meets health and safety requirements**	AC3.1 Describe personal safety **responsibilities** in the workplace AC3.2 Identify **risks** to personal safety in hospitality and catering AC3.3 Recommend personal safety **control measures** for hospitality and catering provision	10–26
LO4 **Know how food can cause ill health**	AC4.1 Describe food-related **causes** of ill health AC4.2 Describe the **role** and **responsibilities** of the Environmental Health Officer (EHO) AC4.3 Describe food safety **legislation** AC4.4 Describe **common types** of food poisoning AC4.5 Describe the **symptoms** of **food induced ill health**	10–27
LO5 **Be able to propose a hospitality and catering provision to meet specific requirements**	AC5.1 Review options for hospitality and catering provision AC5.2 Recommend options for hospitality provision	10–25

Command words and what they mean

There are a number of **command** words used throughout the Assessment Criteria, shown in yellow in the chart on the previous page.

The chart below lists all the command words that could appear in the e-assessment. Each command word requires a different type of response. Some command words will require a response that is a **short sentence** or a one-word answer and other command words will need your answer to be longer, with **full sentences** which are linked back to the data or statement in the question.

The chart below outlines what each command word means and what the examiner is looking for when they are marking the e-assessment.

The command words have been colour coded, starting from green (easiest) at the bottom of the chart, through to red (harder questions which require more information).

Command word	Meaning
Analyse	Examine or study in detail, in order to write information about it.
Justify	Review to give reasons why you think something is better than something else, and to support those reasons with evidence.
Explain	Write about something in a very clear way, giving examples to illustrate your answer, to show that you understand what you are writing about.
Describe	Identify distinctive features: give a description and factual details. No explanations are needed for just 'describe' unless the command word states, 'describe and explain'. Look at it as painting a picture with words.
Review	Review is to explain/evaluate: e.g. write about and assess the importance, quality or value of the topic.
Identify	To show that you know and understand something by being able to give its key features and characteristics.
Suggest	Give reasons or evidence to support your opinion.
Recommend	Put forward or suggest an answer that is suitable for the question.
List	Provide the information in a list rather than in continuous writing.
State	Give a short, accurate and clear list.
Name	Identify/indicate/mention/select who or what.

How will the e-assessment be structured?

1 hour 30 minutes	90 marks	40% of the qualification

The layout for the online e-assessment will be set out in a similar style to the one given in the example e-assessment, which shows the **different styles** of questioning you can expect to see. There are usually a mix of short answer, stimulus, graduated lead-in, free response and data response questions.

All questions in the e-assessment are **compulsory**, which means you must answer all the questions.

Here is an example of an e-assessment with the different styles of questioning explained for you.

Example e-assessment

1. Hospitality and catering providers offer a range of services.

   (b) (Describe) the services provided by an airline. [4]

   Command word

   > The text box will expand
   > the more you type
   > ↓

*Question 1 is an example of a **short-answer question**.*

***Important:** Always look at the marks allocated to each question which appears in brackets next to each question. The number of marks available will give you a good idea of how much you are expected to write for each answer. You would be expected to write more for a six-mark question compared to a three-mark, for example.*

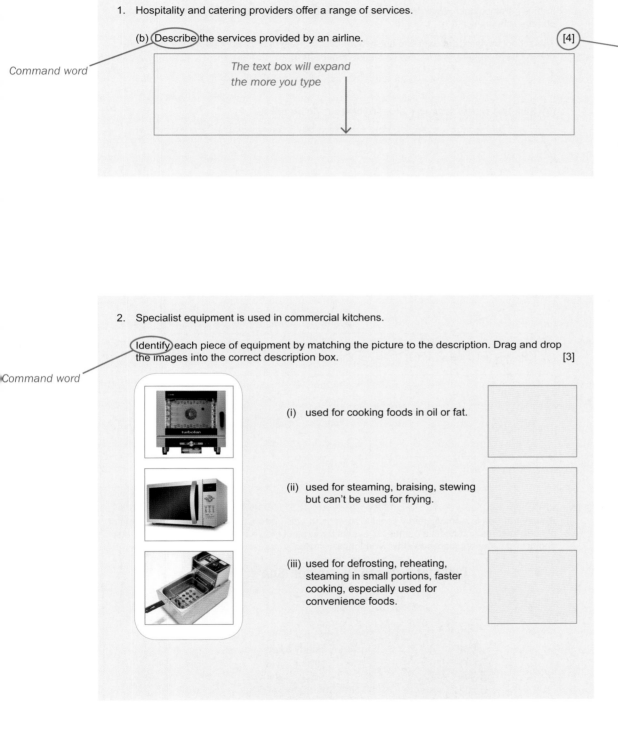

2. Specialist equipment is used in commercial kitchens.

   (Identify) each piece of equipment by matching the picture to the description. Drag and drop the images into the correct description box. [3]

   Command word

   (i) used for cooking foods in oil or fat.

   (ii) used for steaming, braising, stewing but can't be used for frying.

   (iii) used for defrosting, reheating, steaming in small portions, faster cooking, especially used for convenience foods.

*Question 2 is an example of a **stimulus question**. In the e-assessment you would need to **drag and drop** the correct image to the correct statement.*

*Question 3 is an example of a **graduated lead-in** question. These types of questions will follow on from a written statement, as you can see. The first question is normally a short answer, worth 1–2 marks, leading into longer answer questions, which are worth more, normally 4–8 marks.*
This question includes 'data', information that you need to read carefully and link your answers to.

Command words

3.   There are different types of contract of employment within the Hospitality and Catering industry.

Kate is a trained chef. She has two children who need to be dropped off and collected from primary school each day.

The school day starts at 9am and finishes at 3.25pm. Kate cannot work on weekends as she doesn't have anyone else to help look after her children.

(a) State the type of contract that would best suit Kate's needs.   [1]

(b) Describe how this contract meets Kate's needs.   [4]

(c) Kate has got a job as a chef. Describe the dress code required.   [4]

*Question 4 is an example of a **data response question**. These types of questions will include visual or written data such as a graph, recipe or newspaper article, which you will need to carefully analyse and respond to. This example shows a pie chart which contains information about a fictional place called 'Remington Spa'.*

4.   Remington Spa is a small, quirky seaside town. It attracts visitors all year round as it has lots of historic features and hosts a number of events throughout the year. It has several fish and chip shops and cafes but places to stay overnight are limited.

Types of vistor to Remington Spa

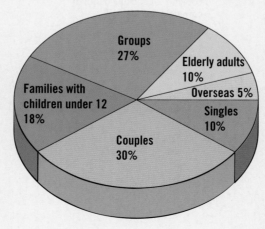

Groups 27%
Elderly adults 10%
Overseas 5%
Families with children under 12 18%
Singles 10%
Couples 30%

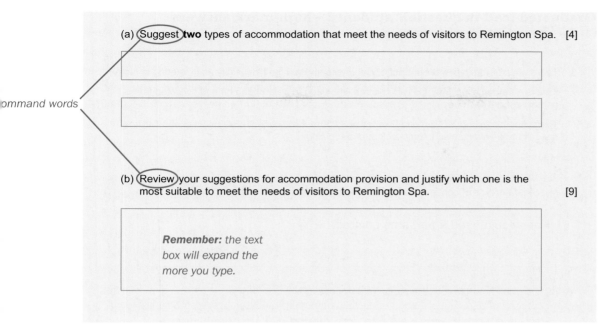

(a) (Suggest) **two** types of accommodation that meet the needs of visitors to Remington Spa. [4]

command words

(b) (Review) your suggestions for accommodation provision and justify which one is the most suitable to meet the needs of visitors to Remington Spa. [9]

> **Remember:** the text box will expand the more you type.

*Question 4b is an example of a **free response question**. These are usually longer questions with more marks available. They frequently use command words such as **justify**, **explain**, and **evaluate**. These command words will appear throughout the exam and are normally linked to questions where there are more marks available, such as this one, which is worth 9 marks.*

Worked examples

Now that we have seen the types of question that will be used in the e-assessment, we will have a look at some examples of how these questions could be answered. Below is the **graduated lead-in question** with examples of answers from two different students. The first example shows a low-mark answer and the second example demonstrates what a higher-mark answer might look like.

Graduated lead-in question: student 1 – low-mark answers

3. There are different types of contract of employment within the Hospitality and Catering industry.

Kate is a trained chef. She has two children who need to be dropped off and collected from primary school each day.

The school day starts at 9am and finishes at 3.25pm. Kate cannot work on weekends as she doesn't have anyone else to help look after her children.

(a) State the type of contract that would best suit Kate's needs. [1]

> Part-time contract ✓ [1]

(b) Describe how this contract meets Kate's needs. [4]

> Part-time will fit around picking kids up and having weekends off. ✓ [1]

Student 1 has only given one answer to question 3b. This means they have missed out on 3 marks.

(c) Kate has got a job as a chef. Describe the dress code required. [4]

> Chef hat, chef whites, apron, non-slip footwear. ✓ [2]

*This answer is a **pass**, the answers are **basic** and are **listed**. Maximum marks available are 4 but this student has only been awarded 2.*

Graduated lead-in question: student 2 – high-mark answers

3. There are different types of contract of employment within the Hospitality and Catering industry.

Kate is a trained chef. She has two children who need to be dropped off and collected from primary school each day.

The school day starts at 9am and finishes at 3.25pm. Kate cannot work on weekends as she doesn't have anyone else to help look after her children.

(a) State the type of contract that would best suit Kate's needs. [1]

> Kate would need a part-time contract ✓ [1]

(b) Describe how this contract meets Kate's needs. [4]

*Student 2 has **described** four different ways in which the contract meets Kate's needs 3(b) meaning they have **full marks** for this.*

> Part-time work means Kate can drop off and pick up her children at school, which will cut down on childcare costs ✓ for Kate. Part-time means less than 40 hours a week, ✓ which will fit around family routine. ✓ Maybe Kate can apply for working tax credit. ✓ [4]

(c) Kate has got a job as a chef. Describe the dress code required. [4]

*Student 2 has **described** the dress code in detail and has answered the question with four good responses, which means they have **full marks**.*

> Kate would need clean, ironed chef whites, worn with a clean, ironed white chef apron. ✓ She would need to wear a hair net if her hair is longer than collar length, with a chef's hat over the top. ✓ Kate would need chef trousers to match the rest of her uniform. ✓ Including black non-slip shoes and a neckerchief. ✓ [4]

Data response question: student 1 – low-mark answers

4. Remington Spa is a small, quirky seaside town. It attracts visitors all year round as it has lots of historic features and hosts a number of events throughout the year. It has several fish and chip shops and cafes but places to stay overnight are limited.

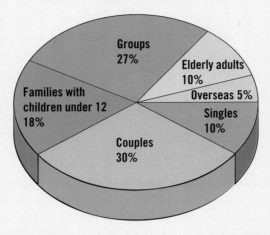

Types of vistor to Remington Spa

(a) Suggest **two** types of accommodation that meet the needs of visitors to Remington Spa. [4]

Bed and Breakfast ✓ [1]

Hotel ✓ [1]

(b) Review your suggestions for accommodation provision and justify which one is the most suitable to meet the needs of visitors to Remington Spa. [9]

> A bed and breakfast could be good for the needs of the visitors as they are cheaper than hotels, so if anyone in the group is on a budget there will be different price range for different rooms. ✓ This may be used by the groups of people who will visit, they could book up the whole B&B and have it as a group.
>
> The hotel would be good for visitors as it would be better for the families and couples. This is because they could have family rooms in the hotel, so large enough for children and parents. ✓ The couples 31% may find a hotel more special and romantic than a B&B, which can be budget. ✓
>
> I think the B&B is the best choice as it can cater for most of the visitors and would be ideal as the sizes of the room are normally different in the B&B and it would be cheaper than a hotel. ✓ [4]

*Question 4a is worth 4 marks. It is asking for **suggestions** of two types of accommodation that **meet the needs** of the visitors. This student has listed suggestions but not given details of how these will meet the needs of the visitors and has lost 2 possible extra marks.*

Student 1 has given a simple outline for reasons of choice for Question 4b. They have used information from the data chart to give basic justification (reasons why) for the choice of accommodation. Student 1 has made five basic statements and has used the information from the data and related this in the answer. This would be a Pass grade which is between 4 and 6 marks.

*Student 1 has been awarded 4 out of a possible 9 marks.

Data response question: student 2 – high-mark answers

4. Remington Spa is a small, quirky seaside town. It attracts visitors all year round as it has lots of historic features and hosts a number of events throughout the year. It has several fish and chip shops and cafes but places to stay overnight are limited.

Types of vistor to Remington Spa

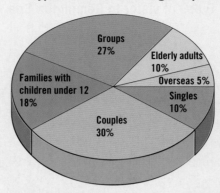

*Question 4(a) is worth 4 marks. The question is asking for **suggestions** of two types of accommodation that meets the needs of the visitors and student 2 has listed suggestions with reasons why their choices will meet the needs of the visitors. They have been awarded maximum marks available.*

(a) Suggest **two** types of accommodation that meet the needs of visitors to Remington Spa.   [4]

> Chained budget hotel ✓ will have different-sized rooms for families and couples. Could suit group visitors too due to a number of rooms on offer. ✓   [2]

> For the couples and overseas visitors a boutique hotel would be a good choice for Remington spa. ✓ This is because they may want something special and unique. ✓   [2]

*Student 2 has outlined clearly and given detailed explanations for the reasons for their choice of accommodation provision; this is based on information sourced from the chart and data. Evidence contains detailed reasons of how the provision would meet the needs of the visitors to Remington Spa. Suggestions have been communicated with a logical and clear structure. Key points have been highlighted from the data provided by the chart. Selection and rejection are evident and reasoning as to why. This answer would be a **Merit**, which is between 7 and 9 marks*.*

*Due to the detailed justification and reasoning behind student 2's choices, they have been awarded the maximum 9 marks.

(b) Review your suggestions for accommodation provision and justify which one is the most suitable to meet the needs of visitors to Remington Spa.   [9]

> I have suggested a chain budget hotel for families and OAPs, which is roughly 28% of visitors to Remington Spa. I have also suggested a unique boutique for Remington Spa. I have chosen a unique boutique hotel provision for the visitors of Remington Spa as the data clearly ✓ shows that there are a lot of couples (30%) who visit Remington Spa.
>
> This accommodation provision would be ideal; as the boutique hotel ✓ would also meet the needs of single, overseas and the couples visiting the area. (46% of visitors in total. ✓) May also appeal to the OAPs ✓ too as there would be limited families or groups staying at this provision. This would cater for 56% of visitors. ✓
>
> As it is boutique it would be unique and special for those couples wanting a romantic break away or time to relax. The boutique hotel is also less appealing to families; this would be ideal for couples as there would be less noise, more chance of a relaxing stay within the hotel. ✓ The least likely provision I would suggest is a B&B, this is because B&Bs are normally family run and quite limited with the number of rooms. ✓ Couples that are the highest visitor count to Remington Spa would probably not stay at a B&B, as it may seem less private and not romantic. ✓ The needs of a couple for hotel would be privacy, less noise, somewhere they can relax and be pampered.
>
> The boutique could offer special services such as turn-down service, spa treatments or packages linked to sightseeing and day trips in the town. ✓   [9]

The text box has expanded the more student 2 has typed.

Activity 14.1

Imagine you are a new examiner. Look at the following two example e-assessment answers from different students and mark the examples with the help of the mark scheme provided and the description of the command words listed on page 112. You will need to be prepared to explain and justify your reasons for the marks you have awarded, just like a real examiner.

Example 1

5. The James family want to stay in a hotel in London. Mr James is a wheelchair user and he has two children, one aged 6 years and the other 18 months. This is the family's first visit to the city and they want to make the most of the attractions on offer.

The Kenyon Hotel

 Air conditioning

 24-hour room service

 Concierge

 Babysitting

 Disabled accessibility

 Free Wi-Fi

 Storage of belongings after checkout

 Cots available

 Free parking

(a) Explain how the accessibility in this hotel will meet the needs of the James family. [6]

> Mr James is in a wheelchair and the hotel provides disabled accesses. Mr James would not have problems with accessing the room or hotel building.

(b) Explain how the free Wi-Fi service in this hotel will meet the needs of the James family. [4]

> - Free Wi-Fi for kids
> - Check social network sites
> - Check for family attractions
> - Check Internet for opening times

Example 2

5. The James family want to stay in a hotel in London. Mr James is a wheelchair user and he has two children, one aged 6 years and the other 18 months. This is the family's first visit to the city and they want to make the most of the attractions on offer.

The Kenyon Hotel

 Air conditioning

 24-hour room service

 Concierge

 Babysitting

 Disabled accessibility

 Free Wi-Fi

 Storage of belongings after checkout

 Cots available

 Free parking

(a) Explain how the accessibility in this hotel will meet the needs of the James family.   [6]

Mr James is wheelchair bound and would have difficulty with steps and space restrictions due to the size of the wheelchair and the amount of room needed to move around freely. The hotel offers disabled access, so this would not include steps but ramps would be used to aid with movement. There would be handrails to aid with movement in the bathroom, the possibility of a wheel-in shower or wet room available. Doorways within the hotel are wheelchair friendly, with designated disabled toilets available on the ground floor. There may be an alarm in the room or disabled toilet if Mr James is in need of help. The bedroom may contain power points and a desk of wheelchair height in order to make sure Mr James's stay is without problems.

(b) Explain how the free Wi-Fi service in this hotel will meet the needs of the James family.   [4]

The free Wi-Fi would meet the needs of the James family for several reasons. They could research online attractions that London has to offer. Use the free Wi-Fi to book these attractions or to check their email for vouchers in relation to the attractions. Possibly use websites such as Voucher code or Groupon to find the best deals for the James family. They could use the free Wi-Fi to checkout disability access within each attraction and the prices. It could meet the needs of the James family who may wish to use the Wi-Fi facilities to entertain the children by downloading a film or games apps. Helps the James family to stay connected, they could use to FaceTime/Skype relatives/Facebook or via other social networks.

Mark scheme for Activity 14.1

Question	Marks	Answers
5(a)	6	Award 1–2 marks. Outlines in general, basic explanation of how disabled accessibility meets the needs of the James family. Response is limited in detail mainly listed. Award 3–4 marks. Clear explanation of how the hotel meets the needs of the James family in relation to the disability accessibility. Statements that are relevant, with detailed reasoning to the needs met for the James family. Award 5–6 marks. Clear and detailed explanation of how the hotel meets the needs of the James family in relation to the disability accessibility. Statements that are relevant, with detailed reasoning to the needs met for the James family. Award 0 marks. No response or quality of response is not sufficient for a mark to be awarded.
5(b)	4	Award 1–2 marks. Outlines a general, basic explanation of how Wi-Fi accessibility meets the needs of the James family. Response limited in detail, mainly listed or bullet pointed. Award 3–4 marks. Clear explanation of how the hotel meets the needs of the James family in relation to the Free Wi-Fi. Statements that are relevant, with detailed reasoning to the needs met for the James family.

Peer and group work

- Discuss with the people on your table the marks you have awarded to each question and why.
- Did you award the same marks?
- Justify why you gave those marks for each question.
- After listening to your peers, would you keep your marks the same or change them?

This is what happens in the moderation process. All examiners meet and discuss the marks that they have awarded. This is to make sure that the marking is consistent and fair.

Activity 14.2   Create command word cards

Command word

Review

Review is to
explain/evaluate:
e.g. write about
and assess the
importance, quality
or value of the topic.

Word cards or flash cards are small cards to help you to remember words and what they mean.

- On one side write down the command word and on the other side write down the meaning.

- Store the cards (in your folder or bag) and when you have a spare 5 minutes you can use them to test yourself.

- Ask a friend to help you revise by showing you the front of the card and telling you if your answer is correct or not.

- You can add an image to your cards if this would help you to remember words.

Stretch and challenge

Below are three questions from an e-assessment. Write these questions down on a piece of paper. You now have **5 minutes** to highlight the different command words in each question and explain what each is asking you to do.

You then have **10 minutes** to answer the questions.

1. Name *two* responsibilities of the Environmental Health Officer. *(2 marks)*

2. Describe *one* way in which stock control is managed in a popular restaurant. *(2 marks)*

3. In 2008–2009 the UK was hit by a recession and sales in the hospitality industry decreased.
   Explain why sales within the hospitality sector could drop during a recession. *(6 marks)*

I am the examiner

- Exchange your answers to these questions with the person sitting nearest to you.

- Using the mark scheme below and the command words above, mark the questions and the command word description from the other student.

- Give a reason for your mark awarded.

- Give the question back again and explain to them why you have awarded those marks.

- Do they agree with you? If not give a logical and clear argument. You can change the marks if you feel that perhaps you have marked wrongly.

- Give both sets of answers to your teacher who will give the final mark.

Mark scheme for Stretch and challenge

Question	Marks	Answers	
1. Name *two* responsibilities of the Environmental Health Officer.	2	Award 1 mark for each correct responsibility. These could be: • Carrying out routine inspections to ensure compliance with health and safety • Providing advice and assistance to businesses • Taking photos, producing drawings • Removing samples, investigating complaints from the general public • Carrying out food hygiene and food standards inspections • Investigating accidents at work • Investigating complaints about poor standards of health and safety • Investigating outbreaks of infectious disease • Taking water samples to maintain and improve standards • Issuing licences for food providers • Advising on planning and licensing applications • Giving talks at public enquiries, meetings and exhibitions • Taking enforcement action, initiating legal proceedings • Preparing and giving evidence in court • Advising on health and safety issues in relation to new businesses	
2. Describe *one* way in which stock control is managed in a popular restaurant.	2	**Award 1 mark** Outlines in general terms (basic) – this may be in bullet points **Award 2 marks** One way stock control is managed, with a description	
3. Explain why sales within the hospitality sector could drop during the recession.	6	**Award 1–2 marks** Outlines in general (basic) the factors affecting the Hospitality and Catering industry (H&C). Response is limited in detail, mainly listed. **Award 3–4 marks** Clear explanation of how a recession could affect the Hospitality and Catering industry. Statements are included which are relevant, with detailed reasoning for the effects of a recession on the Hospitality and Catering industry. **Award 5–6 marks** In-depth explanation of the effect the recession had on the Hospitality and Catering industry. Evidence contains detailed reasoned statements, which are relevant to the effects the recession had on the Hospitality and Catering industry. **Award 0 marks** No response, or quality of response is not sufficient for a mark to be awarded.	**Example answer 1–2 marks** A recession may reduce spending on eating out/holidays/going out to pubs and clubs. **Example answer 3–4 marks** During a recession spending is restricted on luxury items/travel/eating out. People are more careful with their money. People may lose jobs during a recession, so limited spending within the Hospitality and Catering industry. Credit crunch could be mentioned, with simple explanation. H&C businesses closing down due to lack of financial support. **Example answer 5–6 marks** A recession will restrict spending by most on 'luxury' items such as holidays/eating out and breaks away. People may lose jobs during a recession, so money will not be freely available for 'luxuries' such as holidays/eating out/takeaways. It can cause a slowdown in economy, meaning less spending. Less money being spent equals jobs being lost in hospitality and catering and other industries. Credit crunch causes shortages/limited finance and disposable income, loss of confidence in financial sector. No credit being given, hospitality and catering businesses suffering as not being able to expand or be helped out during the downturn.

Chapter 15

Nutrients

What will I learn?

In this chapter you will learn about the **functions** of nutrients in the body (why the body needs them) and which foods contain them. This will help you to understand how useful different foods are when you are planning menus for groups of people with specific needs.

Key terms

- **Balanced diet** – a diet that provides a person with the right amount of nutrients for their needs

- **Diet** – the food people eat every day

- **Good nutrition** – eating a wide variety of foods (mainly plant foods), that are mostly unprocessed (whole foods) and drinking plenty of water

- **Nutrients** – natural chemical substances in foods that are essential for body growth, function and health

- **Nutrition** – the study of what people eat and how all the nutrients in foods work together in the body

- **Sources** – the foods in which nutrients are found

- **Whole foods** – foods that have not had any nutrients removed during processing

Introduction

All living things, including people, need food and water. People eat foods that come from plants (vegetables, fruits, cereal grains, nuts, beans, seeds) and animals (meat, fish, dairy foods, eggs).

Foods contain many thousands of natural substances that give them characteristics such as colour, flavour and texture. Some of these natural substances are essential for our bodies to grow, work properly and stay healthy – they are called nutrients. There are five groups of nutrients: protein, fat, carbohydrate, vitamins and minerals.

Although water is not classified as a nutrient, it is vital for the health of the body, so you will also learn about why the body needs it.

Nutrition is the study of what people eat and how all the natural substances (including nutrients) in foods *work together* in the body to enable it to grow, stay healthy and work properly.

Good nutrition throughout life enables people to stay healthy. A definition of good nutrition is:

> *Eating a wide variety of foods (mainly plant foods), that are mostly unprocessed (whole foods), and drinking plenty of water.*

The food people eat every day is called their diet. A balanced diet is one that provides a person with the right amount of nutrients for their needs. There are also special diets, e.g. a low-salt diet or a high-fibre diet.

All foods contain nutrients. The amounts of each nutrient in different foods vary considerably.

Whole foods, such as whole grain cereals (wheat, oats, rice, etc.), beans and whole milk are sometimes called 'nutrient rich' or 'nutrient dense' as they contain the most nutrients. This is because they have not had any nutrients removed by processing. For example, wholemeal flour contains every part of the wheat grains (seeds), which have been turned into flour during milling, and is nutrient dense. White flour is less nutrient dense, even though it has also been made from wheat grains. This is because it has lost some of the nutrients and fibre the wheat grains contained during the milling process, as it is sieved to remove the outer layers of the wheat grains.

Nutrient-rich foods

Some foods contain large amounts of a particular nutrient and are called a 'rich source' of that nutrient. For example, papayas, oranges, kiwi fruit, peppers (capsicums), peas, tomatoes and broccoli are all rich sources of vitamin C.

The functions of nutrients in the body AC1.1

The table below describes the functions of each of the nutrients and shows which foods contain them (the sources of nutrients). Remember that the nutrients **all work together** in the body, but to help you learn about them, they are described separately.

PROTEIN

Nutrient function (Why the body needs it)

- **Growth** of the body
- **Repair** of the body when it is injured
- Giving the body **energy**

Which foods contain it (Sources)

HBV protein foods:
meat, poultry, fish, eggs, milk, cheese, yogurt, quark, soya beans, quinoa

LBV protein foods:
beans, peas, lentils, cereals (rice, wheat, oats, barley, rye, millet, sorghum) and cereal products (bread, pasta, etc.), nuts, seeds, gelatine

High protein foods made from plants:

- Tofu, tempeh, textured vegetable protein (TVP) – all made from soya beans
- Mycoprotein – made from a high protein fungus, e.g. Quorn

Further information to help your understanding:

- Protein is made up of 'building blocks' called **amino acids**

- Some amino acids are **essential** for children and adults

- We must get **essential amino acids** ready-made from food

- Some foods contain all the essential amino acids – they are called **high biological protein foods (HBV)**

- Some foods are missing one or more of the essential amino acids – they are called **low biological protein foods (LBV)**

- If you eat two or more LBV protein foods together, you will get all the essential amino acids. This is called **protein complementation**: e.g. beans on toast, lentil soup and bread, rice and peas, nut butter on bread, rice and bean salad

Carbohydrate

Nutrient function (Why the body needs it)

- This is the main source of **energy** for the body to enable it to move, produce heat, make sound, digest food, use the brain, etc.

- Dietary fibre helps the body get rid of **waste products (faeces)** from the intestines

Further information to help your understanding:

- Carbohydrate is made by green plants during **photosynthesis**

- Plants store carbohydrates in their roots, seeds, stems, leaves and fruits

- When animals eat plants, they take in the carbohydrates stored in the plants and use them in their body

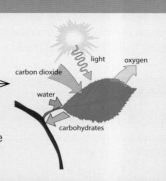

Which foods contain it (Sources)

There are two groups of carbohydrates:

Group 1 – Sugars:

- **Glucose:** ripe fruits and vegetables (e.g. apples, onions, beetroot, parsnip, sweet potato)

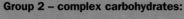

- **Fructose:** fruits, vegetables and honey

- **Galactose:** milk from mammals

- **Maltose:** barley, a syrup (malt extract), added to breakfast cereals, biscuits, hot drink powders, confectionery (sweets)

- **Sucrose:** 'sugar' from sugar cane and sugar beet is used in cooking and many processed foods, drinks and confectionery

- **Lactose:** milk and milk products

Group 2 – complex carbohydrates:

- **Starch:** cereals (e.g. wheat, rice, oats, barley, maize [corn]), cereal products (e.g. breakfast cereals, pasta, bread, cakes, pastry, biscuits); starchy vegetables (e.g. potatoes, yams, sweet potatoes, parsnip, pumpkin, butternut squash, peas, beans, lentils); seeds, quinoa

- **Pectin:** some fruits, e.g. oranges, lemons, limes, apples, apricots, plums, greengages and some root vegetables, e.g. carrots

- **Dextrin:** formed when starchy foods (e.g. bread, cakes, biscuits) are baked or toasted

- **Dietary fibre / non-starch polysaccharide (NSP):** wholegrain cereals and cereal products, e.g. breakfast cereals, bread, pasta, flour; fruits and vegetables, especially with skins left on (e.g. peas, beans, lentils); seeds, nuts

Fat

Nutrient function (Why the body needs it)

- Gives **energy** which is stored in the body under the skin and elsewhere
- **Insulates** the body from the cold
- **Protects** the bones and kidneys from physical damage
- Provides **'fat soluble' vitamins A,D,E,K**

Further information to help your understanding:

- Fats are solid at room temperature
- Oils are liquid at room temperature
- Fats and oils have the same **energy value**
- Fats and oils contain **essential fatty acids** which must come ready-made from food

Which foods contain it (Sources)

- **Essential fatty acids:**
  found in oily fish, plant oils, seeds, eggs, fresh meat

- **Solid fats**:
  e.g. butter, lard, suet, block vegetable fat, ghee, the fat in meat, palm oil, coconut and chocolate

- **Liquid plant oils:**
  e.g. olive, rapeseed, sunflower and corn; and also oily fish, avocado pears, nuts, seeds and some vegetable fat spreads

- **Visible fats and oils:**
  fats/oils in a food that you can easily see: e.g. fat in meat, oil in tuna, butter, lard, suet, block vegetable fat, ghee, plant oils such as olive, palm, sunflower oil

- **Invisible fats and oils:**
  fats/oils in a food that you cannot easily see: e.g. in cakes, pastries, potato crisps, chips, biscuits, chocolate, nuts, cheese, fried foods, meat products, etc.

Vitamins

Vitamin A (fat soluble)

Nutrient function (Why the body needs it)	Which foods contain it (Sources)
• To keep the skin healthy • To be able to see in dim light • To enable children to grow • To keep the mucus membranes that line the mouth, throat, lungs and digestive system moist and healthy • Antioxidant, which helps prevent the development of heart disease and cancers	• **Animal foods (retinol):** milk; cheese; butter; eggs; liver, kidney; oily fish, vegetable fat spreads (added by law) • **Plant foods (beta-carotene):** cabbage, spinach, kale, lettuce; peas; orange/ yellow/red vegetables and fruits (e.g. carrots, apricots, mango, papaya, peppers, tomatoes)

Vitamin D (fat soluble)

Nutrient function (Why the body needs it)	Which foods contain it (Sources)
• Helps the body absorb the mineral calcium during digestion • Helps calcium to be laid down in the bones and teeth for strength	• The action of sunlight on skin produces an important amount of vitamin D • It is also found in oily fish, meat, eggs, butter, vegetable fat spreads (added by law), fortified breakfast cereals

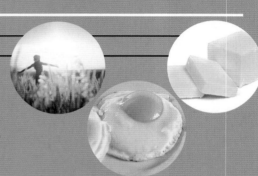

Vitamin E (fat soluble)

Nutrient function (Why the body needs it)	Which foods contain it (Sources)
• Antioxidant, which helps prevent the development of heart disease and cancers	• Soya beans, corn oil, olive oil, nuts, seeds, whole wheat, vegetable fat spreads

Vitamin K (fat soluble)

Nutrient function (Why the body needs it)	Which foods contain it (Sources)
• Helps the blood clot after an injury	• Green, leafy vegetables, liver, cheese, green tea

Vitamin B₁ (water soluble)

Nutrient function (Why the body needs it)	Which foods contain it (Sources)
• Allows energy to be released from carbohydrates in the body	• Meat, especially pork, milk, cheese, eggs, vegetables, fresh and dried fruit, wholemeal bread, fortified breakfast cereals, flour

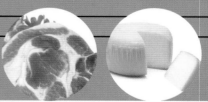

Vitamin B₂ (water soluble)

Nutrient function (Why the body needs it)	Which foods contain it (Sources)
• Allows energy to be released from carbohydrates, fats and proteins in the body	• Milk and milk products, eggs, fortified breakfast rice, mushrooms

Vitamin B₃ (water soluble)

Nutrient function (Why the body needs it)

- Allows energy to be released from carbohydrates, fats and proteins in the body

Which foods contain it (Sources)

- Beef, pork, wheat flour, maize flour, eggs, milk

Vitamin B₉ (water soluble)

Nutrient function (Why the body needs it)

- Helps to make healthy red blood cells
- Helps to prevent spinal cord defects in unborn babies, e.g. spina bifida

Which foods contain it (Sources)

- Green leafy vegetables, yeast extract (e.g. Marmite); peas, chickpeas, asparagus; wholegrain rice; fruits; added to some breads and breakfast cereals

Vitamin B₁₂ (water soluble)

Nutrient function (Why the body needs it)

- Helps to make healthy red blood cells
- Helps to make healthy nerve cells

Which foods contain it (Sources)

- Liver, meat, fish, cheese, fortified breakfast cereals, yeast

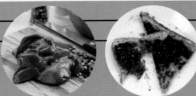

Vitamin C (water soluble)

Nutrient function (Why the body needs it)

- Helps the body to absorb the mineral iron during digestion
- Helps to maintain connective tissue, which binds body cells together
- Antioxidant, which helps prevent the development of heart disease and cancers

Which foods contain it (Sources)

- Fruits and vegetables, especially citrus fruits (e.g. oranges, lemons, limes and grapefruit), blackcurrants, kiwi fruit, guavas, Brussels sprouts, cabbage, broccoli, new potatoes, milk, liver

Minerals

Calcium

Nutrient function (Why the body needs it)

- Helps to make and strengthen **bones** and **teeth**

- Makes **nerves** and **muscles** work

- Helps **blood to clot** after an injury

Which foods contain it (Sources)

- Milk, cheese, yogurt; green leafy vegetables; canned fish; enriched soya drinks; white flour (added by law)

Iron

Nutrient function (Why the body needs it)

- Makes **haemoglobin** in **red blood cells** to pick up and carry **oxygen** to all body cells in order to produce **energy**

- Prevents **iron deficiency anaemia**

Which foods contain it (Sources)

- Red meat, kidney, liver; wholemeal bread, added by law to wheat flour (except wholemeal); green leafy vegetables (e.g. watercress, spinach, cabbage); egg yolk; dried apricots; lentils; cocoa, plain chocolate; curry powder; fortified breakfast cereals

Sodium

Nutrient function (Why the body needs it)

- Controls the amount of **water** in the body

- Makes **nerves** and **muscles** work properly

Which foods contain it (Sources)

- Salt (**sodium** chloride); salted foods; cheese, yeast extract, stock cubes, gravies and seasonings, snack foods (e.g. crisps), canned fish, bacon, ham, dried fish, soy sauce, salted butter, fast foods and many ready meals; baking powder (cakes, biscuits, baked desserts); takeaway foods

Fluoride

Nutrient function (Why the body needs it)

- Strengthens **tooth enamel** and bones

- Helps to prevent tooth decay

Which foods contain it (Sources)

- Seafood, fish, tea, some water supplies

Iodine

Nutrient function (Why the body needs it)

- Makes the hormone called **thyroxin** in the thyroid gland (in the neck) to control the **metabolic rate** (the speed of chemical reactions in the body)

Which foods contain it (Sources)

- Seafood, vegetables, dairy foods

Phosphorus

Nutrient function (Why the body needs it)

- Helps to make strong **bones and teeth**

- Helps to release **energy from food** in the body

- Makes **cell membranes**, especially in the brain

Which foods contain it (Sources)

- Found in a wide range of foods

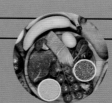

Water

What water does in the body (its functions)

- Controls body temperature to keep it at 37°C
- It is needed for thousands of chemical reactions in the body
- It removes waste products from body
- It keeps the mucous membranes moist and healthy
- It keeps the skin moist and healthy
- It is needed for all body fluids, e.g. blood, joints, etc.
- It is found in all body cells

Further information to help your understanding:

- Heat is removed from the body by sweating
- Waste products leave the body in the urine (made in the kidneys) and faeces (made in the large intestine)
- Water controls the concentration of substances (e.g. sodium) in the blood

Which foods contain it (Sources)

- Drinking water (tap water)
- Naturally found in many foods – milk, milk products, fruit, vegetables, meat, fish, eggs
- Added to many foods – soup, sauces, pastries, breads, boiled rice, pasta, beans, pulses, etc.

Further information to help your understanding:

- Tap water is good quality and safe to drink in the UK and much cheaper than bottled water
- Discarded plastic water bottles have a major impact on environmental sustainability and pollution

What happens if you do not have enough water (dehydration)

- You become thirsty
- A headache often starts
- **Dehydration** – the urine becomes very dark in colour
- You feel weak and sick
- The body overheats
- You become confused
- The blood pressure and heart rate change

Further information to help your understanding:

- Headaches may be caused because the blood has become too concentrated
- The urine is a good indicator of dehydration:

1		Good
2		Good
3		Fair
4		Dehydrated
5		Dehydrated
6		Very dehydrated
7		Severe dehydration

- Chemical reactions in the body may be affected
- If the body rises above 37°C, this is dangerous
- The brain becomes affected by lack of water
- The volume of the blood decreases, which affects the blood pressure and heart rate

What happens if you have too much water

- Substances in the blood become over-diluted
- Vital organs in the body start to fail, e.g. heart, kidneys
- May cause death

Further information to help your understanding:

- It is a rare cause of death, but it has happened to some people who have done a lot of exercise and then had a lot of water to drink in one go

What is the recommended amount of water per day

- In the UK: 1–2 litres of water or other fluids a day (6–8 average glasses)

Further information to help your understanding:

- More water will be needed in hotter climates and when doing a lot of physical activity

Put it into practice

Plan and make a two-course lunch for two people in their early twenties.

One of the two people has iron deficiency anaemia and has been advised by their doctor to try to obtain more iron in their diet.

Explain how you will ensure that the meal is nutritionally balanced and how you have catered for the person with anaemia.

Activity 15.1

Match each nutrient function to the correct nutrient:

Function	Which nutrient?
Repairs the body when injured	Iron
The main source of energy for the body	Iodine
Insulates the body from the cold	Protein
Helps you see in dim light	Vitamin C
Helps the body absorb calcium	Vitamin B$_{12}$
Helps the body release energy from carbohydrates	Sodium
Helps prevent spinal cord defects in unborn babies	Phosphorus
Helps make healthy nerve cells	Fluoride
Helps the body absorb iron	Carbohydrate
Makes haemoglobin in red blood cells	Vitamin A
Controls the amount of water in the body	Fat
Strengthens tooth enamel	Vitamin B$_9$
Makes the hormone thyroxin	Vitamin D
Makes cell membranes in the brain	Vitamin B$_1$

Scenario

A new chef has been employed in a primary school to cook meals for the children and teaching staff. The school wants to increase the number of children eating cooked meals provided by the school, and the chef has been asked to provide a menu that is appealing to the children as well as being nutritionally balanced.

Design a lunch menu for five school days. There should be a vegetarian option available each day.

Explain how you have made sure that the menu is nutritionally balanced and why you think it will appeal to children.

Practice questions

1. Explain what a 'balanced diet' means. *(1 mark)*

2. Why are whole foods described as being 'nutrient dense'? *(1 mark)*

3. Give three reasons why water is essential in the diet. *(3 marks)*

Stretch and challenge

1. Explain, with reasons, how you can ensure that a vegetarian meal provides all the essential amino acids. Give two examples in your answer. *(4 marks)*

2. Explain, with reasons, why a person may not realise that they are consuming a lot of fat when they choose to eat biscuits, cakes, chips and pastries. *(3 marks)*

3. There are two vitamins which each help the body to absorb a different mineral during digestion. Which are they and what do they do in the body? *(4 marks)*

LO1 Understand the importance of nutrition when planning menus

You have learned about the nutrients that are found in different foods and why the body needs them. In this chapter you will learn about the nutritional needs of specific groups of people at different life stages and the dietary guidelines and Eatwell Guide that have been produced by the government to help people choose what to eat. This information will help you to plan menus for different people.

What will I learn?

Key term

Life stages – stages of development that people go through during their life: i.e. infancy (babyhood), childhood, adolescence (teenagers), adulthood and later adulthood

Dietary guidelines:

1. Base your meals on starchy foods

2. Eat lots of fruit and vegetables

3. Eat more fish – including a portion of oily fish each week

4. Cut down on saturated fat and sugar

5. Eat less salt – no more than 6g (1 level teaspoon) a day for adults

6. Get active and be a healthy weight

7. Don't get thirsty – drink plenty of water

8. Don't skip breakfast

(Source: Public Health England '8 tips for eating well', 2016)

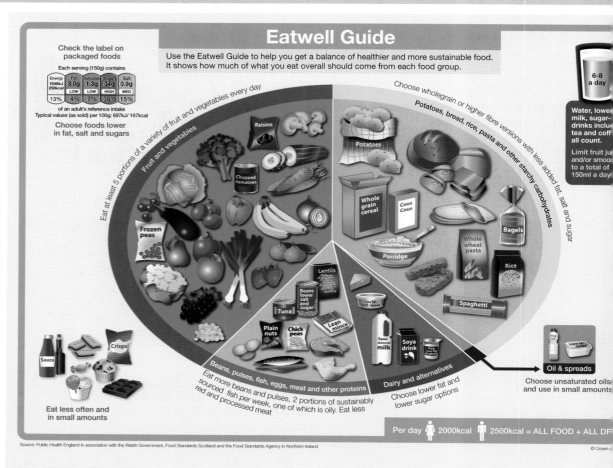

The Eatwell Guide

- The Eatwell Guide is based on the five food groups.

- The size of the segments for each of the food groups shown in the Eatwell Guide matches the government's recommendations for a diet that would provide all the nutrients needed by a healthy adult or child over the age of 5 years.

- From the age of 2–5 years, children should gradually start eating a greater variety of foods as shown in the Eatwell Guide.

The Eatwell Guide also recommends that:

- Sweet, salty and fatty foods such as crisps, chips, cakes, biscuits, chocolate, ice cream and sauces should be eaten less often and in smaller amounts.

- People should drink 6–8 cups or glasses of fluid a day (water, lower fat milk, sugar-free drinks, unsweetened tea/coffee). Fruit juice and/or smoothies should be limited to 150ml a day.

- People should check the nutritional labels on packaged foods and choose foods lower in fat, salt and sugars.

Nutritional needs of specific groups of people (AC1.2)

Pre-school children 1–4 years

Body growth and development are rapid at this stage.

A lot of energy is used in physical activity.

Nutritional needs

- All nutrients are important, especially protein, vitamins and minerals
- Limit the amount of free sugars and salt in foods and drinks

Children 5–12 years

Growth continues in 'spurts'.

Children should be physically active most of the time, but increasing numbers become sedentary (inactive) if they use computers, social media or watch TV a lot, which can lead to them becoming overweight or obese.

Nutritional needs

- All nutrients are important especially protein, vitamins and minerals
- Limit the amount of free sugars and salt in foods and drinks

Adolescents (teenagers)

The body grows rapidly at certain times and develops from a child into an adult.

This is an important life stage when minerals are taken into the bones and teeth so that the skeleton reaches peak bone mass when they are adults.

Girls start to menstruate (have periods), which may mean they do not have enough iron and become anaemic.

Staying up late and pressures of school may lead to lack of energy, poor concentration and tiredness.

Nutritional needs

- Protein, vitamins A, B group, C, D, E, carbohydrate (starch and fibre; limit free sugars), fats – especially essential fatty acids, all minerals
- Calcium and vitamin D
- Iron and vitamin C
- Vitamin B group, iron and vitamin C

Key terms

- **Free sugars** – sugars, honeys, syrups and fruit juices/concentrates that are added to foods and drinks by manufacturers, cooks/chefs and consumers to sweeten them during preparation, processing, cooking and serving

- **Peak bone mass** – when bones have the maximum amount of minerals and are at their strongest and most dense

Adults

The body does not grow any more in height after approximately 21 years of age.

The body needs to be maintained to keep it free from disease, strong and active.

The metabolic rate gradually slows down.

Weight gain can occur if the energy intake of the diet is unbalanced and insufficient physical activity is taken.

The skeleton continues to take up minerals until peak bone mass is reached at around 30 years of age.

Women continue to menstruate (have periods) until the menopause (approximately late 40s to early 50s), which may mean they do not have enough iron and become anaemic.

Nutritional needs

- Protein, vitamins A, B group, C, D, E, carbohydrate (starch and fibre; limit free sugars), fats – especially essential fatty acids, all minerals

- Calcium and vitamin D

- Iron and vitamin C

Older adults

Body systems such as digestion, blood circulation, etc., start to slow down.

Blood pressure may increase.

The body needs to be maintained to keep it free from disease, strong and active.

The metabolic rate gradually slows down, so weight gain may happen if energy balance is wrong.

The appetite usually gets smaller.

The sense of smell and taste may be lost.

Short- and long-term memory may become poor.

The eyesight may weaken.

The skeleton gradually starts to lose minerals and become weakened, which becomes worse in women after the menopause. This can develop into osteoporosis in men and women.

Nutritional needs

- Protein, vitamins A, B group, C, D, E, carbohydrate (starch and fibre; limit free sugars), fats – especially essential fatty acids, all minerals
- Iron and vitamin C: (especially women) to avoid scurvy (see page 143) and anaemia (see page 144)

- B group vitamins: to help the body use energy and to help prevent memory loss
- Vitamins A, C and E: to help prevent age-related eye conditions
- Calcium/vitamin D

Special diets for different food choices and medical conditions

If a person has a medical condition or chooses to eat a particular diet for health, religious or other reasons, there will be certain foods they can eat and others that they should avoid, as shown in the chart below:

Type of diet	Reason for following this diet	Foods that can be eaten	Foods to avoid
Vegan	Health, religious, ethical or other	All plant foods Protein alternatives: tofu, tempeh, TVP	All animal foods including fish and shellfish
Lacto-ovo vegetarian	Health, religious, ethical or other	All plant foods Milk and dairy foods, eggs	Any animal food where the animal has been killed, including fish and shellfish
Lacto vegetarian	Health, religious, ethical or other	All plant foods Milk and dairy foods	Any animal food where the animal has been killed, including fish and shellfish, eggs
Gluten free	Coeliac disease	Rice, rice products, soya, maize (corn), cassava (tapioca), linseeds, polenta, beans, peas, lentils, quinoa, sorghum, agar, nuts	Wheat and wheat products, bread, cakes, biscuits, pastries, barley, oats, rye products
Lactose free	Lactose intolerance	Specially produced lactose-free dairy products All foods with no dairy in them	Milk, milk products (cream, yogurt, cheese, butter), foods containing milk products
High fibre	Diseases of the intestines, e.g. constipation, diverticular disease	Fruits, vegetables, wholegrain cereals, breads, pasta, rice, peas, beans, lentils	White flour and white flour products, white rice, smooth fruit juice
Low sugar	Diabetes, weight reduction diet	Fresh vegetables and fruit, milk, unsweetened milk products	Free sugars that have been added to cakes, biscuits, drinks, confectionery, desserts, sauces, ice cream, breakfast cereals, honey, syrup, jam, etc.
Fat reduced	Heart disease, weight reduction diet	Naturally low-fat foods, e.g. fruits, vegetables, cereals, white fish, fat reduced cheese, spreads, milk, etc.	Full-fat dairy foods, pastries, meats, crisps, chips, doughnuts, cakes, biscuits, fried foods, desserts, ice cream
Low sodium (salt)	Heart disease, high blood pressure, kidney disease	Fruits, vegetables, milk, eggs, poultry, unprocessed meat	Yeast extract, cheese, dried fish, canned fish, soy sauce, ketchup, pickles, ready meals, snack foods, cakes, biscuits, scones, ham, bacon, processed meats, e.g. sausages

Key terms

- **Lacto-ovo vegetarian** – a person who chooses to eat only plant foods and milk, milk products and eggs, but no meat, poultry or fish

- **Lacto vegetarian** – a person who chooses to eat only plant foods and milk and milk products, but no eggs, meat, poultry or fish

- **Vegan** – a person who chooses to eat only plant foods and no animal foods

Nutritional needs for different activity levels

Key terms

- Basal Metabolic Rate – the amount of energy needed to keep a person alive and their body working normally. It varies according to age, gender, body size, their Physical Activity Level (PAL)

- Physical Activity Level – how physically active someone is and the amount of energy they need

Energy is needed by the body for:

- Growth
- Movement
- Body warmth
- Production of sound
- Brain function.

Energy comes from foods and drinks that contain carbohydrate, fat and protein.

Glucose (a sugar) is the form of carbohydrate which is used in the body for energy.

Fat is a store of energy in the body and some of it is converted into glucose when there is not enough carbohydrate available.

Protein is only used for energy if there is not enough carbohydrate or fat available.

The recommended amount of energy from different nutrients each day for an average, healthy person is as follows:

- **Carbohydrate**: 50%
- **Fat**: 35% or less
- **Protein**: 15%

For carbohydrate, most energy should come from starch and sugars naturally found in foods and milk.

No more than 5% should come from natural fruit sugars and free sugars added to foods.

Too much energy consumed leads to weight gain.

Too little energy consumed leads to weight loss.

The amount of energy needed by people is influenced by:

- A person's Basal Metabolic Rate (BMR)
- How **active** someone is (their Physical Activity Level – PAL).

Physical activity reduces the risk of someone developing a range of diet-related diseases, e.g. obesity and heart disease. It also improves the strength of their skeleton and muscles and keeps their brain alert.

Physically active people, e.g. athletes, builders, farmers, need enough food every day to give them sufficient energy for their BMR and their PAL. Athletes and sports teams often employ dietitians to plan a healthy diet that provides sufficient energy for their needs.

Sedentary people (people who are not very physically active), who are, e.g., working all day at a computer or driving a vehicle, need to limit the amount of energy they have from food in order to prevent weight gain.

Put it into practice

Plan a day's meals for a young adult who is going to run in a marathon in a week's time, and who does training runs for two hours every day.

Explain how you have ensured that the meals are healthy and well balanced and have sufficient energy for their needs.

Scenario

A chef is asked to plan a lunchtime buffet menu for a conference on coeliac disease. Many of the delegates who will be attending the conference are coeliacs.

Suggest a range of ten menu items for the buffet that will be suitable for all delegates.

Practice questions

1. Which nutrients are especially important for the following?

a) Helping to prevent memory loss in elderly people. *(1 mark)*

b) Helping to prevent age-related eye conditions. *(3 marks)*

c) Reaching peak bone mass in adulthood. *(2 marks)*

d) Preventing anaemia in adolescents. *(2 marks)*

2. For each of the following special diets, list two foods that someone should avoid eating:

a) Low-fat diet. *(2 marks)*

b) Low-salt diet. *(2 marks)*

c) Vegan diet. *(2 marks)*

d) Lactose intolerance. *(2 marks)*

Stretch and challenge

Choose **two** of the following dietary guidelines for healthy eating and find out and explain, with reasons, why they have been given. *(4 marks each for the two chosen guidelines)*

1. Base your meals on starchy foods.

2. Eat lots of fruit and vegetables.

3. Eat more fish – including a portion of oily fish each week.

4. Cut down on saturated fat and sugar.

5. Eat less salt – no more than 6g (1 level teaspoon) a day for adults.

6. Get active and be a healthy weight.

7. Don't get thirsty – drink plenty of water.

8. Don't skip breakfast.

LO1 Understand the importance of nutrition when planning menus

What will I learn?

You have learned about the nutrients and why the body needs them at different life stages. In this chapter you will learn about what happens to the body if it does not have enough or has too much of each nutrient.

The body needs to have just the right amount of nutrients each day to make sure that it grows properly, works correctly and stays healthy. Having too little of a nutrient is called a **nutritional deficiency** and having too much of a nutrient is called an **excess**. For both of these situations, visible signs may develop after a period of time to show that all is not well with the body, e.g. marks on the skin, weight gain or weight loss, bent legs or arms. Non-visible signs may also develop and these can only be detected by medical tests, e.g. x-rays, blood tests, body scans. The person with the deficiency or excess is likely to feel unwell and will not be able to function normally.

People who plan and prepare meals for others need to be aware of the problems and signs associated with nutritional deficiencies and excesses. This is especially important for vulnerable groups of people such as babies and children, elderly adults, people who have been unwell and people with a health condition such as coeliac disease or diabetes.

It is advisable to seek medical advice before taking nutrient supplements, as it is easy to take too many, which could be dangerous for the body.

The characteristics of unsatisfactory nutritional intake AC1.3

The chart below shows what happens to the body if it has too little or too much of a nutrient and the visible and non-visible signs that would happen in the body.

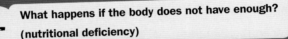

NUTRIENT — What happens if the body does not have enough? (nutritional deficiency)

+ What happens if the body has too much? (nutritional excess)

PROTEIN

Visible signs

A deficiency of protein is rare in the UK, but signs of deficiency are:

- **Children do not grow properly**, because the body cannot grow new cells, bones, etc., without the right amount of protein
- **Hair becomes thin and falls out**, because hair is not essential to how the body works, so it will stop hair from growing if it is short of protein
- **Poor skin and weak nails**, because skin and nails both contain protein, they will weaken without enough protein in the diet

Non-visible signs

- **Infections will develop and make the person very ill**, because the body's immune system, which naturally fights infections that enter the body, needs protein to help it do so
- **Food is not digested properly**, because the digestive system becomes weak without enough protein

Visible signs

- Some excess protein is stored as body fat
- This can lead to weight gain and obesity

Non-visible signs

- Excess protein puts a strain on how well the liver and kidneys work

FAT

A deficiency of fat is rare in the UK, but signs of deficiency are:

Visible signs

- **Weight loss**, because if it does not have enough energy from food, the body will gradually use up the stores of fat in the body to release energy from them

- The person will then **feel cold** because fat stored under the skin helps to insulate the body from the cold

Non-visible signs

- **Bruising of the bones** if they are accidentally knocked, because they are not protected by a layer of fat

- **Lack of vitamins A, D, E and K,** which are supplied by foods containing fat

An excess intake of fat is common in many countries, including the UK and causes several problems:

Visible signs

- Excess fat is stored as body fat under the skin in adipose tissue cells, which leads to health conditions and diseases such as weight gain, obesity, type 2 diabetes, heart disease, high blood pressure, shortage of breath

Non-visible signs

- Internal body organs, such as the liver, store fat in them, which stops them working properly

- Other parts inside the body, e.g. the intestines, can become surrounded by fat, which stops them working properly

- Fat can block up arteries, which stops blood flowing properly to the heart and can lead to coronary heart disease

CARBOHYDRATE

A deficiency of carbohydrate is rare in the UK, but signs of deficiency are:

Visible signs

- **Lack of energy**, tiredness, because carbohydrate is the main source of energy for the body

- **Weight loss**, because the body will use up its fat stores to release energy from them

- Severe weakness

Non-visible signs

- Not enough fibre from wholegrain carbohydrate foods, fruits and vegetables will lead to constipation and other intestinal problems

An excess intake of carbohydrate is common in many countries, including the UK, and causes several problems:

Visible signs

- Excess carbohydrate that is not used for energy is stored as fat, which leads to weight gain and obesity

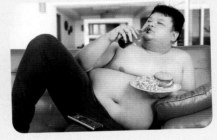

Non-visible signs

- Frequently eating too many **refined and processed carbohydrates** (e.g. white bread, doughnuts, biscuits, cakes, potatoes, white rice, pasta, etc.) and **free sugars** (e.g. sugar, sugary foods, sweet soft drinks, biscuits, cakes) can lead to tooth decay, raised blood sugar levels and type 2 diabetes

VITAMINS

A

−

Visible signs
- Dry and infected skin and mucus membranes
- Poor growth in children

Non-visible signs
- Dry and infected mucus membranes
- **Night blindness** leading to total blindness

+
- Excess vitamin A is poisonous, especially to unborn babies, e.g. if too much is taken by the mother in food or in supplements

D

−

Visible signs
- Bones weaken and bend because not enough calcium is being absorbed to strengthen them
- This condition is called **rickets** in children and **osteomalacia** in adults

+
- Excess vitamin D can cause too much calcium to be absorbed into the body, which will affect the kidneys and other organs. It is rare.

E

−
- A deficiency is rare

+

K

−
- A deficiency is rare, but may happen in newborn babies, who are given some vitamin K when they are born to prevent this

+

B₁

−

Visible signs
- A condition called **beriberi** can develop, which affects how the nerves and muscles work

+

B₂

−

Visible signs
- A deficiency is rare, but can lead to sores at the corners of the mouth

+

B₃

−

Visible signs
- A condition called **pellagra** can develop, which can cause diarrhoea, dementia (unable to think or remember properly) and dermatitis (skin sores and infections)

+

VITAMINS

B9

Invisible signs

- A condition called **megaloblastic anaemia** can develop, which causes the red blood cells to become too big. This means they cannot work properly to deliver oxygen to the cells of the body

- Possibly **spina bifida** will develop in unborn babies, which may affect the baby's ability to sit and walk properly and can cause brain damage

B12

Invisible signs

- A condition called **pernicious anaemia** can reduce the amount of vitamin B$_{12}$ the body can absorb, and this affects how well the red blood cells can work

C

Visible signs

- Bleeding under the skin – which shows as red spots under the skin

- Loose teeth, which can then fall out because the gums have weakened

- Wounds not healing properly

- The condition is called **scurvy**

Invisible signs

- **Iron deficiency anaemia** due to not absorbing enough of the mineral iron – this leads to tiredness and weakness

MINERALS

CALCIUM

Visible signs

- The bones in the legs and arms bend because they are weak, which in later life can lead to a condition called osteoporosis

Invisible signs

- The bones and teeth weaken
- Nerves and muscles don't work properly
- Blood will not clot and form a scab after an injury

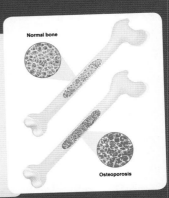

IRON

Visible signs

A condition called **iron deficiency anaemia** develops which causes:

- Pale skin complexion and pale pink colour inside the eyelids
- Weak and spilt nails
- Tiredness and lack of energy
- Weakness

Excess iron is poisonous if too much taken, e.g. in supplements

SODIUM

Visible signs

- Muscle cramps

Excess sodium (salt) can lead to high blood pressure and heart and blood vessel disease

FLUORIDE

Invisible signs

- A deficiency of fluoride can lead to weak tooth enamel, which means there is more chance of tooth decay

Excess fluoride may lead to discoloured teeth, which develop brown bands on them

IODINE

Visible signs

- A condition called a goitre develops as a swelling in the neck. It is caused by the thyroid gland enlarging

PHOSPHORUS

A deficiency is rare

Practice questions

1. List three visible/non-visible signs that show that a child has a protein deficiency. *(3 marks)*

2. Name three health conditions that can develop if someone has too much fat in their diet. *(3 marks)*

3. Give two signs of iron deficiency anaemia. *(2 marks)*

4. What is the name of the condition where the bones in the arms and legs bend, and the names of the vitamin and mineral that are involved in its development? *(3 marks)*

Stretch and challenge

1. Using your knowledge about nutrients and life stages, explain (with reasons), why people are advised to limit the amount of fat and sugar they eat over a period of time. *(6 marks)*

2. Using your knowledge about nutrients and life stages, explain the reasons for the development of the following health conditions:

   a) Scurvy *(5 marks)*

   b) Rickets *(5 marks)*

   c) Obesity *(5 marks)*

Chapter 18

The impact of cooking methods on nutritional value

LO1 Understand the importance of nutrition when planning menus

What will I learn?

An important part of the skill of food preparation and cooking is to understand how different cooking methods affect the nutritional value of foods, and to use methods that conserve (save) nutrients and enhance (improve) how they are digested and absorbed by the body. In this chapter, you will learn how this can be put into practice when preparing and cooking meals for people.

Key terms

- **Coagulated** – the heat causes lots of denatured proteins to join together and change the appearance and texture of food, e.g. when an egg is cooked, the white changes from a clear liquid to a white solid and the yolk changes from a liquid to a solid

- **Denatured** – the heat has caused protein to change its chemical nature

- **Gelatinised** – the heat causes the starch granules in the food, e.g. in a white sauce, to swell with the water they have absorbed, and the sauce starts to thicken. When the sauce reaches boiling point, the granules burst and release the starch – this is called gelatinisation

Foods, such as fruit and vegetables, contain the most nutrients at the point when they are harvested. The longer they are stored and exposed to the air before being eaten, the more nutrients, such as vitamins, they will lose. Some nutrients are easily lost during food preparation or damaged by heat during cooking, and therefore cannot be used by the body. Some other nutrients become much easier for the body to use when the food they are in is cooked.

How cooking methods affect nutrients in food **AC1.4**

Different cooking methods use water, oil or dry heat to transfer heat to foods. The chart below shows how different cooking methods affect nutrients in food:

Cooking method	How nutrients are affected
Boiling	• Up to 50% of vitamin C is damaged when green vegetables are boiled in water • Vitamins B_1, B_2 and B_3 are damaged by heat and also dissolve in the water • Some calcium and sodium dissolves in the water that food is boiled in • Starch (carbohydrate) is gelatinised when cooked in a liquid, which makes it easier for the body to use
Steaming	• Steaming is the best method for conserving vitamin C, as only about 15% is lost because the food does not come into direct contact with the boiling water
Poaching	• Vitamins B_1, B_2 and B_3 are damaged by heat and dissolve in the water
Baking	• The high heat used in baking can easily over-cook protein and damage B vitamins and vitamin C
Grilling	• When food such as meat is grilled, up to 40% of B vitamins can be damaged • The high heat used in grilling can easily over-cook protein
Stir frying	• The fat used in stir frying increases amount of vitamin A the body can absorb from some vegetables • The heat will damage some vitamin C and B vitamin but, as they are only cooked for a short time, the damage is minimal
Roasting	• The high heat used in roasting will destroy most of the vitamin C and some B vitamins
All cooking methods	• Protein is denatured and coagulated by heat, which makes it easier for the body to use • Protein can be over-cooked, which will make it harder and more difficult for the body to use • Fat/oil is damaged by repeatedly being heated to fry foods, and it breaks down into substances that are harmful to the body

Practical tips

When you are cooking, you can reduce the amount of loss and damage to nutrients in a variety of ways.

During food storage:

- Store food away from heat and light
- Store food in airtight containers
- Store food for as little time as possible

During food preparation:

- Avoid buying damaged and bruised fruits and vegetables as some of their nutrients will have been destroyed
- Cut, grate, squeeze and chop fruits and vegetables just before cooking and serving
- If possible, avoid peeling fruits and vegetables as many of the nutrients are found just under the skin and will be lost if it is removed

During cooking:

- Use only a little water for cooking, so only small amounts of nutrients dissolve in the water
- Boil the water first, then add the foods so that they start to cook quickly
- Cook (simmer) vegetables for a minimum time until they are just tender
- Steaming, instead of boiling vegetables, saves more vitamins
- Serve cooked food straightaway – avoid keeping the food hot as more nutrients will be destroyed
- Save the cooking water from vegetables and use it in gravy/soup/sauces
- Cook meat and fish for the shortest time possible so that the protein they contain is tender and not over-cooked
- Oil that is used for frying should be changed frequently

You will learn more about different cooking methods and foods that are suitable to be cooked by each of them in Chapter 25.

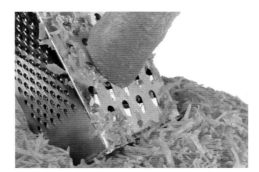

Put it into practice

Make a batch of burger mixture using 500g of, e.g., minced beef, lamb or pork. Add a finely chopped onion and a little salt and pepper to season it.

Divide the mixture into four equal-sized pieces.

Shape each piece into a burger – make sure all four burgers are the same size, shape and thickness.

Cook the burgers as follows:

Burger #1. In a frying pan with a little oil until cooked through to the centre – turn the burger over several times during cooking.

Burger #2. In the oven – gas 5/ 190°C for approximately 15–20 minutes until cooked through to the centre.

Burger #3. In the microwave oven for 3–5 minutes until cooked through to the centre.

Burger #4. Under the grill for 8–10 minutes on one side, then turn it over and cook for 8–10 minutes on the other side, until cooked through to the centre.

Save any juices that come from each burger.

Analyse the results:

1. What has happened to the size, shape and colour of each burger?

2. Which looks the most appetising and why?

3. Comment on the flavour and texture of each burger and how many juices have been produced.

4. Which cooking method is likely to have caused the most and the least nutrient damage and why?

5. Which cooking method for burgers would you recommend and why?

Practice questions

1. List two vitamins that are damaged by heat. *(2 marks)*

2. Name two vitamins that dissolve in water. *(2 marks)*

3. a) Describe what happens to a raw egg when it is cooked. *(2 marks)*

   b) Which nutrient is responsible for the changes when the egg is cooked? *(1 mark)*

4. Why is steaming a good choice of cooking method for green vegetables such as broccoli and cabbage? *(3 marks)*

Stretch and challenge

1. Explain, in detail, what would happen to the protein in a piece of meat that was cooked for too long, at too high a temperature under the grill. *(4 marks)*

2. Explain, with reasons, why and how making a white sauce makes the carbohydrate it contains more useful to the body. *(4 marks)*

3. Describe and explain how you would store, prepare, cook and serve fresh green vegetables (e.g. Brussels sprouts, broccoli, cabbage, kale) in a way that would conserve as much vitamin C as possible. *(4 marks)*

LO2 Understand menu planning

Menus

A **menu** is a list of food items (dishes) that are prepared by restaurants and other catering businesses and offered to customers to choose a meal from.

Menus are usually planned for a set period of time, e.g. a day, a week, a month, then they are changed. This adds variety to keep returning customers interested and prevents boredom for the chefs.

To be 'customer friendly', menus need to:

- Be easy to read and understand
- Be clearly set out
- Have clear descriptions/images of the menu items.

A menu should include the following information:

- The name of each food item
- A description of each food item and its accompaniments
- Food allergy/intolerance advice
- Suitability for specific groups, e.g. vegetarians, religious groups
- The price of each menu item.

What will I learn?

In this chapter you will apply the information that you have learned so far in Units 1 and 2 to learning how catering businesses choose dishes when planning menus.

Activity 19.1

Find each of the types of information on the following sample menu:

Menu

Starters

Cream of mushroom soup V £ 4.95
Served with wholegrain bread roll and butter
A Contains cream

Prawn salad £ 6.95
Served with wholegrain bread and butter
A Contains seafood

Liver paté and salad £ 5.95
Served with wholegrain toasted bread
A Contains butter

Spiced hummus Vg £ 4.95
Served with wholegrain toasted bread
A Contains fresh chilli pepper

Mains

Homemade chicken and leek pie £ 11.95
Free-range, locally produced pieces of chicken encased in a leek and white sauce, with a flaky pastry lid Served with a choice of vegetables in season and creamed potatoes
(Halal chicken available – please ask the waiter)
A Contains cream and butter

Roasted pork steak with apple sauce £ 10.95
Locally produced pork steak, served with roasted root vegetables, crackling, savoy cabbage and gravy
A Gravy contains wheat flour

Bean casserole Vg £ 9.95
A comforting winter vegetable casserole made with cannellini, butter and kidney beans, chickpeas, tomatoes, garlic, leeks and root vegetables. Served with a choice of crusty bread, jacket potato or roasted potatoes.
A Contains celery

Desserts

Raspberry and chocolate cheesecake V £ 5.95
A delicious combination of dark chocolate and fresh raspberries on a chocolate biscuit base, drizzled with raspberry coulis
A Contains cream, cream cheese, butter and eggs

Lemon posset V £ 4.95
A velvety, smooth dessert served with homemade ginger shortbread bites
A Contains cream and butter

Apple crumble V £ 4.95
Made with our own home-grown apples and served with a choice of custard, ice cream or cream
A Crumble may contain traces of nuts

A = Allergy/food intolerance advice
V = Suitable for lacto-ovo vegetarians
Vg = Suitable for vegans

In the catering industry, there are different types of menus, as shown below.

À la carte

Description

- All the food items/dishes are listed under different headings and sub-headings:
  - **Starters:** soups, hot starters, cold starters
  - **Main courses:** (mains/entrées) – *may be divided into fish & shellfish, meat & poultry, vegetarian, pasta, etc.*
  - **Accompaniments/sides:** e.g. vegetables, salads, breads, rice, items such as onion bhajis
  - **Desserts:** hot and cold with different accompaniments offered, e.g. cream/ice cream/custard

Notes

- A type of menu often used in restaurants
- Usually has a wide choice of food items
- Food items are listed and priced separately, so the customer can make up their meal by choosing individual items
- Food is cooked to order

Menu

Starters

Hand-dived Oban scallop £10
kohlrabi, gooseberry, sea aster, elderflower hollandaise

Wild sea trout £9
salt-baked Jersey Royals, buttermilk, grelot onions, ramsons

Winchcombe lamb tartare £9
Evesham peas, mint jelly, charcoal, Berkswell

Courgette flower tempura £7
Laverstoke buffalo ricotta, broad beans, Summer truffle

Mains

Cornish hake £22
hen crab claw, scrumps, fennel, lemon, seashore greens

Cornish plaice £21
roasted cauliflower, cep mushrooms, summer truffle, romanesco

Devonshire duckling £24
Broadway honeycomb, turnip, pickled cherry, pak choi

Poached duck egg £18
polenta, black olive, spinach, heritage tomatoes

Sides

Summer beans, pancetta

Heritage carrots, lovage emuls

Triple cooked chips, black tru

Desserts

Primrose Vale raspberries
white chocolate textures, tofu, p

Poached white peach £
bavarois, maple ice cream, g

Local artisan cheese with apple
fermented beetroot, celery, wheat wafers, fig
Choose three from Rosary, Penard B
Duddleswell, Lincolnshire Poac
Merry Wyfe, Beauvale, Aber

Or share a board for two

Choose three scoops of our homema
or sorbets with a honeyc

Coffee and petit fours £

Cyclic menu

Description

- A set of menus, each with limited choices, that are rotated every week, every two weeks or once a month

Notes

- Often used in hospital and school meals catering, where budgets have to be carefully planned and managed

	Week 1	Week 2
Monday	Margherita Pizza Vegetable Bolognaise Jacket Potato with Tuna Mayo Carrots & Garden Peas Fruit Crumble with Custard Yoghurt/Fresh Fruit Platter	Margherita Pizza Quorn & Vegetable Rice Jacket Potato with Tuna Mayo Roasted Peppers & Sweetcorn Berry & Apple Strudel & Custard Yoghurt & Fresh Fruit Salad
Tuesday	Spaghetti Bolognaise (made with Organic Mince Beef) Vegetable Pasta Bake Filled Baguette with Ham/Cheese/Tuna or Egg Sweetcorn & Broccoli Chocolate & Beetroot Brownie Yoghurt/Fresh Fruit Salad	Chicken Fajita with Jacket Wedges Macaroni Cheese Filled Baguette with Ham/Cheese/Tuna or E Peas & Coleslaw Lemon Drizzle Cake Yoghurt/Fresh Fruit Platter
Wednesday	Roast Gammon with Roast Potatoes & Gravy Quorn Roast with Roast Potatoes & Gravy Jacket Potato with Beans Seasonal Vegetables Cheese & Biscuits Jelly/Fresh Fruit Platter	Roast Pork with Roast Potatoes & Gravy Vegetable Pasty with Roast Potatoes Jacket Potato with Beans Seasonal Vegetables Cheese & Biscuits Oaty Cookie/Fresh Fruit Salad

Du jour menu

Description

- A menu that changes each day or is served only on certain days of the week
- A **plat du jour** is a dish of the day – sometimes called 'chef's special' or 'specials'

Notes

- Often used in small restaurants or pubs, where they may serve a particular type of cuisine on one night of the week, e.g. curries on a Thursday; fish and chips on a Friday

THURSDAY NIGHT is CURRY NIGHT

A curry and a pint £8.95

Function menu

Description

- Similar to a Table d'hôte, but with a more limited choice
- Set price per head (person) is charged

Notes

- Used for functions such as weddings, parties, conferences
- A range of menus may be offered, with a scale of prices per head, to reflect the types and cost of ingredients used and the skills involved in making the dishes

THE RIVERSIDE HOTEL & RESTAURANT
WEDDING BREAKFAST MENU (£30 per head)

Canape selection

Welsh rarebit tartlet, tomato relish
Smoked salmon and dill crème fraiche roulade
Mini fish and chip with pea puree
Individual sausage roll
Mini Yorkshire pudding, roast beef and horseradish
Battered halloumi, confit red pepper sauce
Black olive and goats cheese bon-bon, roasted almonds
Beetroot, cream cheese and fennel seed turnover
Crisps, nuts and olives

Meal menu

Description

- Menu choices for specific meals: breakfast, brunch (late breakfast/early lunch), lunch, afternoon tea, dinner (evening meal)

Notes

- Often used in hotels and in some restaurants and cafés

UNTIL MIDDAY, WEEKENDS UNTIL 1PM

Bry's Breakfasts

AVOIDING GLUTEN? ASK TO SEE OUR MENU

Bry's Big Breakfast £8.95

Fried free range eggs, Cumberland sausage, smoked streaky bacon, pesto roasted plum tomatoes, mushrooms and toast

Bry's Vegetarian Breakfast V £8.95

Poached free range eggs, pesto roasted plum tomatoes, mushrooms, tomato hummus, smashed avocado, sweet chilli sauce, basil and toast

Bry's Granola Sundae V | N £5.50

Bry's granola with yogurt, banana, strawberries, berry compote, honey and pomegranate seeds

Cumberland Sausage or Smoked Streaky Bacon Sesame Bun £4.75

+ Fried Egg £1.30

Speciality menu

Description

- For target groups, e.g. children, pensioners, ethnic groups, special diets

Notes

- Used in fast food outlets, some restaurants and cafés

Table d'hôte

Description

- The menu is set to two or three courses and has a set price for a meal
- Each person pays the same price no matter which choices they make from the set menu

Notes

- Limited choices within each course
- Faster service than à la carte and usually less wastage, because of the limited menu choices
- Often used in cafes, smaller restaurants and function rooms in places such as hotels, conference rooms, sport stadiums

LUNCH SET MENU

2 courses £11   3 courses £14

2 or 3 courses including a glass of wine
Add a bottle of wine for £16

STARTERS

SMOKED COD ROE Toasted sesame seeds, Scottish oatcakes
FISH SOUP Saffron aioli, gruyere cheese, granary bread
BRITISH HAM HOCK   Piccalilli, wholegrain mustard dressing, granary toast
CHARGRILLED COURGETTES (V) Gremolata, olive oil

MAINS

HERRING SALAD Beetroot, egg, horseradish, heritage potatoes
KING PRAWN SPAGHETTI Roasted chilli oil, lemon, garlic
COD LOIN FISH FINGERS Tartare sauce
BRITISH CHARGRILLED 8oz BEEFBURGER Seeded brioche bun, gherkin, dill mayonnaise, Cheddar cheese

Key terms

- **À la carte** — a menu where the dishes are all listed and priced separately under different headings

- **Cyclic menu** – a set of menus with limited choices that are rotated every week, two weeks or month

- **Du jour menu** – a menu that changes each day

- **Entrée** – a French word, which in the UK, USA and Canada often means a main course on a menu. In some other countries, entrée means the dish served before the main course – i.e. a starter

- **Menu** – list of food items (dishes) to choose from

- **Table d'hôte** – a set menu with limited choices, which has a set price for the meal (e.g. a two- or three-course meal)

Menu styles

Menu styles vary according to the image that a restaurant wants to portray to potential customers, e.g. fine dining/banqueting, informal/social, family, fast food, organic/locally sourced/environmentally sustainable.

Menus are presented in a variety of formats:

- Paper/card hand-held menus
- Menu boards, including:
  - chalk board
  - wall poster
  - digital board
  - interactive online menu
  - sandwich board outside.

Factors to consider when proposing dishes for menus AC2.1

It is important to plan menus carefully in advance and to take into consideration a number of factors:

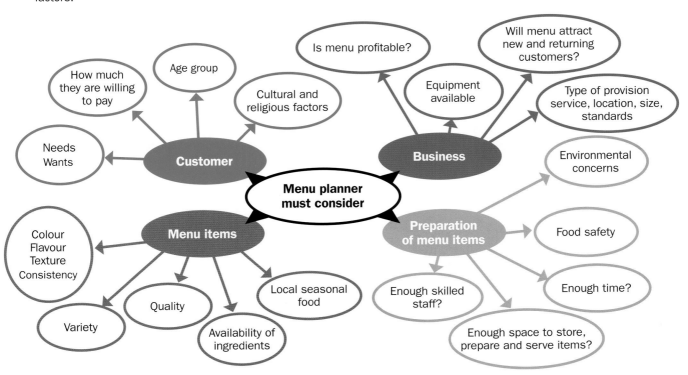

The advantages of careful menu planning are outlined below.

For the customer, menus will:

- Be balanced: flavour, texture, colour, temperature and variety of foods

- Provide sufficient vegetarian and 'free-from' options (e.g. gluten free)

- Meet cultural and religious dietary requirements, e.g. Kosher and Halal

- Meet nutritional requirements and recommendations of health advisors, especially in schools and hospitals.

For the business, menus mean:

- Being able to plan the whole budget more accurately

- Being able to provide a varied menu that will attract customers and encourage them to recommend it to others and return as customers themselves

- Helping the business to keep up to date with trends in food choices and food preparation techniques and presentations.

For the menu items on offer, careful planning:

- Allows ingredients and materials to be ordered in advance

- Means being able to make use of foods in season and local foods as they become available

- Allows the business to be prepared for busy times during annual festivities e.g. Christmas, Diwali, and seasonal and special occasions, e.g. summer weddings, Mothering Sunday, the tourist season

- Means having alternative menus ready, should problems arise with a planned menu, e.g. unavailability of ingredients.

For the preparation of menu items:

- Plan ahead, so that the kitchen knows about and is prepared for the ingredients it needs to order, how the work/skills will be divided between the staff, and the equipment needed

- Make a time plan for the kitchen, by working out how long dishes will take to prepare and cook, and which can be pre-prepared and regenerated (heated ready to serve) (see Chapter 22).

Scenario

Hembledown is a popular tourist village, situated three miles from a fishing port and surrounded by farmland. There is one public house in the village, which serves a limited range of bar food from 12 till 4pm. A new, medium-sized restaurant is going to open for six days a week, in the centre of the village. The restaurant will have access to locally produced vegetables, dairy foods (cheese, milk, cream) and eggs, as well as fish from the nearby fishing port.

1. Suggest the types of service that the new restaurant could offer to customers and create a menu for it.

   Write statements to explain how the following will affect your menu planning:

   a) The time of year/availability of ingredients/seasonal foods.

   b) The customer base – who are they likely to be?/how much are they likely to want to spend?/what types of food would they like to see on the menu?/how will the restaurant cater for their various dietary needs?

   c) The skills of the staff.

   d) The available equipment and storage space in the restaurant kitchen.

   e) The time available to prepare and cook the menu items.

2. Work out the cost of three of your menu items and explain how much gross and net profit you would expect the restaurant to make for each.

Practice questions

1. A carefully planned menu will provide customers with plenty of choices.
Give three points to consider when planning a menu. *(3 marks)*

2. The following menu was offered to patients in a hospital:

> ### Menu
>
> *Cream of cauliflower and parsnip soup*
>
> *Baked cod in a white sauce*
>
> *Creamed potatoes and sweetcorn*
>
> *Rice pudding*

   a) Suggest two reasons why this menu was not very popular with the patients. *(2 marks)*

   b) Suggest two ways in which the menu could have been improved to make it more appetising and appealing to the patients. *(2 marks)*

   c) Give two reasons why it is very important that hospital patients eat well and enjoy their food while they are in hospital. *(2 marks)*

3. School meals providers have to cater for a wide variety of dietary needs.

   a) List two special diets that they may have to cater for. *(2 marks)*

   b) List, with reasons, three factors that a school meals menu planner would need to take into account when planning menus for a primary school. *(6 marks)*

What will I learn?

In this chapter, you will learn about environmental issues that are associated with how food is produced, processed, sold, cooked and consumed and why there is concern about their effects on the health of planet Earth.

Having an understanding of these issues will help you to minimise the environmental effects of the menus that you plan. See also Chapter 3.

Key terms

- Climate change – changes in the Earth's temperature that can lead to unusual and extreme weather conditions

- Greenhouse effect – the atmosphere allows solar radiation through to reach the Earth but reflects some of the heat radiated from the Earth back, leading to raised temperatures

- Greenhouse gases – the gases that form a layer around the Earth which traps heat

Food and environmental issues

Research shows that food production has a major effect on climate change.

Many greenhouse gases (e.g. carbon dioxide, methane, nitrous oxide) are produced during food production, packaging, transportation, cooking and food waste.

These gases are released into the Earth's atmosphere where they form a layer around the Earth, which traps heat and raises its temperature (**global warming**). This is called the greenhouse effect and it causes climate change.

Sun

Heat to Earth

Some heat is trapped and returned back to Earth

Insulating layer of gases and water vapour

Greenhouse gases from food production, factories, forest fires, etc., contribute to global warming

Climate change

Climate change leads to many problems that affect the production and supply of food in many parts of the world:

← The effects of climate change on food production and supply

Drought
(lack of rain)

- Plant crops and animals die
- Streams and rivers dry up
- Soil blows away
- Forest fires start easily

Flooding

- Soil/farmland is washed away
- Animals and plant crops are killed
- Water and land become polluted

Hurricanes Severe storms

- Animals are killed
- Farm property is damaged
- Plant crops are damaged

Higher or lower temperatures than normal

- Plant-growing season may change
- Plants may not be pollinated by insects at the right time
- Pests (insects, animals, moulds) may attack crops
- Animals may die out

The carbon footprint of food production

When food is produced and processed, very large amounts of non-renewable energy from fossil fuels (coal, oil, gas) and water are used.

As fossil fuels are burned to release the energy they contain, large quantities of the greenhouse gas, **carbon dioxide (CO_2)**, are released.

The term carbon footprint is used as a measure of the amount of CO_2 gas that is released into the atmosphere from the activities of people, communities, industry, transport, etc.

The carbon footprint of food measures how much CO_2 and other greenhouse gases are released throughout the whole process of producing and consuming food.

Meat, dairy foods and egg production has the **highest carbon footprint**.

Vegetable, fruit, nut, bean and cereal production has the **lowest carbon footprint**.

How to plan menus that have the least impact on the environment AC2.2

Ingredients used

It is important to carefully consider the provenance of the food (where it comes from) you use in your menus and how it is produced. Many plant and animal foods are grown by a method called **intensive farming**, where large numbers of the same plant crop or livestock (animals, birds, fish) are grown together in one place, e.g. in a very large field, in cages inside a barn or in a large tank.

Many farmers spray the plant crops with chemical **pesticides** in order to stop them being attacked by insects and moulds, and to prevent weeds from growing. Also, artificial **fertilisers** are often added to the soil they grow in, because intensive farming removes lots of nutrients that need to be replaced quickly in order to grow another crop.

Having lots of livestock together in one place can lead to **animal welfare** concerns, including the spread of diseases and pests, so livestock have to be given medicines or chemical sprays to prevent this. The livestock may also fight and injure themselves or become very stressed, because they are not used to living in such crowded conditions.

Key terms

- Carbon footprint – a measure of how much food production contributes towards the production of greenhouse gases

- Food provenance – where food and the ingredients in them originally come from before they reach the Hospitality and Catering industry

- Fossil fuels – fuels such as coal, oil and gas that were created over millions of years by fossilised plants and animals

- Non-renewable energy – energy produced from fossil fuels, which cannot be renewed once they are used up

Organic food production does not allow the use of artificial fertilisers for plant crop production, and severely restricts the use of pesticides, medicines and chemical sprays for animals and plants. Many people choose to buy organically produced food, and in the UK, the **Soil Association** is the organisation that oversees organic food production standards and awards its logo to foods that meet these standards.

157

Food miles

The distance that food is transported from the time it is produced until it is eaten is measured in **food miles**. Nearly half of the foods we eat travel hundreds or thousands of miles before they reach the shops in the UK.

There is concern about the environmental impact of food miles because of the huge amounts of **non-renewable energy** used to transport foods by land, sea and air, and the **pollution** that is caused by these forms of transport.

To have the least impact on the environment when you are planning menus:

- Try to use ingredients that have been grown locally and have travelled only a short distance.

- Try to plan the menus so that the food can be delivered to the kitchen in as few journeys as possible, e.g. buy food in bulk; buy from one supplier.

- Try to use foods that are in season in the UK, so that they do not have to be imported from other countries.

- Where possible, try to use ingredients that have been grown organically or are 'free range' (livestock that has had access to the outside).

↑ Examples of disposable plastic items that are used widely throughout the Hospitality and Catering industry.

Packaging

Most foods sold in shops and to the catering industry have some form of packaging, often made from plastic. Also, many disposable plastic items are used in the Hospitality and Catering industry, as the image shows.

A lot of non-renewable energy from fossil fuels is used in the manufacture of packaging, especially for plastics, and leads to the release of greenhouse gases. A large proportion of household rubbish is food packaging. Some food packaging can be recycled, but if it is contaminated with food waste or formed of different layers of material (e.g. as in some long-life food cartons and disposable hot drinks cups), it can be difficult to recycle. Some plastics are **biodegradable** – they will eventually break down by the action of micro-organisms, usually bacteria.

There is a major concern about the amount of plastic that ends up in the oceans, where it kills wild animals in large numbers.

Food manufacturers, catering businesses and retailers are being encouraged to reduce the amount of plastic packaging they use.

↓ Plastic waste building up in the ocean

Did you know?

The UK uses 13 *billion* plastic water bottles every year, only 3 billion of which are recycled.

Many of these bottles end up polluting land and waterways, especially the sea.

Water UK is supporting the national roll-out of a scheme whereby every shop, hospitality and catering business and other businesses will offer free water refill points in every major town and city in England by 2021. This means people will be able to refill their water bottle instead of buying a new one.

To have the least impact on the environment when you are planning menus:

- Use ingredients that have as little packaging as possible.

- Use ingredients such as spices, flavourings, sauces, etc., that come in refillable or recyclable catering-sized containers.

- Avoid serving individually packaged portions of condiments such as seasonings, sauces, salad dressings, butter and other spreads, jams, marmalade, etc., with menu items.

Sustainability of food production

In order to be sustainable, when food is produced it should:

- Support the work of farmers in every country.

- Protect all the varieties of plants and animals, so that food production does not just depend on only a few types, which could become diseased and have nothing to replace them.

- Protect the welfare of farmed and wild species of plants and animals.

- Avoid damaging or wasting natural resources such as land, fresh water, the sea and the countryside.

- Avoid contributing to climate change through the emission of greenhouse gases.

- Give social benefits to everyone, especially to farmers and their families in developing countries, e.g. safe, healthy and good-quality food, educational opportunities, employment, good housing and stable communities.

- Reduce food waste and food packaging.

Key term

Sustainable – producing food in a way that can be maintained over a long period of time and protects the environment

Food storage, preparation and cooking methods

Many food products are refrigerated or frozen. People eat lots of chilled and frozen foods (e.g. drinks and snacks), as well as lots of meat and dairy foods that require refrigeration or freezing because they are high-risk for food safety (see Chapters 9 and 10).

To have the least impact on the environment when you are storing and preparing cold foods:

- Make sure refrigerators and freezers are located in cool areas of the kitchen. If they are in hot areas, their motors have to work very hard, which uses more energy.
- Make sure the refrigerator/freezer door seals are in good condition, so that warm air is kept out.
- Avoid opening the door of the refrigerator or freezer too often.
- Do not put hot food into a refrigerator or freezer – cool it down first.
- Defrost refrigerators and freezers regularly to make sure they work efficiently.

Cooling food down in a refrigerator or freezer causes the release of lots of greenhouse gases, and there is a big push for the refrigeration industry to produce more energy-efficient refrigerators and freezers.

A lot of energy is wasted by inefficient cookers and hobs. Gas and electric ovens use only a small amount of the energy they use to actually bake the food – the rest escapes as heat into the area surrounding them.

Hobs are more energy-efficient, because most of the heat goes directly into the pan to cook the food, providing the pan base completely covers the gas flame or electric ring.

To have the least impact on the environment when you are cooking foods:

- Make sure that the oven door seals are in good condition, as they minimise the amount of heat that escapes when the oven is on.
- Try to fill up the oven with items to cook to make full use of the energy used to heat it.
- Cook more meals on the hob – make sure that the pans fit properly over the gas flame/electric ring.
- Keep pan lids on to minimise heat loss.
- Use an electric induction hob, microwave oven or slow cooker where possible, which all use small amounts of electricity.
- Use quick methods of cooking, e.g. stir frying, sautéing, to minimise the amount of gas/electricity used.
- When cooking several types of vegetable, place them in different sections of a tiered steamer, so only one hob ring is used to cook them.

Food waste

Research by the charity WRAP has shown that every year in the UK:

- Approximately 3,415,000 tonnes of food waste is produced by the Hospitality and Catering industry.
- Approximately 41% of the waste from fast food restaurants, hotels, pubs and restaurants is food waste.
- 75% of food wasted in the Hospitality and Catering industry is avoidable.

There are many reasons why food is wasted, including:

- Not planning meals properly – buying more food than is needed.
- Serving portions of food that are too large.
- Not storing food properly.
- Misunderstanding the use-by and best before dates on food packaging.

Food waste produces a lot of the greenhouse gas methane when it is left to rot in landfill sites.

Much of the food that is wasted is good enough to be eaten. Some chefs are opening restaurants and developing menus that make use of wasted food from the food industry, e.g. The Real Junk Food Project, where meals are made from left-over food donated by local supermarkets and restaurants and customers decide how much they want to pay for their meal.

Food retailers, e.g. supermarkets, have been criticised for the demands they place on farmers and growers to supply only 'good looking' fruits and vegetables, i.e. those that meet a rigid set of criteria for shape, colour and size. It is estimated that between 20 and 40% of perfectly edible, nutritious fruits and vegetables have been wasted every year because they did not meet the criteria and were misshapen or had variable colours and sizes.

There have been some recent campaigns to highlight the issue of food wastage, and encourage supermarkets to sell misshapen fruits and vegetables and for consumers and the catering industry to buy and use them.

Put it into practice

Plan and make a soup from misshapen vegetables (usually available in most supermarkets or vegetable shops/market stalls) and another using the same recipe, but using non-misshapen vegetables.

Keep the skins on as many of the vegetables as you can, rather than peeling them.

Work out the costs of both soups and comment on the results.

Carry out a sensory analysis of the soups and comment on the results.

Suggest some other recipes where you could use misshapen vegetables.

To have the least impact on the environment when you are cooking foods:

- Avoid buying too much food by planning menus as accurately as possible.
- Avoid serving very large portions to cut down on food waste.
- Store food correctly.
- Make use of misshapen fruits and vegetables, which are generally cheaper to buy and are just as nutritious and well flavoured.
- Serve some fruits and vegetables with their skins left on to avoid unnecessary food waste.
- Send food waste to be composted so that it can be used to grow more plants.
- Send food waste to charities who collect left-over food for people in need.

Practice questions

1. List three ways in which climate change affects the production and supply of food. *(3 marks)*

2. Name three foods that have the highest carbon footprint during their production. *(3 marks)*

3. Name three foods that have the lowest carbon footprint during their production. *(3 marks)*

4. List three ways in which you can avoid wasting energy when cooking foods. *(3 marks)*

5. Suggest two ways in which a restaurant can reduce the amount of food that gets wasted when they are planning their menus. *(2 marks)*

Stretch and challenge

1. The Hospitality and Catering industry uses a lot of plastic in its operations.

   Explain why the use of plastic has become an increasingly urgent environmental issue.

   Suggest some practical ways in which the Hospitality and Catering industry can improve its environmental reputation by reducing its use of plastic. *(5 marks)*

2. Plan a lunch menu for a medium-sized restaurant that incorporates and explains the following goals to address environmental issues:

   a) A reduction in the use of non-renewable energy. *(2 marks)*

   b) A reduction in the amount of food waste. *(2 marks)*

   c) The use of foods with a lower carbon footprint. *(2 marks)*

3. A local charity wants to set up a cafe serving breakfasts and light lunches using left-over foods donated by local shops and restaurants.

   Explain how the cafe workers will ensure that they meet the requirements of food safety rules when storing, preparing and cooking the foods they receive. *(4 marks)*

What will I learn?

In this chapter, you will learn about how to plan menus that meet the needs of customers.

Planning and writing a menu is a very important part of running a restaurant. A menu needs to be appealing to people so that they become customers and provide the restaurant with an income. In order to be appealing, the menu needs to meet the needs of its customers.

What are the needs of customers?

Nutritional

One of the key factors in menu planning is **balance**. This means planning a menu that has a variety of foods and dishes at different prices, cooking methods, cultural dishes and is nutritionally balanced.

Many people choose to follow a healthy lifestyle and want themselves and their children to be able to eat food in a restaurant that meets current dietary and nutritional recommendations, such as that provided by the Eatwell Guide (see Chapter 16).

A menu needs to be planned so that the overall balance of the foods on offer is approximately in line with the amounts of different food groups a healthy person should eat, as suggested in the dietary guidelines, i.e.:

- 37% complex carbohydrates (rice, potatoes, pasta, bread)
- 39% fruit and vegetables
- 12% beans, pulses and meat/fish
- 8% dairy foods
- 1% fats and oils
- 3% occasional foods such as chocolate and savoury snacks.

A menu should also offer some dishes with ingredients and cooking methods that suit people with special nutritional and dietary requirements, or that can be adapted to suit them, e.g.:

- Dairy free
- Gluten free
- Nut free
- Low salt, low sugar, low fat
- High fibre
- Vegetarian/vegan
- Religious dietary restrictions, e.g. followers of Islam do not eat pork, pork gelatine or drink alcohol; Jewish people do not eat pork or shellfish; Hindus do not eat beef.

This means that in order to meet customers' needs and be successful, restaurants and their menus must be **flexible**. For example, many restaurants offer **substitutions** (alternative dishes or ingredients) for customers, e.g. soya milk instead of cow's milk; gluten-free bread rolls; a vegan version of a menu item; boiled or baked potatoes instead of fried chips. This makes customers satisfied with the service they receive, because they feel that their needs are understood and are being catered for.

Many restaurants print the substitutions they have available on the menu and will indicate which menu items are suitable for different dietary needs. This helps customers to navigate their way through the menu and make suitable choices.

Some restaurants print nutritional information on the menu, such as the energy values, protein, fat, salt and sugar content of different menu items, which many customers find useful.

Many restaurants also offer smaller portions for children and elderly customers and bigger portions to suit customers with larger appetites.

Activity 21.1

Plan a menu for some evening meals for a small restaurant, which is in line with the dietary guidelines of the Eatwell Guide.

- Plan four starters, six main courses and four dessert choices.
- Include additional menu items (sides) e.g. bread, sauces, salads.
- To help you to see how well your menu is balanced, highlight the menu items that contain the foods in each section of the Eatwell Guide, in the colours it uses, i.e.:
  - Fruit and vegetables – **green**
  - Complex carbohydrates (starchy foods) – yellow
  - Beans, pulses, meat, fish – pink
  - Dairy foods – **blue**
  - Fats and oils – purple

Explain how the menu can be adapted for different special nutritional and dietary requirements.

Organoleptic

The word organoleptic means the qualities of food that people experience with their senses. Eating good food is one of life's pleasures and its enjoyment is dependent on all the body's senses working together.

There are five senses involved in the organoleptic qualities of food: **sight**, **smell**, **taste**, **touch** and **sound**. The enjoyment of food is the result of a mixture of all these senses working together. If one of the senses is not working correctly, it can affect the whole eating experience; e.g. if you have a cold and your nose is blocked, it is likely that you will not be able to taste your food properly, because you cannot smell it.

To enable people to enjoy their food, it is important that the menu planning, preparation, cooking and serving of food is carried out well so that the food is appetising (makes people want to eat it) and appeals to their senses. This is why, when you are learning to cook, you need to develop good skills in each of these areas.

If your senses are not all working together, food can seem unappetising and tasteless.

Key terms

Appetising – food prepared, cooked and served so well that people want to eat it

Organoleptic – the qualities of food that people experience with their senses

Senses – the ability of the body to react to things through sight, taste, sound, smell and touch

The chart below explains which organoleptic qualities of food are linked to the different senses and how menus can be planned and menu items cooked to meet customer needs for the organoleptic qualities of food.

Sight

Organoleptic qualities of food linked to this sense	How menus can be planned and menu items prepared and cooked to provide these organoleptic qualities
Food looks appetising because of: Colour, shape, pattern, neatness, presentation on the plate, quantity served, cleanliness First impressions	Present, decorate and garnish food neatly and creatively Make use of colours – natural food colours, serving dishes, table settings Cut, shape and form food into decorative shapes and presentations Make sure plates and dishes are cleaned before serving the food, to remove drips and splashes, and that the food fits on them neatly

  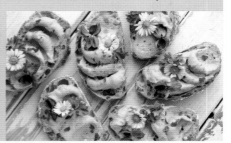

Sound

Organoleptic qualities of food linked to this sense	How menus can be planned and menu items prepared and cooked to provide these organoleptic qualities
The sound of food makes it appetising because: Foods have a particular sound to do with their texture, e.g. roasted potatoes sound crisp and crunchy on the outside; iceberg lettuce, celery and fresh apples are crunchy; biscuits are crisp and snap when broken; carbonated drinks are fizzy, and foods being fried make a sizzling sound If foods go stale, they lose their sounds because they either wilt as they lose water (e.g. lettuce and celery) or soften because they have absorbed water from the air (e.g. biscuits and potato crisps)	Plan menus to include a variety of textures Cook foods correctly to develop their texture and therefore their sounds Store food correctly to keep it fresh and maintain its texture, e.g. salad foods should be stored in a cool place; dry foods, such as biscuits, should be kept in an airtight tin away from moisture

Touch

Organoleptic qualities of food linked to this sense	How menus can be planned and menu items prepared and cooked to provide these organoleptic qualities
The texture and mouthfeel (how food or drink feels in the mouth) make the food appetising because: The food is fresh The food has been well prepared and cooked so that there are no unexpected textures in it, e.g. lumps, egg shell, bones, fruit stalks, grit	Plan menus to include a variety of textures Use fresh foods – stale foods, e.g. vegetables, fruits, fish, lose their texture quite quickly Prepare food well to remove inedible parts, e.g. shells, bones, stalks, tough skins, seeds/fruit stones, small stones and grit Cook food well to avoid unexpected textures, e.g. lumps in a sauce, undercooked egg white, undercooked cake mixture, overcooked and tough meat Cook food at the correct temperature and for enough time to allow textures to develop, e.g. when melting chocolate, baking a cake or bread, frying chicken

Taste

| Organoleptic qualities of food linked to this sense | How menus can be planned and menu items prepared and cooked to provide these organoleptic qualities |

The taste (flavour) of food is appetising because:

The nose and mouth (tongue) work together to produce the sensation of flavour (see below)

There are five basic flavours that are detected by taste buds on the tongue: **salty, sweet, bitter, sour and umami (savoury)**

Fresh ingredients and a combination of flavours have been produced and the food is well cooked

Use fresh food – stale food loses its flavour

Cook the food carefully to avoid damaging flavours, e.g. overcooking can make some flavours become bitter, such as those in spices and green vegetables

Use cooking methods that develop ('bring out') flavours, e.g.:

- Sautéing vegetables in butter or oil

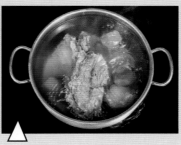

- Making stock from meat, poultry or fish bones plus vegetables, herbs, peppercorns and other spices

- Roasting root vegetables (e.g. carrots, beetroot, onions, garlic, parsnips), which intensifies (strengthens) their flavour by evaporating water from them and caramelising the natural sugars they contain

- Reducing a sauce (allowing water to evaporate by heating it) so that the flavours in the sauce intensify and become concentrated

Make use of natural flavours, e.g. citrus fruit zest, fresh herbs and spices e.g. rosemary, sage, basil, ginger, mint and lemongrass

Take care not to add too much when using intense flavours such as fresh chilli peppers, fish sauce and soy sauce, as they can easily overpower the other flavours in the food and make it unpleasant to eat

Take care not to overpower delicate flavoured foods, such as fish, with too many other flavours

Experiment with combining a few different flavours, but be careful: too many flavours together may not work, because the tongue and brain will become confused

Always taste food before you serve it so you can check the flavour and adjust the seasoning if needed: REMEMBER FOOD HYGIENE! Do not taste the food and put the spoon you have licked back into the food without washing it first!

Smell

Organoleptic qualities of food linked to this sense	How menus can be planned and menu items prepared and cooked to provide these organoleptic qualities
The smell (aroma) of food is appetising because: Fresh ingredients have been used; a combination of aromas has been produced and the food is well cooked Aromas stimulate the appetite and make the mouth water, so that a person is ready to eat and enjoy the food	Plan to use a combination of foods to produce a mixture of aromas, but avoid using too many, as the overall effect will be spoiled Ensure that food is cooked correctly – aromas are released when food is heated, but they can easily be spoiled if the food is overcooked Make sure that only fresh ingredients are used – stale foods lose their ability to produce good aromas Make use of natural foods that produce robust (strong/definite) aromas, e.g. fresh and dried herbs and spices, garlic, orange and lemon zest and cooking methods that develop aromas, e.g. grilling, roasting, baking, frying

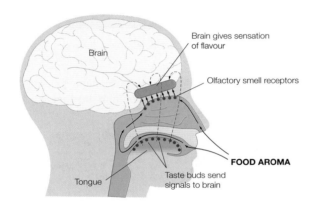

Brain gives sensation of flavour

Brain

Olfactory smell receptors

FOOD AROMA

Tongue

Taste buds send signals to brain

How do smell and taste work together?

Many different natural chemicals are released from food, especially when it is cooked. These are detected by the nose and make the food appetising. When food is put into the mouth and chewed, these chemicals go up into the nose, where special **olfactory (smell) receptors** pick them up and send messages to the brain about what they smell like.

Different areas in the brain then combine the information from the taste buds on the tongue and the olfactory receptors in the nose, to give the sensation of different flavours. About 80% of what people taste as flavour actually comes from the information provided to the brain by the olfactory receptors in the nose.

Cost

When planning menus, it is important to carefully work out the cost of each menu item in order to make sure that the restaurant makes a profit and that prices are affordable for customers (see Chapter 3). There are computer software programs available that enable the price of menu items to be worked out accurately and take into account seasonal price fluctuations and wholesale price changes for ingredients. It is necessary to update the menu prices on a regular basis so that they remain accurate.

It is a good idea for the menu to offer a mixture of lower- and higher-priced menu items to suit different customer needs. Customers like to feel they are getting value for money, so it is a good idea to do some market research in the local area and ask people what they like to eat and what they would be prepared to pay for a particular meal. It is also a good idea to have a look at the prices charged by competing restaurants to give an idea of what customers are prepared to pay.

Restaurants can attract customers by offering a range of price deals, e.g.:

* Discount prices for pensioner, student and children's meals

* Special events (limited menu), e.g. a curry night, Sunday roasts, for a fixed price

* Vouchers for money off the cost of another meal

* 'All you can eat' buffet for a fixed price

* Free delivery for take away meals.

Activity 21.2

Look at the images below of some menu items.
Describe in detail how you would make each of them look more appetising – you can draw a diagram if you wish.

Cauliflower cheese

Carrot and butternut squash soup

Panna cotta

Vanilla cheesecake

Chocolate mousse

Tagliatelle with mushroom sauce

Put it into practice

Plan, cook and present a two-course lunch for one person (starter and main course OR main course and dessert).

Decide with your teacher how much money can be spent on ingredients for the meal.

Explain how your lunch menu does the following:

- Is nutritionally balanced
- Meets customer needs for the organoleptic qualities of foods
- Meets customer needs for value for money.

Practice questions

1. Suggest three substitutions that a restaurant can make to its menu items to meet the needs of customers with special nutritional or dietary requirements. *(3 marks)*

2. List three things that make a menu balanced. *(3 marks)*

3. Why is it important for a chef to taste food before it is served to customers? *(1 mark)*

4. List two cooking methods that can bring out the flavour of foods. *(2 marks)*

5. List three ways in which a restaurant can attract customers by offering price deals and discounts. *(3 marks)*

Stretch and challenge

Explain in detail, giving reasons and examples, why the following are important in meeting customer needs for the organoleptic qualities of foods:

a) Using fresh foods. *(3 marks)*

b) Using different cooking methods. *(3 marks)*

c) Being thoughtful and careful when flavouring foods. *(3 marks)*

d) Colour, shape and neatness. *(3 marks)*

e) Correct storage of food. *(3 marks)*

Chapter 22

The production of dishes for a menu

What will I learn?

In this chapter you will learn why it is necessary and important to plan how the dishes for a catering menu are produced, so that they are of a high standard, meet customers' needs and are served in good time.

Introduction

No matter how big or how small they are, catering kitchens are busy places. Menu items have to be prepared, cooked and served within a short space of time so that customers are not kept waiting too long for their food. If a kitchen is disorganised, it will be inefficient and will cause all the people who work in it a lot of stress and wasted energy. It will also be bad for the success of the business.

So, the most important factor for making a catering kitchen efficient, successful and pleasant to work in, and the production of dishes for a menu at a high standard, is **good planning and organisation**.

Planning the production of dishes for a menu

The production of dishes for a menu needs to be carefully and thoroughly planned, and everyone who works in the kitchen needs to do their jobs correctly and work as a team.

The following chart shows the different stages of planning the production of menu dishes.

Plan the menu

What needs to be done?	**Why is it important for the production of dishes for the menu?**	**Who needs to do it?**
Give clear details of: • The recipes – ingredients (commodities) and method used in each one • The number of portions a recipe yields (makes) • The number of portions of each recipe that need to be made each day • How each recipe is to be served/presented/garnished/decorated	• To give the stock controller (see pages 46–47) an accurate list of ingredients and materials that need to be ordered • To make sure that every chef in each section (partie) of the kitchen knows exactly what they are required to do • To make sure that food is not wasted because portions sizes are too big • To meet customers' needs and expectations for choice, variety, portion size and cost	Head chef and assistant **Health and safety points** There must be adequate storage space to store high-risk foods safely **Contingencies** Prepare alternative menus in case certain ingredients are not available

Key term

Contingency – a backup plan to deal with either an emergency situation (e.g. the cooker breaks down or a special ingredient is not available) so that customer service can be restored as soon as possible; or a seasonal peak in business (e.g. Christmas) so that extra staff and equipment can be hired to cope with the increase in customers

Order

What needs to be done?

- All materials and ingredients required for a menu to be prepared must be ordered in advance

- Take in, check and organise deliveries of ingredients and materials

Why is it important for the production of dishes for the menu?

- To ensure that there are no key ingredients or materials missing

- To be able to advise the Head Chef in advance if any ingredients or materials are not available, so that menu changes can be made

Who needs to do it?

Stock controller

Kitchen porter

Health and safety points

Food deliveries must be checked to ensure that they are at the right temperature and of the quality expected

Contingencies

Buy ingredients from a range of suppliers, so that if one cannot provide an ingredient, another supplier might be able to

Store

What needs to be done?

- Ingredients, materials, tools and equipment need to be stored tidily, so that they can be easily found and used by the chefs

- Make sure tools and equipment are clean and in working order, e.g. knives sharpened, food processor accessories are in place, etc.

Why is it important for the production of dishes for the menu?

- To enable the chefs to have everything to hand when they are cooking the dishes

- To enable the stock controller to make sure that stocks do not run out

Who needs to do it?

Stock controller

Kitchen porter

Health and safety points

Food storage temperatures must be regularly checked

Oldest ingredients must be used first (First In First Out)

Contingencies

Keep a list of companies who can hire out emergency refrigeration units in case one breaks down in the storeroom

Mise en place

What needs to be done?

- This means having everything (ingredients, tools and equipment) **ready and in place** before starting to cook

- It also means reading a recipe thoroughly before you start cooking, to make sure that you know what you need to do to make a dish, and so that nothing is forgotten

- Ingredients need to be prepared ('prepped'), e.g. chopping vegetables and herbs, preparing garnishes, weighing ingredients, jointing poultry, filleting fish, measuring out liquids, spices and seasonings, etc. This can be done several hours before the dish is to be cooked and the prepared ingredients stored in the refrigerator

- Ensuring that a minimum amount of waste is produced

Why is it important for the production of dishes for the menu?

- Mis en place saves time, energy and avoids stress, because everything is organised, ready and in place

- Mis en place also helps the chef to understand and visualise (picture in their mind) what the finished dish will look and taste like

- Prepping ingredients in advance (e.g. garnishes, salad accompaniments), means that they are ready to be used at short notice when a customer order comes into the kitchen

Who needs to do it?

All chefs and their assistants

Health and safety points

Foods, e.g. vegetables, must be washed thoroughly before being prepared

Prepared foods must be stored in appropriate containers and at the right temperatures until they are needed

Contingencies

Have some extra ingredients ready in case there are more orders for a particular dish than originally planned

Sequencing

What needs to be done?

- This means preparing and cooking dishes in a logical order, so that everything is ready to serve on time

- Dishes that take a long time to prepare and cook should be dealt with first, e.g.
  - Bread dough that has to rise
  - Casseroles that have a long, slow cooking time
  - Cold desserts that need to set or freeze
  - Stock and sauces that need time to develop flavour or reduce
  - Fish or meat that has to marinate
  - Dishes that need time for their flavours to develop, e.g. curries, spicy dips
  - Dishes that need to be served cold, e.g. chilled soups, pâtés, salads

- Ingredients/foods that would be spoiled if they are cooked too far in advance should be prepared/cooked last, e.g.:
  - Green vegetables such as broccoli, cabbage and kale will lose vitamins, texture, flavour and colour if they are cooked too early and then kept hot
  - Baked soufflés will collapse if left too long after being removed from the oven
  - Pan-fried fish may dry out and harden if cooked too early
  - Pizzas will lose their crispy texture if kept for too long after baking

- Many foods can be prepared in advance and are fine to either keep hot, heat up from cold storage or serve when required, e.g.:
  - Soups, stews
  - Salads
  - Roasted vegetables
  - Pies and quiches
  - Pâtés
  - Sandwich and roll fillings

Who needs to do it?

Head chef and assistant

Health and safety points

The use of temperature probes and correct storage conditions will help ensure that foods prepared early in the day remain safe and hygienic until used

Food that needs to be reheated for service should be heated to a minimum core temperature of 75°C and only heated once

Contingencies

Keep a list of how long it takes for different dishes/processes to be prepared, cooked and served, for chefs to refer to

Why is it important for the production of dishes for the menu?

- To make the workflow in the kitchen as stress-free as possible

- To meet customers' needs and expectations for food quality and organoleptic features of dishes

- To make the service of foods to customers flow smoothly and efficiently

- To make sure that there is sufficient oven and hob space available to cook foods, such as steaks, fish, soufflés, and vegetables, just before service

Sequencing is also known as '**dovetailing**'. This means fitting together the different stages of a plan into a logical order. You will need to do this when you write a **time plan** for making two or more dishes. This is what you need to do:

- Print a copy of each of the recipes you are going to use.

- Highlight in the method section of each recipe, every activity you will need to do, e.g. make a dough, whisk eggs and sugar together, etc. Use a different colour highlight for each recipe to make it easier to follow.

- Work out and show on your time plan which activity for which recipe you will do first – usually something for a recipe that requires the longest time to be completed, e.g. setting a cold mousse in the refrigerator, leaving a bread dough to rise, making some pastry and letting it rest, or cooking something for a long time.

- Show which activity from another dish you will do next while you are waiting for the first recipe to be ready to move on to the next stage and so on, until every activity has been included.

- When you are dovetailing the activities, remember to allow enough time for, e.g. water to boil when cooking vegetables, meat to tenderise when you are making a stew or enough time to chop up some ingredients.

- Remember to show when you would expect to remove something from the oven and how you would check to see that it is ready.

Cooking

What needs to be done?

- Ensuring that food is cooked correctly so that the outcome is a high-quality product that meets customer needs and expectations

- Ensuring that food is cooked in accordance with food safety and hygiene regulations

- Ensuring that the minimum amount of waste is produced

Why is it important for the production of dishes for the menu?

Cooking the food correctly is important:

- To make the business profitable and successful

- To ensure that the health of customers is not affected

- To prevent food waste

Who needs to do it?

All chefs and supervisors

Health and safety points

Chefs should 'clean as you go' – i.e. clear away and clean work surfaces and equipment throughout the preparation and cooking process to prevent cross-contamination of micro-organisms

Make use of temperature probes to make sure the food is thoroughly cooked

Timing

What needs to be done?

- The length of time it takes for different stages of a dish to be made should be measured, e.g.:
  - How long it takes to peel and chop a large amount of vegetables/fruits
  - How long it takes to fillet a large quantity of fish
  - How long it takes to remove bones/prepare joints of meat or poultry
  - How long it takes for a large pan of potatoes to reach boiling point and then cook the potatoes
  - How long a large sponge gateau takes to bake and cool down before it can be decorated with cream and fruit
  - How long it takes for a batch of home-made ice cream or mousse to freeze/set
  - How long it takes to plate up, garnish/decorate and prepare a large number of dishes for service
  - How long it takes for cooked foods to cool down so that they can be safely stored before reheating for service

Why is it important for the production of dishes for the menu?

Timing how long dishes take to prepare and cook is necessary and important because:

- Timing gives accurate information about how long the menu is going to take to prepare and serve, and therefore how many staff are required at each stage of the process, and whether enough equipment is available at crucial stages

- When there are many portions of a dish to make, it may be more cost-effective and efficient to make use of kitchen equipment and machinery, e.g. an electronic potato peeler, a dough-making machine, an electronic pastry/pasta/icing rolling machine

- It may also be more cost- and time-effective to use some ready-made ingredients and products that have been manufactured elsewhere, e.g. puff pastry, vol-au-vent cases, pasta sauces, partially baked bread rolls, ice creams and sorbets, frozen chips, mayonnaise

Who needs to do it?

All chefs and their assistants

Health and safety points

Cooked foods need to be cooled as quickly as possible to prevent the growth of micro-organisms

Cooling/hot holding

What needs to be done?

- Ensuring that cooked food is kept safe and palatable by cooling it in good time (within 1½ hours to 8°C or below) if it is to be used later and keeping hot food for service to customers at the right temperature (63°C or above)

- Equipment such as large shallow food trays and blast chillers can cool food rapidly

Why is it important for the production of dishes for the menu?

Correct cooling/hot holding is important:

- To make the business profitable and successful

- To ensure that the health of customers is not affected

- To prevent food waste

Who needs to do it?

All chefs and supervisors

Health and safety points

Temperature probes should be used to regularly check the core temperatures of high-risk foods

Completion and serving

What needs to be done?

- Finishing off dishes ready for service, e.g. garnishing, decorating, serving on plates, adding accompaniments such as salad and sauces
- In larger establishments this happens in a finishing kitchen
- There needs to be access to refrigerators, worktops and equipment for keeping dishes hot, e.g. a bain-marie for sauces and custards, electric heating lamps, etc.

Why is it important for the production of dishes for the menu?

Completion and serving are important:

- To make sure the dish is at the correct temperature and has all the elements of the dish in place, e.g. sauces, garnish, vegetables, seasoning
- To make the dish look appetising, creative and neat
- To make sure that customers' orders at a restaurant table are complete and all ready to serve together

Who needs to do it?

Chefs and assistants

Health and safety points

Temperature probes should be used to regularly check the core temperatures of high-risk foods

Serving tongs, disposable gloves and other serving equipment should be used to prevent cross-contamination

Cooked and raw foods should be kept separate from each other

Contingencies

Have some extra garnishes and accompaniments available in case there are more orders than originally planned

Waste

What needs to be done?

- Food waste needs to be minimised at all stages of the production of dishes for a menu
- Any left-over ingredients need to be assessed to see if they can be used in another dish, e.g. raw or cooked vegetables could be used in a soup; cooked meats could be used in a pie; soft fruits could be used in a fruit sauce
- Left-over ingredients need to be stored correctly to keep them safe and hygienic
- Food waste needs to be properly disposed of to prevent pest infestation

Why is it important for the production of dishes for the menu?

- Wasted food means a loss in profits
- Wasted food has to be disposed of properly, which costs a business money
- Some wasted/left-over foods can be used for other dishes so that money is not wasted

Who needs to do it?

All chefs and assistants

Health and safety points

Waste foods need to be disposed of in proper bins outside of the kitchen

Left-over foods should be labelled with the date they were made and stored correctly; they should be used as soon as possible

Contingencies

Make an agreement with a local charity that collects left-over food, so that food is not wasted

Activity 22.1 Dovetailing two recipes

Here are the methods for two recipes:

Bread rolls

Method

1. Set the oven: Gas 7/220°C (200°C for fan ovens).

2. Add the yeast directly to the flour.

3. Add the salt to the flour and stir well.

4. Add the warm water to the flour and stir well with a wooden spoon until mixed to a dough.

5. Knead the dough on a lightly floured worktop for at least 5 minutes. The dough should be stretchy and smooth.

6. Leave the dough in a covered mixing bowl in a warm place to prove (rise) for 1 hour, until doubled in size. Tip the dough out onto the worktop and knead thoroughly for a few minutes.

7. Cut and shape the dough into rolls and leave in a warm place to rise again for 15 minutes before baking.

8. Glaze with either beaten egg, milk or oil and sprinkle with poppy, sesame seeds, pumpkin seeds or oats if wanted.

9. Bake for 15–20 minutes until well risen and golden brown. The cooked rolls should sound hollow when you tap them underneath with your finger.

Spicy lentil soup

Method

1. Peel and chop the carrot and onion or leek into small pieces. Peel and crush the garlic.

2. Heat the oil in a large saucepan; add the chopped onion or leek and sauté on a low heat for about 5 minutes with the pan lid on.

3. Add the garlic, chopped carrots, chilli powder, oregano and cumin, and then cook for 2 minutes with the pan lid on.

4. Stir in the lentils, tomato puree, the water and the stock cube.

5. Bring to the boil, and then simmer gently for approximately 20 minutes, stirring occasionally.

6. Blend the soup with an electric hand blender, taste, and adjust the seasoning with some ground black pepper.

7. Serve the soup with crusty bread or croutons (toasted or fried squares of bread) or a savoury cheese scone.

8. Garnish (decorate) the soup with finely chopped parsley or coriander.

Show how you would dovetail these two recipes in a time plan (use the template below).

You have **two hours** in which to prepare the two dishes.

Time plan template:

Time	Order of Work	Health and Safety / Special Points

Practice questions

1. Give three reasons why it is important to plan a menu carefully. *(3 marks)*

2. List two things that should be done in mis en place. *(2 marks)*

3. Give three examples, with reasons, of how sequencing should be done when preparing dishes for a menu. *(6 marks)*

4. Give two reasons why the completion and serving of a menu dish should be carried out carefully. *(2 marks)*

Stretch and challenge

Study the following menu and then explain, with reasons, the following:

1. The order (sequence) in which a kitchen would produce the menu items. *(4 marks)*

2. Which ingredients the chefs would prepare during mis en place and how they would store them until they were required. *(4 marks)*

3. How the chefs would garnish/decorate each menu item. *(4 marks)*

Menu

Starters

Cream of mushroom soup, served with croutons and a crusty bread roll and butter

Chicken liver pâté and melba toast

Melon and ginger cocktail

Main courses

Roasted free range chicken

Roasted potatoes and parsnips

Seasonal vegetables

Locally produced pork sausages in a red wine gravy with creamed potatoes and peas

Deep fried haddock in a crispy batter, with chips and salad accompaniment

Roasted vegetable quiche tart with jacket potato or chips, served with green salad and coleslaw

Desserts

Lemon meringue pie

Apple tart

Strawberry mousse

Baked vanilla cheesecake with fruit coulis

All served with either homemade ice cream, custard or whipped cream

---

LO3 Be able to cook dishes

Commodities

The following chart describes the different commodities and their uses in catering, the quality points to look out for when buying/using them, and how they should be stored.

What will I learn?

The word 'commodities' means the basic materials that are used in a trade or business. In catering, 'commodities' means the foods/ ingredients that are used to make menu dishes. In this chapter you will learn about the different groups of commodities, how they are used in catering, the quality points they should have, and how to store them correctly.

Key terms

- **Freezer burn** – when frozen food has not been properly wrapped, it becomes damaged and dried out by the cold air and oxygen inside the freezer, which spoils its flavour, texture and appearance

- **Pasteurisation** – this means heating fresh milk to 72°C for 15 seconds in order to kill pathogenic micro-organisms that may be in it

- **Rancid** – unpleasant odours (smells) and flavours that develop in old, stale foods that contain fat

- **Tainted** – when a food picks up the smell of another food being stored close to it, e.g. eggs in a refrigerator can be tainted by uncovered fish being stored nearby

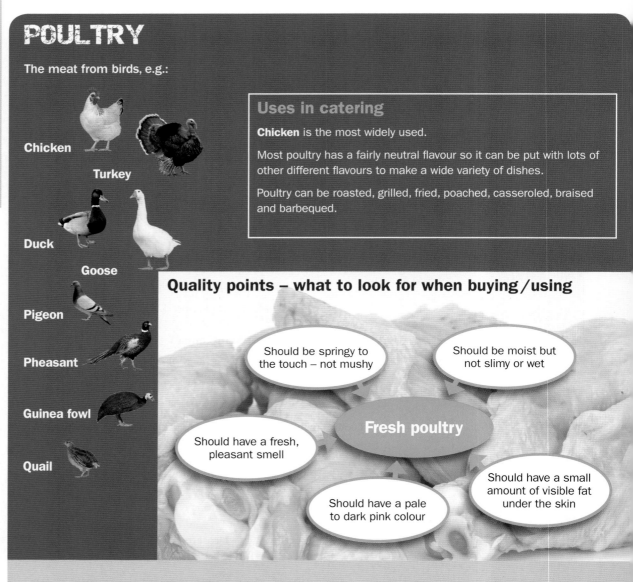

POULTRY

The meat from birds, e.g.:

Chicken

Turkey

Duck

Goose

Pigeon

Pheasant

Guinea fowl

Quail

Uses in catering

Chicken is the most widely used.

Most poultry has a fairly neutral flavour so it can be put with lots of other different flavours to make a wide variety of dishes.

Poultry can be roasted, grilled, fried, poached, casseroled, braised and barbequed.

Quality points – what to look for when buying/using

- Should be springy to the touch – not mushy
- Should be moist but not slimy or wet
- Should have a fresh, pleasant smell
- **Fresh poultry**
- Should have a pale to dark pink colour
- Should have a small amount of visible fat under the skin

How it should be stored

Fresh poultry is a high-risk food, so it must be stored in a refrigerator between 0°C and 5°C, or frozen.

To defrost frozen poultry, place it on a tray at the bottom of the refrigerator (to prevent any drips from it contaminating other foods) and allow several hours for it to defrost.

If frozen, it should be well wrapped to protect it from freezer burn.

MEAT

Meat is the muscle from animals such as:

Pigs (pork, ham and bacon)

Cows/bulls (beef)

Sheep (lamb [young sheep], mutton [older sheep])

Other animals are used for meat, e.g. goats, rabbits and hares

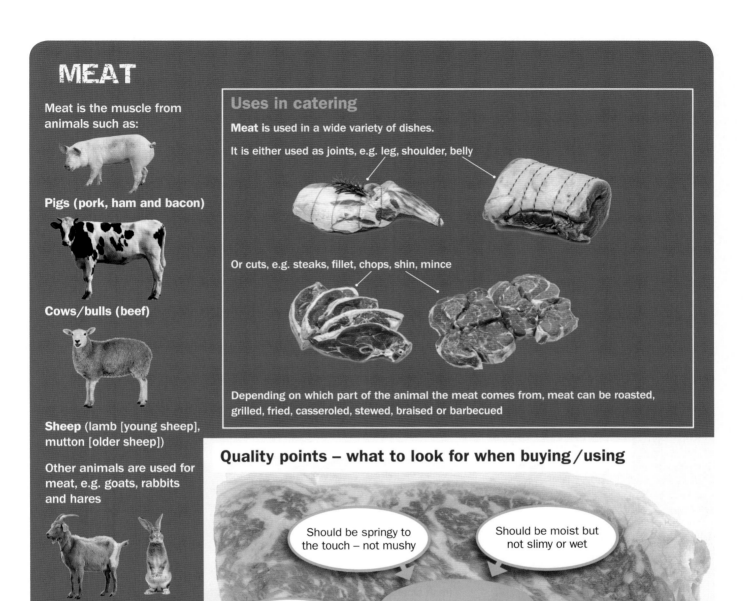

Uses in catering

Meat is used in a wide variety of dishes.

It is either used as joints, e.g. leg, shoulder, belly

Or cuts, e.g. steaks, fillet, chops, shin, mince

Depending on which part of the animal the meat comes from, meat can be roasted, grilled, fried, casseroled, stewed, braised or barbecued

Quality points – what to look for when buying/using

Fresh meat

Should be springy to the touch – not mushy

Should be moist but not slimy or wet

Should have a fresh, pleasant smell

Should have some visible fat under the skin and some in between the muscle fibres (called 'marbling')

Should have a good red colour (beef, lamb and goat) or a pale pink colour (pork, rabbit, hare)

How it should be stored

Fresh meat is a high-risk food so it must be stored in a refrigerator between 0°C and 5°C, or frozen.

To defrost frozen meat, place it on a tray at the bottom of the refrigerator (to prevent any drips from it contaminating other foods) and allow several hours for it to defrost.

If frozen, it should be well wrapped to protect it from freezer burn.

FISH

Different types of fish are classified according to their shape and whether or not they have oil in their flesh.

Flat fish: e.g. plaice, Dover sole, halibut, turbot

Round fish: e.g. cod, haddock, whiting, pollock, mackerel, herring, sardine, sea bass, sea bream, salmon, trout

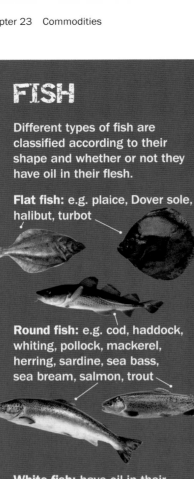

White fish: have oil in their liver, e.g. cod, haddock, whiting, sea bream, sea bass

Oily fish: have oil in their flesh, e.g. mackerel, salmon, herring, tuna, sardine

Seafood: these are shellfish, e.g. mussels, scallops, cockles, etc., and

Crustaceans: e.g. shrimps, lobsters, crabs, prawns, etc.

Uses in catering

Fish generally have a delicate flavour and only require a short time to be cooked as their flesh is very tender compared to meat.

Fish can be left whole (their guts [intestines and other internal organs] are removed for food safety reasons), or they may be cut into:

Fillets

Supremes

Loins

Darnes/cutlets

Goujons

Quality points – what to look for when buying/using

Fresh fish

Should have bright red gills (the flaps behind the eyes)

Should have moist skin, but not slimy

Firmly attached scales – not loose and flaking off

Should have a fresh smell

Firm flesh, slightly springy to the touch

Clear, shiny eyes, not dull and sunken

How it should be stored

Fresh fish and seafood are high-risk foods, so they must be wrapped well (to prevent their smell from tainting other foods, i.e. making them smell like fish) and stored in a refrigerator between 0°C and 5°C, or frozen.

To defrost frozen fish, place it on a tray at the bottom of the refrigerator (to prevent any drips from it contaminating other foods) and allow several hours for it to defrost.

If frozen, it should be well wrapped to protect it from freezer burn.

EGGS

Eggs from a variety of birds are eaten:

Quail

Hen

Duck

Goose

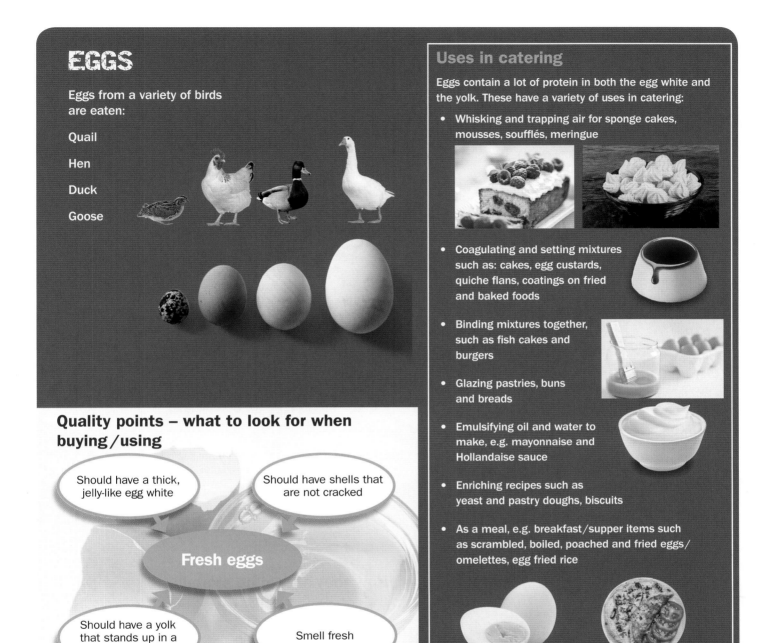

Uses in catering

Eggs contain a lot of protein in both the egg white and the yolk. These have a variety of uses in catering:

- Whisking and trapping air for sponge cakes, mousses, soufflés, meringue

- Coagulating and setting mixtures such as: cakes, egg custards, quiche flans, coatings on fried and baked foods

- Binding mixtures together, such as fish cakes and burgers

- Glazing pastries, buns and breads

- Emulsifying oil and water to make, e.g. mayonnaise and Hollandaise sauce

- Enriching recipes such as yeast and pastry doughs, biscuits

- As a meal, e.g. breakfast/supper items such as scrambled, boiled, poached and fried eggs/omelettes, egg fried rice

Quality points – what to look for when buying/using

Fresh eggs

- Should have a thick, jelly-like egg white
- Should have shells that are not cracked
- Should have a yolk that stands up in a dome shape
- Smell fresh

How they should be stored

Store in the refrigerator away from strong smells, as the egg shells are porous (they have tiny holes in them) and odours from other foods will taint the eggs.

Check the best before date on the egg carton, or check with the supplier when the eggs were laid.

Eggs become very watery as they get older and are not so easy to cook with.

If egg shells are soiled with chicken faeces, store them away from other foods to prevent cross-contamination. Do not wash them until just before you are going to use them, otherwise you will wash off the natural invisible protective coating on the shells that stops bacteria getting into the egg.

Always crack an egg into a separate dish before you add it to a mixture, in case the egg is bad (rare – but it can happen).

Always wash your hands after handling raw eggs to avoid cross-contamination.

DAIRY PRODUCTS

These are milk and milk products, i.e. cheese, butter, cream, yogurt, buttermilk

Cow's milk is the most commonly used milk, but milk from goats and sheep is also used

Types of cow's milk:

1% fat

Semi-skimmed
1.5–2% fat

Skimmed
0.5–0.9% fat

Whole milk
3.9% fat

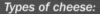

Types of cheese:

Hard, e.g. Cheddar, Parmesan

Soft, e.g. Brie, Camembert

Cottage cheese

Cream cheese

Types of cream:

Clotted – 55% fat

Double – 48% fat

Whipping – 35% fat

Single – 18% fat

Soured cream

Types of yogurt:

Stirred – has a soft texture and often has fruit added

Set – has a more solid texture

Greek – has a thick, creamy texture

Natural yogurt – has no added flavourings

Buttermilk is a by-product from butter making. When cream is churned (stirred) to make butter, it separates out into butter fat and buttermilk. Buttermilk is used in scones, sauces, drinks, cakes and desserts.

Uses in catering

Milk and dairy products are used in many different sweet and savoury dishes and drinks.

Quality points – what to look for when buying/using

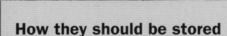

Butter should smell and taste fresh

Cream should smell and taste fresh, not sour

Milk should not smell sour

Soured creamed should have an acidic smell and flavour

Dairy products

Yogurt should have a slightly acidic smell and flavour

Cheese should not be mouldy

Buttermilk should smell fresh

How they should be stored

Many dairy products are heat treated (e.g. by pasteurisation) to destroy pathogenic (harmful) bacteria. Untreated milk and milk products can also be bought. Check the use-by dates.

Fresh dairy foods should be kept in a refrigerator and used by the use-by date.

Some can be frozen.

If it is not stored correctly, butter will develop 'off' flavours and go rancid.

Some products, e.g. long-life (Ultra Heat Treated – UHT) milk, cream, are heat treated and stored safely in cartons at room temperature for many weeks. Once these are opened they must be refrigerated and treated as fresh milk.

Cheeses will go mouldy, even when stored in a refrigerator, so they need to be checked and used within a short time.

Cream and milk will turn sour (due to bacteria) after a while, so should be used up within date.

CEREALS

Cereals are the seeds (grains) from different types of cultivated grasses. They are turned into different products, e.g. pasta, flour, breakfast cereals, etc.

If the whole of the seed is used from a cereal plant, the product that is made is called 'wholegrain' or 'wholemeal'. All of the nutrients and fibre in the seed will be in the product.

If some of the seed is taken away, e.g. the outside layers of bran, the product is called 'refined', e.g. white flour and white rice. These do not have as many of the nutrients from the seed as wholemeal products.

There are several types of cereal that are used:

Wheat

Rye

Rice

Maize (corn)

Barley

Oats

Uses in catering

Cereal flours, particularly wheat, are used for many types of baked products including breads, pastries, cakes, biscuits and pasta.

Rice is a main (staple) food for many cultures around the world and the different types are used for many savoury and sweet dishes. It is also made into products such as rice flour, rice wine vinegar and pasta.

Maize is used as a vegetable (sweetcorn), snacks (popcorn, fried maize snacks), corn bread, tortillas, corn oil, cornflour, etc.

Barley is used to produce malt (a type of sugar) and in the brewing industry to make beer, etc.

Oats are used in porridge, muesli, biscuits, cakes, etc.

Rye is used to make a dark coloured, dense bread, e.g. pumpernickel.

Quality points – what to look for when buying/using

Cereal products should be stored correctly otherwise they can develop moulds

Cereal products

There should be no evidence of insects, e.g. weevils, maggots and moths in cereal foods

Wholemeal flours should smell sweet – if they smell sour, it means they are starting to go rancid

How it should be stored

Store in a cool, dry place that is well ventilated, inside airtight containers with well-fitting lids so that flying insects cannot get into the foods and lay eggs.

Use up wholegrain products by the best before date, as they will start to become stale and unpalatable.

VEGETABLES

Various parts of plants are used as vegetables:

Leaves: cabbage; salad leaves; herbs such as basil, parsley and coriander; Brussels sprouts

Stems: celery, chard, asparagus

Roots; carrots, parsnips, beetroot, turnips, swede, kohlrabi, celeriac, turmeric, ginger, radishes

Bulbs: onions, garlic, shallots, leeks, spring onions (scallions), chives, fennel, water chestnuts

Tubers: potatoes, sweet potatoes, yam, cassava, Jerusalem artichoke

Seeds (legumes/pulses):
Beans (broad, French, runner, kidney, borlotti, black-eyed, haricot, edamame [soya] beans);

Lentils (orange, green puy, brown);

Peas (green, chickpeas, mange tout, snow peas, yellow split peas)

Vegetable fruits: courgettes (zucchinis), cucumber, peppers, tomatoes, butternut squash, okra (lady's fingers), avocados

Uses in catering

Vegetables are used widely in catering:

- As part of menu dishes, e.g. potato topping on cottage pie; roasted vegetables in a quiche flan, cauliflower cheese, beans in vegetarian burgers, lentils in hummus, etc.

- To flavour dishes, e.g. onions, garlic, ginger, etc. in soups, stews, curries, etc.

- In soups and chowders

- In salads

- As side dishes for main courses

- To add colour to meals

- In garnishes.

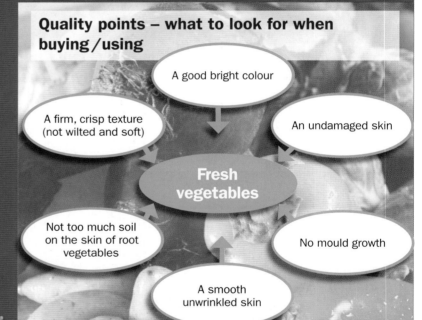

Quality points – what to look for when buying/using

- A good bright colour
- A firm, crisp texture (not wilted and soft)
- An undamaged skin
- **Fresh vegetables**
- Not too much soil on the skin of root vegetables
- No mould growth
- A smooth unwrinkled skin

How they should be stored

Wash vegetables thoroughly to remove grit, soil, dust, etc.

Do not store dirty vegetables next to other foods, to prevent cross-contamination of bacteria.

Do not use mouldy vegetables.

Do not use potatoes that have turned green during storage as they contain a natural poison (toxin) that can cause illness if eaten.

If using raw/dried kidney beans, they must be soaked in cold water for several hours then boiled in fresh water for at least 15 minutes to destroy a natural poison (toxin) they contain that can cause illness if eaten.

FRUITS

Fruits are classified into the following groups:

Stone: plums, peaches, nectarines, apricots, mangoes, cherries, greengages, lychees

 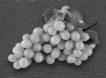

Soft berries: strawberries, raspberries, blueberries, blackberries, tayberries, loganberries, boysenberries, gooseberries, grapes

Currants: blackcurrants, white currants, red currants

Citrus fruits: lemons, oranges, grapefruit, limes, tangerines, clementines, satsumas, **kumquats**

Hard fruits: apples, pears

Other/exotic fruits: kiwi fruit, pomegranates, pineapple, banana, dragon fruit, guavas, paw paws, melon, passion fruit, figs, papaya, persimmon (Sharon fruit), physalis (cape gooseberry)

Stem: rhubarb (strictly speaking a vegetable but used in sweet dishes)

Uses in catering

Fruits are used widely in catering:

- As a starter for a meal, e.g. melon cocktail, citrus fruit cocktail
- As an ingredient in dishes, e.g. apple pie, pear and chocolate tart; mousses, ice creams and sorbets, trifle, fruit salad
- To add colour to meals
- To use as garnishes and decorations
- Drinks, e.g. smoothies, fruit cocktails, juices
- In sauces, e.g. coulis
- Fresh pineapple, kiwi fruit and papaya contain enzymes that will not allow a jelly (gelatine) to set.

Quality points – what to look for when buying/using

A good bright colour

A good texture (not too soft)

An undamaged skin

Fresh fruits

A unwrinkled skin – apart from passion fruit, which become wrinkly as they ripen

No mould/yeast growth

How they should be stored

Wash fruits thoroughly before being used/eaten, to remove dust, bacteria (from being handled by people).

Store soft fruits in a refrigerator to make them last for longer.

Remove any mouldy fruit as the mould will spread to other nearby fruit.

SOYA PRODUCTS

Tofu (soya bean curd) – made from treated soya milk, sold as soft (silken), firm or smoked

Tempeh – made from fermented whole soya beans

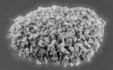

TVP (textured vegetable protein) – made from soya bean flour (after the soya oil has been removed), sold as chunks or mince

Uses in catering

Soya beans and soya products have a high protein content and are used in a wide range of vegetarian recipes in place of meat or fish.

They have little flavour on their own, but readily take up other flavours.

Quality points – what to look for when buying/using

These should all smell fresh and have no evidence of mould

Soya products

How they should be stored

Use within the use-by/best before date.

Store correctly – some is sold fresh and should be refrigerated.

Some tofu is sold in long-life cartons. Follow the storage instructions and use as fresh once the carton has been opened.

Dried TVP should be stored in a cool, dry place in an airtight container.

Practice questions

1. List two quality points to look for when buying each of the following foods: *(2 marks each)*

   a) Meat

   b) Fish

   c) Vegetables

   d) Eggs

2. Give four uses of eggs in catering. *(4 marks)*

3. Explain how poultry or fish should be defrosted, giving a reason for your answer. *(2 marks)*

Stretch and challenge

Choose **one** of the following commodities and write a short report about why it is such an important and useful commodity to the catering industry. Give detailed reasons and examples in your answer. *(8 marks)*

Chicken

Eggs

Milk

LO3 Be able to cook dishes

Techniques AC3.1 AC3.5

Weighing and measuring ingredients

Measuring ingredients accurately is important because:

- Recipes will be made accurately and it is less likely that mistakes will be made.

- Measuring enables the stock controller to keep an accurate record of the ingredients being used from the store cupboard and those that need ordering and replacing.

- It is possible to work out how many portions will be made from a recipe if the ingredients are accurately measured.

Measuring equipment and techniques

Technique 1: Using digital scales

1. Turn the scales on and wait for the display to show 0.0. If the bowl goes onto the scale and it is then turned on, an error may occur, especially if the bowl is a heavy one.

2. Place the bowl onto the scales and press the re-set button to 0.0.

3. Watch the digital display carefully when adding an ingredient. If you add too much, you can remove some until you get exactly the correct amount.

Technique 2: Using measuring spoons

1. A set of measuring spoons is a very helpful piece of equipment. When you use them, make sure that you fill them right up to the top.

2. For a level spoonful, level a heaped spoonful off with a knife.

3. A heaped spoonful is as much as the spoon will carry.

Technique 3: Measuring liquids in a measuring jug

1. Place the jug on a flat surface so that you get a level measurement.

2. Check that you have the correct amount of liquid by looking directly at the measuring scale on the jug whilst it is standing on the flat surface.

Knife skills: chopping and slicing

There are many types of knife for use with different foods. You should always choose the correct knife for the job. Make sure the knives are kept sharp – a blunt knife does not work effectively and is dangerous because more pressure has to be applied to it, which could result in the blade slipping and causing a deep cut in the hand.

Technique 1: Bridge hold to cut an onion using a vegetable knife

1. Place the onion on a chopping board.

2. Cut the onion in half lengthways, from root to tip, cut the top off.

3. Peel the skin away from the onion.

4. Place the onion flat-side down on the chopping board.

5. Cut vertically, making two or three cuts. Make sure you keep the onion intact – do not cut through the root.

6. Grip the onion using the bridge hold with your fingers on one side and your thumb on the other.

7. Cut the onion finely downwards from the top of the onion to the bottom, then cut off the root.

Technique 2: Claw grip to cut a stick of celery into slices using a chef's knife or vegetable knife

1. Place a clean stick of celery on a chopping board.

2. Make a claw with your hand by partly curling your fingers together, and place on top of the celery.

3. Tilt the knife and slice through the celery, using the fingers of your other hand as a guide.

4. Slide your fingers back as you work, keeping your grip on the celery, and continue slicing carefully.

Technique 3: Slicing a carrot into batons and julienne using a chef's knife or vegetable knife

1. Wash and peel the carrots.

2. Place a carrot on the chopping board and cut a thin slice lengthways to create a flat side and prevent the carrot from rolling about.

3. Chop the top and the bottom tip from the carrot.

4. Cut the carrot into sections approximately 4cm long.

5. Using the claw grip, cut each section of the carrot into thin slices along its length.

6. Place the carrot slices flat-side down on the chopping board.

7. Cut the carrot slices lengthways into strips. These are known as batons.

8. Slightly thinner strips, the thickness of matchsticks, are known as julienne.

Technique 4: Segmenting an orange using a serrated knife

1. Slice off the top and bottom of the orange.

2. Place the flat bottom of the orange on the chopping board.

3. Using a gentle sawing action, slice the skin and white pith away from the flesh of the orange.

4. Remove as much of the pith as you can.

5. Separate the segments from the orange by cutting carefully between the membranes that are between each segment. There should be no membrane left on the segment.

Peeling

Many fruits and vegetables are peeled to remove their outer skin before being cooked or eaten raw.

Peeling can be done with a sharp vegetable knife by someone who is skilled enough to only remove a thin layer of skin. Vegetable peelers can also be used, and there are mechanical and electrical peelers available for catering kitchens.

Awkwardly shaped foods, such as root ginger, can be peeled with the rounded end of a teaspoon, which glides over the uneven surface and scrapes off the skin more effectively than a knife or vegetable peeler.

Zesting is a form of peeling. It is used to remove the coloured outer layer of citrus fruit skin (the zest), which contains lots of intensely flavoured essential oils. Zest can be added to recipes to give them additional flavour. The citrus fruit should be unwaxed and thoroughly washed before zesting.

Types of zester

Melting ingredients

Some recipes require some of the ingredients to be melted, e.g. fat, syrup, sugar, creamed coconut, chocolate. If you are melting sugar, syrup and fat in a saucepan, e.g. to make flapjack or gingerbread, it is important to keep the heat very low and stir the ingredients all the time to prevent them from burning.

Some recipes suggest that ingredients are melted in a double saucepan: a smaller pan that fits into a bigger pan. Water is put in the lower pan and the ingredients to be melted are put in the smaller top pan. The water is heated and the heat melts the ingredients.

A bain-marie can also be used to melt ingredients, e.g. chocolate.

Melting chocolate

1. Put some water in the bottom of a pan.

2. Heat the water until it is gently simmering. It is very important **not** to have the water boiling.

3. Put the chocolate into a heatproof bowl and place it on top of the saucepan with the simmering water. This is called a 'bain-marie' or water bath.

4. Stirring constantly, move the chocolate around until it begins to melt.

5. Chocolate is very easily overcooked, so do not stop stirring.

6. Continue stirring until the chocolate has fully melted; the whole process should take 5–10 minutes.

Whisking

Whisking is carried out in order to trap air into a mixture. Various tools can be used to whisk, e.g. a fork, a hand spiral or balloon whisk, an electric hand whisk or an electric free-standing food mixer:

Eggs have the ability to trap a lot of air because of the protein they contain in the egg white and yolk. Eggs are therefore used on their own or with sugar to trap air, which will make a mixture light (e.g. mousses) and enable it to rise when baked (e.g. cakes and soufflés). This technique is also used to make a whisked sponge and meringue.

Technique for making a whisked sponge – used for making, e.g. Swiss rolls, a sponge gateau, sponge finger biscuits (see recipes in Chapter 27)

1. Place the eggs into a bowl and whisk lightly. Fresh eggs will trap more air than older eggs.

2. Add caster sugar to the eggs and whisk the mixture for at least 5 minutes until it is pale in colour and thick in texture. This change is caused by thousands of air bubbles becoming trapped in the mixture.

3. Run a trail of the mixture coming from the whisk across the surface. It should leave a trail that you can see for at least 5 seconds. If you cannot see the trail, the mixture is too thin and needs more air whisked into it.

4. Sieve the flour onto a plate or piece of greaseproof paper. Then sieve the flour again into the whisked mixture in three stages.

5. At each stage, gently fold the flour into the mixture, using a metal spoon in a figure-of-eight pattern. If you beat it too hard, you will burst the air bubbles that have been trapped and the mixture will go flat.

6. When all the flour has been carefully folded in, pour the mixture into the prepared tin. Tip the mixture to allow it to flow into all the corners to make sure it is evenly spread.

7. Place in the oven and bake for the required time. The finished result should be spongy to the touch and have started to shrink away from the edges of the tin.

Technique for making meringues

1. Pre-heat the oven to gas 2/150°C (140°C if using a fan oven).

2. Separate the eggs and put the egg whites into a clean, grease-free glass or china bowl. **Make sure there is no egg yolk in the egg whites or they will not whisk**.

3. Weigh the caster sugar accurately and place in a small bowl. The proportion of sugar is always **50g for each egg white**.

4. Whisk the egg whites on a slow speed for about 2 minutes, or until they have become bubbly and frothy.

5. Whisk on a medium speed for a further minute and then continue whisking at the highest speed to the soft-peak stage, where peaks of meringue remain on the whisk when you remove it from the bowl.

6. Once the egg whites have reached the soft-peak stage, start to whisk in the sugar, a tablespoon at a time, making sure the whisk is set at fast speed.

7. Whisk for about 30–60 seconds after each addition of sugar.

8. Continue to add the sugar and continue whisking until you have a stiff and glossy mixture with a satin sheen.

9. Spoon the mixture into a piping bag and gather up the top.

10. Hold the bag vertically and pipe the mixture onto a baking sheet lined with baking parchment, leaving space between the meringues.

11. Place into the pre-heated oven and then immediately reduce the temperature to gas 1/140°C (130°C if you are using a fan oven).

12. Bake for 1½–1¾ hours in a conventional oven, 1¾ hours in a fan oven, until the meringues sound crisp when tapped underneath.

Rubbing in (shortcrust pastry)

'Short' dough mixtures such as shortbread and shortcrust pastry have a very tender, 'melt in the mouth' texture when they are baked. This is because they contain quite a lot of fat, which is 'rubbed in' the flour with the fingertips. As the fat is rubbed in, the particles of flour are coated with a waterproof layer of fat. When water is added to the mixture to make it into a dough, the waterproof layers of fat prevent long gluten molecules (the protein from the flour) from forming. Only short ones can form. Rubbing in is also used in recipes such as scones, rock cakes and crumbles. Here is the technique for making shortcrust pastry:

Making shortcrust pastry

1. Add 100g of plain flour to a mixing bowl.

2. Cut 50g of chilled, hard fat into the flour and distribute it evenly.

3. Rub the fat into the flour, using your fingertips as lightly and gently as possible.

4. If you shake the bowl, any large pieces of fat will come to the surface.

5. When the fat has been rubbed in, make a well in the centre and add 25ml of cold water. Then use a knife to mix in the water.

6. Bring the dough together, cutting and turning, so it starts to combine.

7. Then bring it all together with your fingertips making a firm, smooth dough.

8. Remove the dough and knead it very lightly on a lightly floured work surface until it becomes smooth.

9. When the dough is ready, cover it and leave in the refrigerator for about 30 minutes.

10. Once rested, the pastry is ready to be rolled out and used as needed, for example, to line a pastry case or make pies or pasties.

Sieving

The technique of sieving is used for a variety of reasons:

1. To separate particles of ingredients that have different sizes, e.g. separating raspberry seeds from the raspberry flesh in order to make a smooth fruit coulis sauce.

2. To remove lumps from ingredients such as flour and icing sugar.

3. To trap air between particles of flour when it is sieved, in order to add lightness to a mixture.

4. To evenly distribute a mixture of dry ingredients through a sieve, e.g. flour, plus baking powder, plus dry powdered spices or cocoa powder, for a cake mixture.

5. To make a smooth soup or sauce by rubbing cooked ingredients through a sieve. This is very time consuming, so in modern kitchens, it is usually done by using an electric blender.

Shaping

Many foods are shaped in particular ways to give them an interesting appearance and make them more appealing to eat.

Foods can be shaped by hand, e.g.:

Making a plaited bread roll

Shaping some meat pasties

Making meat balls

Modelling sugar-craft decorations

Foods can be shaped with the help of tools, e.g.:

Using a piping bag

Using a pasta shaping machine

Using a knife to shape vegetables and fruit

Using cookie cutters

Blending

Blending means to mix a substance with another substance so that they merge together. For example, when a cornflour or arrowroot sauce is made, the first stage is to blend the liquid gradually into the cornflour/arrowroot, using a wooden spoon, until a smooth liquid, without any lumps, is formed. Blending allows time for the dry ingredient (the cornflour or arrowroot) to merge thoroughly with the liquid.

The word blending is also used to describe how different types of the same substance, e.g. types of tea leaves or fruit juices, are put together to create a particular flavour. 'Juice flights' are now popular in some restaurants. These are blended fruit juices that are served with different courses of a meal to complement the flavour of the foods, in a similar way to how different wines are served with different parts of a meal.

Electric blenders are machines that are designed to mix together a variety of ingredients, e.g. fruit, vegetables, at high speed to turn them into a smooth liquid with a uniform appearance and taste.

Hydrating

Hydrating means the absorption of water by a food, e.g. dried peas and beans are soaked in cold water for several hours to allow them time to hydrate and become ready to be boiled. Once they have been soaked, the soaking water should be thrown away and they should be boiled in fresh water.

Other foods will take up water, e.g. dried fruits, lentils, nuts, dried mushrooms, noodles, dried TVP (see page 184), dried milk, cereal grains, seeds, cous cous and salted fish.

Soaking fresh fruits and vegetables in cold/iced water can help to refresh them if they have wilted in hot climates.

Practice questions

1.   Give three reasons why foods are sieved. *(3 marks)*

2.   Give two reasons why it is important to weigh and measure ingredients accurately for a recipe. *(2 marks)*

3.   Give two reasons why eggs are used in whisked mixtures such as sponge cakes. *(2 marks)*

4.   Explain what zesting is and why it is used as a technique. *(2 marks)*

5.   How is fat rubbed in flour and why is it done? *(2 marks)*

Stretch and challenge

You are working as a chef in a restaurant kitchen and have been asked to teach a young trainee chef a range of techniques.

Your task is to write out a set of instructions for each of the following techniques, for the trainee to follow. The instructions should explain clearly how each technique is carried out, giving reasons, where appropriate. You can use illustrations or images to help explain them.

1.   Preparing a courgette (zucchini) for a stir fry. *(5 marks)*

2.   Making a Swiss roll. *(5 marks)*

3.   Melting some chocolate and dipping fresh strawberries into it. *(5 marks)*

There are various different ways in which foods can be cooked. Choosing suitable and appropriate methods of cooking for specific foods and recipes is part of the skill and creativity of the chef. In this chapter you will learn about the different cooking methods, how they affect the organoleptic qualities of the food and which foods are most suited to being cooked by each method.

What will I learn?

Different methods of cooking (AC3.3) (AC3.5)

The different methods of cooking are divided into three groups:

- Those methods that use moisture to cook foods, e.g. boiling, steaming.
- Those methods that use dry methods to cook foods, e.g. baking and grilling.
- Those that use oil to cook foods, e.g. frying, roasting.

Different cooking methods affect the organoleptic (sensory) qualities and palatability of foods, as well as their nutritional value. It is important to know and understand how to select an appropriate method of cooking for the different recipes that you make. Understanding what happens to different foods when they are cooked will help you to do this.

The following chart shows the different cooking methods, how they affect the organoleptic qualities of the food and suitable foods that can be cooked by each method.

Cooking methods that use moisture to cook food

Boiling – means cooking food in water at 100°C

Suitable foods:

Eggs, rice, pasta, vegetables such as carrots, potatoes, swede; joints of meat such as gammon (bacon/ham), beans, peas, lentils, vegetable or meat stock

What happens to the ingredients?	What are the effects on the organoleptic qualities of the food?		What are the effects on the nutrients in the food?
	The appearance of the food (colour, size, shape, etc.)?	The palatability of the food (texture, aroma, flavour)?	
• Starch granules in foods such as potatoes, rice, flour and pasta absorb water and gelatinise between 60 and 100°C • Protein coagulates, e.g. egg white protein coagulates at 60°C and egg yolk at 70°C • Fat will melt • Stocks and sauces reduce in volume as water evaporates	• Pasta, rice, beans and lentils swell in size as their starch granules absorb the boiling water • Green vegetables turn bright green for a few minutes, then gradually become a dark olive green if overcooked  • Red/purple fruits and vegetables are affected by acids (makes them a brighter red/purple) and alkalis such as bicarbonate of soda, which makes them turn blue • Egg white becomes opaque and yolk becomes lighter in colour as protein coagulates • Meat/poultry shrink in size as protein coagulates	• Pasta, rice, peas, beans and lentils soften in texture as they absorb the water • Vegetables soften and tenderise – may become mushy and disintegrate if boiled for too long • Meat will tenderise, but can dry out if boiled for too long because the protein coagulates too much and squeezes out the moisture it contains • The flavour of some vegetables intensifies, e.g. carrots become sweeter • Some flavour from meat will go into the water, but if the water is used to make gravy or stock, the flavour will be saved • The flavour of stock and sauces will intensify as the water evaporates	• Vitamin C, B_1 (thiamine) and B_2 (riboflavin) are destroyed by prolonged heating at boiling point • Water soluble vitamins (B group and C) dissolve into the cooking water • Overcooking meat will make the protein less digestible • Vitamin A remains stable when cooked • Starch granules are softened and some starch released, which makes it easier to digest

Braising – means sealing meat/poultry in hot oil, then cooking it slowly in a covered dish with a little liquid

Suitable foods:

Chicken, fish, eggs, fruit, e.g. pears

What happens to the ingredients?	What are the effects on the organoleptic qualities of the food?		What are the effects on the nutrients in the food?
	The appearance of the food (colour, size, shape, etc.)?	The palatability of the food (texture, aroma, flavour)?	
• Starch granules absorb water and gelatinise • Protein coagulates • Meat tenderises • Vegetables tenderise • Fat will melt	• Colour of red meat becomes brown • Meat/poultry shrink in size as protein coagulates • Red cabbage becomes a deep red/purple colour • Glossy sauce develops	• Meat, poultry and vegetables tenderise • Food cooks slowly and absorbs flavours from stock, vegetables, herbs and spices that are added to it	• Vitamin C, B_1 (thiamine) and B_2 (riboflavin) are affected by heat, but the damage may be less than in boiling • Water soluble vitamins (B group and C) dissolve into the cooking liquid, but this is served with the meal • Overcooking meat will make the protein less digestible • Starch granules are softened and some starch released, which makes it easier to digest

Poaching – means cooking food in a shallow pan of water or wine at just under boiling point with only the occasional bubble visible

Suitable foods:

Meat, poultry, tagines, vegetables, e.g. carrots, fennel, red cabbage

What happens to the ingredients?	What are the effects on the organoleptic qualities of the food?		What are the effects on the nutrients in the food?
	The appearance of the food (colour, size, shape, etc.)?	The palatability of the food (texture, aroma, flavour)?	
• Protein coagulates • Cell structure of fruit softens	• Egg white becomes opaque and yolk becomes lighter in colour as protein coagulates • Fish shrinks slightly, becomes opaque and separates into flakes of muscle as protein coagulates	• Fish and poultry tenderise • Fish is less likely to be overcooked because the temperature of the water is just under boiling point and it is easy to see when the protein has coagulated • Some flavour from poultry and fish will go into the water, but if the water is used to make gravy or stock, the flavour will be saved • The time needed to poach fruit, e.g. pears in wine and spices, enables the flavours from the poaching liquid to be absorbed into the fruit	• Vitamin C, B_1 (thiamine) and B_2 (riboflavin) are affected by heat, but the damage will be less than in boiling as the temperature is just below boiling point for poaching • Water soluble vitamins (B group and C) dissolve into the cooking liquid, and will be lost when the liquid is poured away

Simmering – means cooking food in a liquid just below boiling point, so that it bubbles gently

Suitable foods:

Vegetables, soups, stews, fruit, e.g. apples, meat sauces, e.g. Bolognese sauce, curries, chowders (chunky soup)

What happens to the ingredients?	What are the effects on the organoleptic qualities of the food?		What are the effects on the nutrients in the food?
	The appearance of the food (colour, size, shape, etc.)?	The palatability of the food (texture, aroma, flavour)?	
• Starch granules absorb water and gelatinise • Protein coagulates • Fat will melt • Stock reduces in volume as water evaporates • Cell structure of fruit softens	• Colours of ingredients intensify • Volume may reduce	• Meat and poultry tenderise • Vegetables tenderise • Food cooks slowly and absorbs flavours from stock, vegetables, herbs and spices	• Same as for braising

Steaming – means cooking food in the steam rising from a pan of boiling water beneath

Suitable foods:

Green vegetables, e.g. broccoli, cabbage, spinach, kale, Brussels sprouts; white fish; dim sum dumplings; sponge puddings; rice

What happens to the ingredients?	What are the effects on the organoleptic qualities of the food?		What are the effects on the nutrients in the food?
	The appearance of the food (colour, size, shape, etc.)?	The palatability of the food (texture, aroma, flavour)?	
• Starch granules absorb water and gelatinise • Protein coagulates • Fat will melt • Cell structure of fruit and vegetables softens	• Green vegetables turn bright green for a few minutes, then gradually become a dark olive green if overcooked • Fish shrinks slightly, becomes opaque and separates into flakes of muscle as protein coagulates • Rice grains swell as the starch granules they contain gelatinise • Dim sum swell as the starch granules in the flour gelatinise, and the filling coagulates and sets • Sponge puddings rise and set, but do not develop a golden crust because the starch they contain does not turn to dextrin in moist heat	• Food cooks gently and is unlikely to be overcooked • Foods tenderise and develop a soft, moist, easily digestible texture	• Loss of water soluble vitamins (B group and C) is reduced because the food does not come in direct contact with boiling water • Some foods can take a long time to cook, so more vitamin C may be destroyed as a result • Protein is unlikely to be overcooked by this method so is more digestible • Starch granules are softened and some starch released, which makes it easier to digest

Stewing – means to cook food by simmering gently in a covered pot in the oven, on the hob or in a slow cooker

Suitable foods:

Meat, poultry, sausages, casseroles, fruit, e.g. apples, plums, rhubarb

What happens to the ingredients?	What are the effects on the organoleptic qualities of the food?		What are the effects on the nutrients in the food?
	The appearance of the food (colour, size, shape, etc.)?	The palatability of the food (texture, aroma, flavour)?	
• Starch granules absorb water and gelatinise • Protein coagulates • Meat tenderises • Fat will melt • Cell structure of fruit and vegetables softens	• Colours of ingredients intensify, e.g. fruits • Volume may reduce as water evaporates • Glossy sauce develops • Colour of red meat becomes brown • Meat/poultry shrink in size as protein coagulates • Red/purple fruits and vegetables are affected by acids (makes them a brighter red/purple) and alkalis such as bicarbonate of soda, which makes them turn blue	• Same as for braising	• Same as for braising

Cooking methods that use dry heat to cook food

Dry frying – means cooking food that naturally contains oil or fat in a frying pan without adding oil

Suitable foods:

Minced meat, e.g. beef, lamb, pork, nuts, seeds, spices

What happens to the ingredients?	What are the effects on the organoleptic qualities of the food?		What are the effects on the nutrients in the food?
	The appearance of the food (colour, size, shape, etc.)?	The palatability of the food (texture, aroma, flavour)?	
• Starch changes to dextrin • Fat will melt/ natural oils will soften • Protein will coagulate	• Food develops a golden brown colour • The oils in nuts and seeds melt and are released • Meat changes to a brown colour and fat and juices are released from it	• Flavour intensifies • Oils are released and add texture and flavour • Fat in meat melts and drains out of it • Proteins in meat coagulate and squeeze out juices from the meat, which develop flavour	• B vitamins damaged by the heat • Overcooking meat will make the protein less digestible • The fat from meat can be skimmed off to reduce the energy density

Baking – means cooking foods in a hot oven

Suitable foods:

Cakes, breads, biscuits, cookies, scones, pastries, potatoes, pizzas, desserts

What happens to the ingredients?	What are the effects on the organoleptic qualities of the food? The appearance of the food (colour, size, shape, etc.)?	The palatability of the food (texture, aroma, flavour)?	What are the effects on the nutrients in the food?
• Gases from raising agents expand with the heat and make mixtures rise • Protein coagulates • Added sugars melt and form a syrup that softens the gluten • Added sugars eventually caramelise • Fat will melt • Starch granules absorb water and/or melted fat • Starch granules absorb moisture, swell and gelatinise • Alcohol produced by yeast in bread doughs evaporates in the heat of the oven • Yeast is killed by the heat • Gluten, egg proteins and starch set and form a framework around the gas bubbles inside baked products	• Baked foods containing raising agents rise and expand before setting in the heat of the oven  • Starch in the outside crust of baked goods becomes dextrinised and develops a golden brown colour • Caramelised sugars add golden brown colour	• Risen food sets and develops a tender, open/crumbly/spongy texture inside  • A crust develops on the outside • Caramelised sugars add flavour	• Heat damages vitamin B group • Starch is more digestible because of the baking process

Grilling/barbecuing – means cooking foods by intense radiant heat on a metal grid or grill rack, underneath a heated grill element in a cooker or above the glowing charcoal/flames in a barbecue

Suitable foods:

Meat and poultry joints, oily fish, sausages, burgers, toppings for au gratin dishes (cheese sauce), halloumi cheese, tomatoes, sweetcorn cobs

What happens to the ingredients?	What are the effects on the organoleptic qualities of the food? The appearance of the food (colour, size, shape, etc.)?	The palatability of the food (texture, aroma, flavour)?	What are the effects on the nutrients in the food?
• Protein coagulates rapidly • Fat melts and drains away from the food • Starch turns to dextrin • Sugars caramelise	• Meat/poultry will shrink rapidly due to protein coagulating • Fat melts and drains out • Surface of meat/poultry develops a golden brown colour	• Juices from meat and poultry are squeezed out and develop flavour on the surface • If cooked too rapidly, meat and poultry can become dry and chewy due to protein coagulating and squeezing out water • Flavour intensifies as water evaporates	• Vitamin C, B_1 (thiamine) and B_2 (riboflavin) are damaged by the intense heat • Fat melting out of meat, meat products and other foods reduces the energy density of the food • Overcooking meat/poultry will make the protein less digestible

Roasting – means cooking food in some fat or oil in the oven

Suitable foods:

Meat and poultry joints, root vegetables, some fruits, e.g. plums; nuts

What happens to the ingredients?	What are the effects on the organoleptic qualities of the food?		What are the effects on the nutrients in the food?
	The appearance of the food (colour, size, shape, etc.)?	The palatability of the food (texture, aroma, flavour)?	

What happens to the ingredients?	The appearance of the food (colour, size, shape, etc.)?	The palatability of the food (texture, aroma, flavour)?	What are the effects on the nutrients in the food?
• Starch absorbs oil and softens • Natural sugars in vegetables and fruit caramelise • Protein coagulates • Cell structure of fruit and vegetables softens	• Red meat turns brown; poultry turns creamy/white colour • Onions, parsnips, carrots become golden brown due to caramelisation of sugars • Colours of vegetables intensify • Vegetables shrink as water evaporates from them • Skin on poultry and fat on meat, e.g. pork becomes golden brown  • Juices from meat and poultry are squeezed out and develop into a golden/brown glaze in the roasting pan • Meat/poultry shrink in size as protein coagulates	• Vegetables/fruits tenderise inside and develop a crisp outer texture  • Juices from meat and poultry are squeezed out and develop flavour on the surface • Skin/fat on outside of joints of meat/poultry become crisp • Overcooking causes meat/poultry to dry out and become indigestible	• Fat used in roasting adds to energy density • Fat used adds fat soluble vitamins A,D,E,K • Vitamin C, B$_1$ (thiamine) and B$_2$ (riboflavin) are affected by the heat • Overcooking meat/poultry will make the protein less digestible

Toasting – cooking starch-based foods with dry heat from a grill or flame

Suitable foods:

Bread, buns, crumpets and other starch-based products, nuts, seeds

What happens to the ingredients?	What are the effects on the organoleptic qualities of the food?		What are the effects on the nutrients in the food?
	The appearance of the food (colour, size, shape, etc.)?	The palatability of the food (texture, aroma, flavour)?	
• Starch turns to dextrin	• Food develops a golden brown colour	• Flavour intensifies • Crust adds texture to the food	• B vitamins damaged by the heat

Cooking methods that use oil to cook food

Sautéing – means frying food gently in a little oil in order to soften the food and develop the flavour

Suitable foods:

Onions, leeks, peppers, meat/poultry and vegetables used as a base for soups and stews, celery, carrot, butternut squash, sweet potato, courgette

What happens to the ingredients?	What are the effects on the organoleptic qualities of the food?		What are the effects on the nutrients in the food?
	The appearance of the food (colour, size, shape, etc.)?	The palatability of the food (texture, aroma, flavour)?	
• Natural sugars caramelise • Starch granules absorb oil and swell • Protein coagulates	• Onions, parsnips, carrots become golden brown due to caramelisation • Red meat turns brown, poultry turns creamy/white colour • Meat/poultry shrink in size as protein coagulates	• Caramelised vegetables taste sweeter • Flavour intensifies as water evaporates • As meat and poultry cook, protein coagulates and shrinks and juices are squeezed out and form flavour on the surface	• Vitamin C, B$_1$ (thiamine) and B$_2$ (riboflavin) are affected by the heat • Overcooking meat/poultry will make the protein less digestible • Fat/oil used for sautéing adds to the energy density of the food • Fat/oil will add some fat soluble vitamins (A,D,E,K) • Starch granules are softened and some starch released which makes it easier to digest

Shallow frying (pan frying) – means frying food in a shallow frying pan in a little oil

Suitable foods:

Eggs, fish (white or oily), bacon, burgers, sausages, meat cuts such as chops, cutlets, and steaks, pancakes, flat breads, onions, potato slices fishcakes, potato cakes, rissoles, bananas

What happens to the ingredients?	What are the effects on the organoleptic qualities of the food?		What are the effects on the nutrients in the food?
	The appearance of the food (colour, size, shape, etc.)?	The palatability of the food (texture, aroma, flavour)?	
• Starch granules absorb oil and soften • Protein coagulates • Fat will melt • Cell structure of fruit and vegetables softens • Coatings such as egg and breadcrumbs (used for fish, chicken breast, fishcakes, potato cakes), will protect the food inside from drying out and overcooking as the egg protein coagulates and seals the food from the intense heat of frying	• Egg white becomes opaque and yolk becomes lighter in colour • Fish shrinks slightly, becomes opaque and separates into flakes  • Onions, parsnips, carrots become golden brown due to caramelisation • Red meat turns brown, poultry turns creamy/white colour • Meat/poultry shrink in size as protein coagulates	• Foods develop a crispy texture on the outside, especially if the food is coated with, e.g., egg and breadcrumbs • Some vegetables will caramelise and become sweeter • Vegetables/fruits will soften as the starch and cell walls they contain soften • As meat and poultry cook, protein coagulates and shrinks, and juices are squeezed out and form flavour on the surface	• Vitamin C, B$_1$ (thiamine) and B$_2$ (riboflavin) are affected by the heat • Overcooking meat/poultry will make the protein less digestible • Fat/oil used for sautéing adds to the energy density of the food • Fat/oil will add some fat soluble vitamins (A,D,E,K)

Stir frying – means frying food for a short time in a wok, using very little oil and stirring all the time

Suitable foods:

Finely cut vegetables and other foods, e.g. peppers, onion, mushrooms, courgettes, pak choi, spring onions, bean sprouts, mange tout peas, bamboo shoots, root ginger, seafood, meat, poultry, nuts, tofu

| What happens to the ingredients? | What are the effects on the organoleptic qualities of the food? | | What are the effects on the nutrients in the food? |
	The appearance of the food (colour, size, shape, etc.)?	The palatability of the food (texture, aroma, flavour)?	
• Starch granules absorb oil and soften • Protein coagulates • Cell structure of fruit and vegetables softens	• Colours of vegetables intensify • Vegetables shrink as water evaporates from them • Meat/poultry/seafood shrink in size as protein coagulates	• Quickness of stir frying conserves the colour of vegetables • Vegetables tenderise a little but retain a degree of crispness • Meat/poultry/fish cook quickly so must be cut into small pieces in order to be tender and cooked right through	• Little oil is used so energy density is low • Quick cooking minimises loss of vitamin B group and vitamin C

Other methods

Microwaving – means cooking food by electromagnetic waves, called microwaves, in a microwave oven

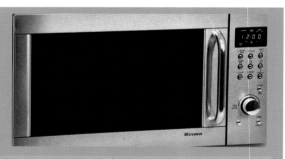

Suitable foods:

Sauces, cake and sponge pudding mixtures, scrambled eggs, vegetables, fruits, fish, soups, melting chocolate and butter

| What happens to the ingredients? | What are the effects on the organoleptic qualities of the food? | | What are the effects on the nutrients in the food? |
	The appearance of the food (colour, size, shape, etc.)?	The palatability of the food (texture, aroma, flavour)?	
• Water molecules will vibrate and transfer heat energy to the food • Protein will coagulate • Fat will melt • Sugar will caramelise and burn easily • Starch will gelatinise in the presence of moisture	• Cakes, sponge puddings, meat and other foods do not develop much colour • Juices and water from meat will leak out as the protein coagulates and squeezes them out	• Meat will not develop flavours on the outside as it does in frying, roasting or grilling • Overcooking may result in sugars burning easily	• Less damage to B group vitamins and vitamin C due to rapid cooking time • Overcooking can make egg, meat and fish protein less digestible

Induction cooking – means a method of cooking where heat energy is transferred quickly to a pan through a specially designed ceramic cooking surface, over an induction coil that creates a magnetic current. Pans that are used on induction hobs must be made from metals that contain iron, e.g. cast iron, magnetic stainless steel or steel

What happens to the ingredients?	What are the effects on the organoleptic qualities of the food?		What are the effects on the nutrients in the food?
	The appearance of the food (colour, size, shape, etc.)?	The palatability of the food (texture, aroma, flavour)?	
• Same as for other methods of cooking carried out on the hob	• Same as for other methods of cooking carried out on the hob	• Same as for other methods of cooking carried out on the hob	• Same as for other methods of cooking carried out on the hob

Important temperatures in catering (AC3.5)

In catering, large amounts of food need to be prepared and cooked in advance so that they are ready to be served to customers on time. It is important to know and understand how to keep food safe to eat and palatable either by chilling, reheating or keeping it hot. The chart below shows the information you need to know.

Food handling process/activity	Safe temperatures you need to know	Food safety notes
Checking the temperature of high-risk foods when they are delivered to the kitchen	Refrigerated foods should be: **0 to 5°C** Frozen foods should be **minus 22 to minus 18°C**	If the temperatures are higher than these, the delivery of food should not be accepted, as bacterial growth and multiplication may have started in the food.
Storing high-risk foods in a refrigerator, cold store or freezer	Refrigerated/cold store foods should be: **0 to 5°C** in England and Northern Ireland, and **up to 8°C** in Wales and Scotland Frozen foods should be: **minus 22 to minus 18°C**	Regularly (every day) check the temperatures of refrigerators and freezers to make sure they are working properly.
Defrosting frozen meat, poultry, fish and seafood	**0 to 5°C**	Defrost on a tray (to prevent drips) in the refrigerator or cold store.
Cooking high-risk foods	Core temperature: **minimum 70°C for 2 minutes**	Cook to destroy any pathogenic (harmful) bacteria. Use a food probe that has been checked (calibrated) for accuracy by placing it in ice to check that it reads 0°C or just under; then placing it in boiling water to check that it reads 100°C.

	Cooling cooked foods	The food should reach **5°C or cooler within 1½ hours**	Fast cooling of cooked food will prevent the growth and multiplication of bacteria.
		Blast chillers and well-ventilated rooms away from the heat of the kitchen will cool food down rapidly.	
		Foods such as cooked rice can be cooled rapidly by rinsing in cold water.	
		Foods such as meat sauces can be poured into large shallow trays. The large surface area helps them to cool more rapidly.	

Blanching

Food is blanched to soften it, or to partially or fully cook it, or to remove something from it, e.g.:

- Nuts can be blanched to remove their skins, e.g. almonds, hazelnuts

- Vegetables such as fresh peas and beans are blanched to destroy natural chemicals called **enzymes**, which would cause vitamin, colour, texture and flavour changes to the vegetables during storage

- Potato chips/fries can be blanched in hot oil (130°C) to cook the inside of the potato. They are then drained, and later fried in hotter oil (190°C) to make the outside really crisp

- Blanching is carried out on some fruits and vegetables before they are frozen to help preserve their colour, texture and flavour

Vegetables can be **blanched** in boiling (100°C) water for a few minutes to destroy enzymes and bacteria, and to preserve their bright colour, texture and vitamin content.

They are then rapidly cooled (refreshed) in iced water and chilled until needed later.

They can be reheated quickly, ready for service.

Blanching helps to destroy bacteria on the surface of the vegetables.

| | Reheating cooked and chilled foods | Core temperature: **minimum 70°C for 2 minutes** in England, Wales and Northern Ireland. In Scotland the core temperature must be a **minimum of 82°C**. | Use the correct temperature to prevent the growth and multiplication of bacteria. Cooked foods should only be reheated **once**. |

| | Hot holding – keeping cooked food hot for service | Core temperature: **minimum 63°C** | Keep at the correct temperature to prevent the growth and multiplication of bacteria. |

| | Cold holding/chilled foods displayed for service | **0 to 5°C** | Keep at the correct temperature to prevent the growth and multiplication of bacteria. |

Practice questions

1. List three cooking methods that use moisture to cook the food. *(3 marks)*

2. Explain two ways in which the organoleptic qualities of food are affected by each of the following cooking methods:

   a) Braising *(2 marks)*

   b) Steaming *(2 marks)*

   c) Baking *(2 marks)*

   d) Stir frying *(2 marks)*

3. Give the correct temperatures for each of the following in catering: *(1 mark each)*

   a) Refrigerated foods delivered to the kitchen

   b) Storing foods in a freezer

   c) Cooking high-risk foods

   d) Cooling cooked foods

   e) Reheating cooked foods

   f) Hot holding cooked food

   g) Cold holding chilled foods

Stretch and challenge

Plan a three-course set dinner menu (starter, main course and dessert) for a hotel restaurant, including accompaniments such as vegetables and sauces.

Use a variety of cooking methods to prepare the meal and explain (giving examples) how you have:

1. Used the cooking methods to develop the palatability of the meal.

2. Used the cooking methods to develop the appearance of the meal.

3. Explain how you would ensure the food safety of your meal, by using the correct temperatures and procedures when preparing the ingredients in advance and holding them until the meal is ready to be served to the customers.

Key terms

- **Coagulate** – when lots of protein molecules in a food join together during cooking and change the appearance and texture of the food

- **Dextrin** – small groups of glucose molecules that are formed when a starchy food is exposed to dry heat, e.g. when toasting a slice of bread

- **Gelatinise** – the swelling of starch granules when they are cooked in a boiling liquid to the point where they burst and thicken the liquid, e.g. in a sauce

- **Gluten** – the protein formed in wheat flour when liquid is added to it, e.g. in bread making, giving the bread dough a stretchy texture.

- **Palatability** – what makes a food acceptable and good to eat

- **Starch granules** – tiny particles found in starchy foods, e.g. rice, flour, potatoes, that contain starch molecules

LO3 Be able to cook dishes

What will I learn?

In this chapter you will learn about how to present dishes so that they are appetising, creative and appealing to customers. You will also learn the importance of portion control to ensure that a restaurant maintains its profit margins.

Presentation techniques AC3.4 AC3.5

The first sense that people use when choosing and enjoying their food is **sight**. Good presentation of a dish will make people want to choose it and it will enhance their enjoyment of eating it. Good presentation also showcases the skills of the chef(s) and encourages people to become regular customers and tell other people about the interesting and creative food at the restaurant.

There are no set rules about how food should be presented – this is down to the individual creativity of the chef and is often influenced by trends and fashions in food choice and eating. However, there are some guidelines for presenting food and plating it up (putting the food on the plate), which are shown below:

1. Have all the ingredients ready and cooked before starting to plate up – this avoids food starting to cool down and lose its flavour and appearance if not everything is ready.

2. Choose a suitable plate/serving platter:

   • Don't use anything too big (which would make the portion of food look too small). ➤

   • Don't use anything too small (which would make the plate look overcrowded).

   • Think of the serving plate or platter as an artist's blank canvas and the food as the 'picture' – the plate is the 'frame' around the food.

   • White or black plates are often used because they are a neutral background to show off the colours of the food.

   • Plates and platters can be made of a variety of materials, e.g. wood, ceramic/china, slate, stone (e.g. granite), stainless steel, banana leaves, bamboo stems, etc.

   • If the food is hot, make sure that the plate has been warmed so that it does not chill the food.

   • Cold food should be served on a cold plate.

   • Wipe the edges of the plate clean of food drips and spills (using a clean cloth or fresh piece of kitchen paper) before serving.

3. Place the ingredients on the plate/platter:

- Do not overcrowd the plate – the plate should frame the food.

- Do not have food hanging over the edges of the plate – it looks messy and makes it difficult for the food servers to handle the plate properly and hygienically.

- Have one ingredient as the **focal point** of the plate, e.g. the protein/main food (e.g. meat, fish or vegetarian main). This is often placed to one side of the dish, rather than directly in the centre, with the rest of the foods around it.

- Imagine that the plate is the face of a clock and place the ingredients like this:

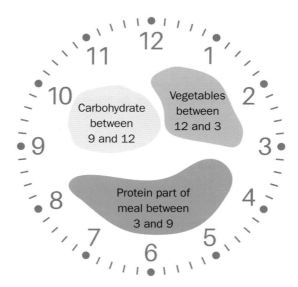

- Ingredients that may move about on the plate when it is carried to the table, e.g. purées, small vegetables (e.g. peas), olives, etc., should be positioned against other ingredients that will hold them in place, e.g. mashed potato, a piece of meat or fish or some bread.

- It is quite common practice to serve up odd numbers of foods (e.g. 3, 5, or 7) such as roast potatoes, meatballs and whole fried mushrooms, as it creates the illusion of there being more food on the plate and is visually more appealing.

Activity 26.1

Here are two plates of vegetable stir fry and noodles.

A is an example of bad plating up of food.

B shows how the food should be plated up.

List the bad points about plate A and the good points about plate B.

4. Be creative:

- Make use of the **natural colours** and **shapes** of foods to make the meal visually appealing.

- Combine different **textures**, e.g. smooth sauces with crunchy chopped nuts; crispy vegetables and soft purées.

- Decorate plates creatively with **sauces**.

- Some **flowers** are edible and make colourful and creative additions to a dish.

  Flowers from these plants are edible: basil, borage, calendula (marigold), chervil, chives, lavender, nasturtium, pansy, rose, sage.

  Any flowers that are used for food must be clean and **must not** have been sprayed with pesticides, fertilisers, or be contaminated with urine or faeces from animals.

- Use **caramelised sugar** to make decorations, e.g. spun sugar.

Ingredients and method for spun sugar

150g caster sugar
75g water
20g glucose syrup

N.B. You need a wooden rod (e.g. long wooden spoon handle), oiled with cooking oil and positioned and secured so that it is protruding over the side of the worktop.

Protect the floor with plastic sacks or other covering. Making spun sugar is a very sticky process!

A spun sugar 'nest' on a cake

Method

1. Place all the ingredients in a small, heavy-based pan and heat gently to make a syrup of the sugar, water, and glucose. Make sure that you wet all of the sugar with the water and wash down the sides of the saucepan with a pastry brush dipped in water.

2. Boil gently until the syrup reaches 160˚C. **DO NOT STIR IT** because it will crystallise if you do.

   WARNING: RISK OF SEVERE BURNS – the syrup is very hot, so extreme care must be taken when making it.

3. Then stop the cooking immediately by carefully plunging the base of the pan into cold water.

4. Allow the syrup to stand for a few minutes until it is slightly cooled and thickened.

5. Dip a spoon or fork in the syrup and tap lightly to remove the excess. Wave or flick the spoon/fork vigorously over the wooden rod so that the sugar is thrown off in fine, long threads.

6. Repeat until the desired amount of spun sugar is hanging from the rod. Carefully lift the mass from the rod.

7. Coil the sugar, or shape as desired for decoration.

8. Use to decorate gateaux or desserts, but do not put in place until just before serving as the sugar will pick up moisture and start to dissolve.

Spun sugar surrounding choux pastry profiteroles, piled into a tower, called a 'croquembouche'

Caramelised sugar can also be used to make decorations by drizzling the hot syrup into shapes onto a heat-proof tray, lined with non-stick silicone baking paper. Allow the shapes to cool and set and then carefully lift them off the paper and use to decorate cakes and desserts.

- Make **chocolate** decorations, e.g. chocolate leaves, swirls, squares, etc.

Instructions for melting chocolate

Use good quality, plain cooking chocolate, with a high percentage of cocoa solids.

1. Put some water in the base of a pan. Place a heat-proof mixing bowl on top. This is called a bain-marie or water bath.

2. Make sure that the bottom of the bowl is not in contact with the water underneath it.

3. Heat the water until it is gently simmering. It is very important not to overheat the water.

4. Add the chocolate to the bowl.

5. Stirring constantly, move the chocolate around until it begins to melt.

6. Chocolate is very easily overcooked, so be careful not to stop stirring.

7. Continue stirring until the chocolate has fully melted; the whole process should take anywhere from 5 to 10 minutes.

8. Ideas for using melted chocolate:

Chocolate shapes can be drizzled or piped onto non-stick silicone baking paper and allowed to cool and set, then lifted off and used as decorations. Keep shapes cool until used.

Spread melted chocolate onto non-stick silicone baking paper and allow it to cool and set at room temperature, then cut out shapes, e.g. squares, triangles, using a sharp knife or metal cutter. Keep shapes cool until used.

Dip fresh fruits into melted chocolate and allow to set.

Instructions for chocolate leaves

1. Wash and dry the leaves.

2. Paint the underside of each leaf generously with the melted chocolate, using a pastry brush.

3. Place the painted leaves on a baking tray lined with parchment paper.

4. Place in the fridge for 15–20 minutes.

5. Wash your hands in cold water when you are ready to decorate your dish.

6. Peel the leaves off the chocolate – working quickly.

7. Keep the leaves in the fridge to keep cool until time to use.

5. Use garnishes and decorations:

- Use garnishes and decorations that complement the other ingredients and add flavour and texture to the meal.

- Place the garnishes and decorations carefully on the plate to add to the creativity of the meal.

- There are many different ways of creating colourful and interesting garnishes. Here are some for you to try.

Vegetable garnishes

Julienne vegetable sticks – use peppers, carrots, courgettes, raw beetroot, cucumber to create various patterns.

The stars were cut using a miniature cutter.

Vegetable spirals – use a spiral cutter for courgettes, cucumbers.

Vegetable curls – use a speedy vegetable peeler to cut long, thin strips of courgette or carrot, then curl them creatively on a plate.

Cucumber twists – use thinly sliced cucumber with the skin left on. Cut a slice almost in half, then twist the slice into an 'S' shape or a cone.

Vegetable tassels – cut thin strips into a piece of celery, a chilli pepper or a spring onion making sure NOT to go all the way to the end.

Place cut vegetables in a bowl of cold water and leave for at least 30 minutes.

The cold water will cause the cut edges of the vegetables to curl, forming tassels.

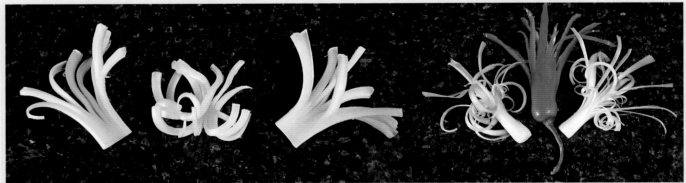

Tomato rose – choose a firm, red tomato. Thinly peel the skin in one long strip from around the tomato, starting at the base. Roll the peeled skin into a coil to imitate the petals of a rose. Secure the rose with a piece of cocktail stick at the base and add a couple of mint, bay or basil leaves.

Vegetable bundles – make bundles of julienne vegetables. Hold together with either a ring of red onion, cucumber or courgette (cut out the middle) or tie with a chive stalk.

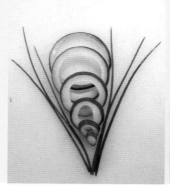

Fruit garnishes

Fruit fans – chose a firm but ripe fruit, e.g. strawberry (with leaf on), mango (peeled, and half the fruit cut in one piece from the stone, lengthways), kiwi fruit (peeled and cut into quarters, lengthways), nectarine (cut in half, lengthways and stone removed).

Make thin cuts through the fruit, but not right through at the end, so the slices you are making all stay attached.

Spread the slices out to form a fan.

Patterns with fruit slices

Lemon and lime twists – formed like the cucumber twists.

- There are various tools that are designed for serving food creatively, including:

  Silicon plating wedge (various shapes available) for spreading sauces and coulis creatively

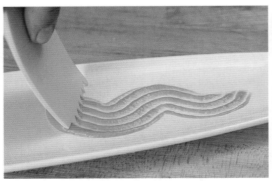

Precision spoon for putting neat drops of sauce onto a plate

Fine tweezers for placing items carefully onto a plate

Ring mould (various sizes and shapes available) for plating cooked rice or mashed vegetables

Double melon baller for making round balls of melon and other suitable fruits

Plastic squeeze bottle for drizzling or dotting sauces onto a plate.

Key terms

Decoration – the process of adding something to a dish to make it look attractive and pretty, e.g. swirls of cream, chocolate shapes, caramel decorations, and spun sugar; usually applied to sweet foods and desserts

Garnish – the process of adding something to a dish to make it look more visually appealing; usually applied to savoury foods

Portion control – serving a standardised portion of food that is the same size each time

Portion control

Portion control means serving a standardised portion of food that is consistently the same size each time. The number of portions that a recipe makes is usually called its **yield**, e.g. a large cheesecake may yield sixteen portions.

Portion control is essential to make sure that a catering business keeps to its profit margins. If just a small amount of extra food is regularly given to customers when they are served, over a period of time the business will struggle to make a profit and may even lose money.

The amount of food that is given in a portion to customers will depend on:

- The type of customer – are they likely to need large portions, e.g. if they are builders working on a nearby building site, or if they are elderly people who may have smaller appetites.
- The type of business – e.g. roadside cafes that tend to sell 'hearty' (larger) portions compared to a fine dining restaurant where portions tend to be smaller.
- How much the food costs the restaurant to buy.
- The quality of the food – better quality food tends to have less waste and therefore provides more portions.
- The knowledge of the food buyer and the chef about what to buy and the number of portion sizes required and expected from different recipes.

How to make sure that portion sizes are controlled:

- Train the kitchen staff to use the correct serving equipment to make sure sizes are consistent.
- Make sure that each recipe clearly indicates how many portions it will yield.
- Use **portion control equipment** that is designed to serve a fixed amount of food, e.g.:

Serving scoop for mashed vegetables, ice cream

Serving spoon

Ladle for serving sauces, soups, stews, etc.

Scoops to serve chips/fries

Double sided cake marker – each side gives a different number of portions

Pie/flan cutters

Healthy food-portion controller

Moulds for e.g. mousses, cakes, muffins, jellies, etc.

Put it into practice

For each of the foods below, suggest how you would finish, present and decorate/garnish each one to make them suitable for a summer celebration party:

Plain cooked chicken

Plain sponge cake cooked in a ring mould

Plain lettuce salad

Whole cooked salmon

Stretch and challenge

You are in charge of planning the catering for a sit-down buffet to serve 50 people at a wedding anniversary party. The customer would like a mixture of savoury and sweet food items. Some of the guests are lacto-ovo vegetarians.

1. Plan eight savoury and four sweet items to be served at the buffet.

2. Name the recipes and list the quantity of ingredients and the expected yield of each.

3. Explain how the portions of each item will be controlled.

Chapter 27

Recipes

What will I learn?

In this chapter you will find lots of recipes and instructions that demonstrate the use of different commodities, techniques and cooking methods that you will use throughout your course. You may want to have a go at making some of them. They are just a selection of the many hundreds of recipes that are available in books, on the Internet, TV and in magazines, or passed on from person to person.

Introduction

The recipes on the following pages are grouped under the different commodities. To help you with your understanding of practical cookery methods, each recipe has a table showing the commodities, techniques and cooking methods used.

Some of the recipes can be made and completed in a one-hour lesson, but there are others that need a longer time and so may need to be prepared over two lessons. You will need to discuss with your teacher how you can do this, e.g. you might make up a pastry dough in one lesson, freeze it, and then use it to make an item in the next lesson. If you did this, you will need to allow time for the pastry to defrost before you can use it. You could put the pastry dough in the refrigerator for a few hours and then use it, but if you leave it any longer, it may start to react with oxygen in the air and change to an unappetising grey colour.

Some of the recipes suggest variations that you could try to make the recipe different.

At the end of the recipes, there is a table with further suggestions for recipes that you could research and make in each commodity group.

It is a good idea to keep a record of all the recipes you have made and make notes about:

- How easy/challenging you found them to make
- How much time they took to make
- Any variations you made to them
- Any feedback you received from people who tasted the results.

This will help you when choosing recipes/menus for your assessments.

Commodity: Poultry

1,2   Wings

3, 4   Thighs

5, 6   Drumsticks

7, 8   Breast portions

9, 10   Winglets

11   Wishbone

12   Parson's nose

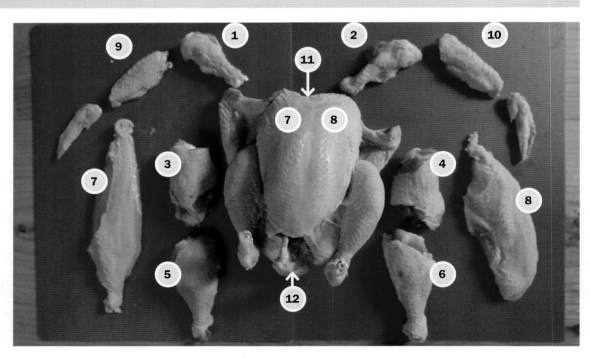

Jointing a whole chicken

A whole chicken can be jointed into ten portions and used in different recipes. Here are the instructions – look at the diagram and images to help you.

1. Wash your hands thoroughly, before and afterwards. **Do not** wash the chicken (washing a raw chicken spreads bacteria around a wide area).

3. **Wings**: Where the wing meets the body of the bird, cut at a slight diagonal around the skin. Then twist until the joint is exposed. Cut through the joint and remove the wings and winglets.

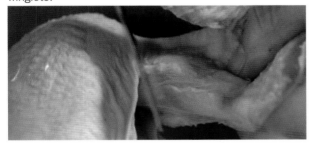

5. **Legs**: Pull the legs gently away from the bird. Cut through the skin where it appears between the thigh and the body.

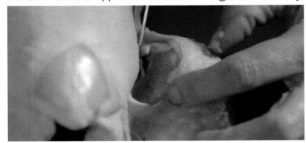

7. Cut through the skin and the joint to remove the leg in one piece. Repeat with the other leg.

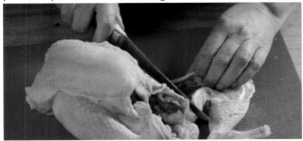

9. **Breast**: Gently cut down one side of the breastbone, using a gentle cutting–slicing motion with the knife. Keep as close to the bone as you can.

2. If the chicken is tied with string, then snip and remove it.

4. Cut through the two joints to separate the wing tips, wings and winglets. Repeat with the other wing.

6. Turn the bird over and pull a leg up. Cut around the joint towards the parson's nose. Turn the bird onto its back and break the hip joint between the leg bone and where it joins the body.

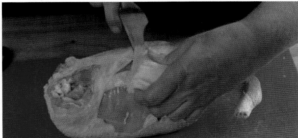

8. Roll the skin away and find the faint white line between the thigh and the drumstick. Cut along this line (the joint) to separate the two parts. Repeat with the other leg.

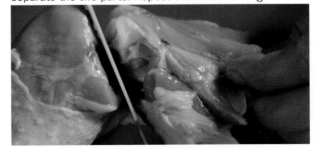

10. Lift the top of the breast away from the carcass and carefully cut to detach it. Repeat with the other breast portion.

Baked stuffed chicken breasts with savoury rice
Serves 2 people

This recipe uses:

Commodities

Poultry – chicken
Rice
Dairy foods – cheese, butter
Vegetables

Techniques

Chopping
Shaping
Peeling
Slicing

Cooking methods

Boiling
Baking
Frying – sautéing

Ingredients

For the stuffed chicken breasts

2 chicken breasts with the skin left on
2 small slices of cooked ham or Prosciutto/Parma ham (Italian dry-cured ham) **[optional]**
50g mozzarella cheese – cut into 4 equal slices
4 fresh basil leaves
Ground black pepper
10g butter or vegetable fat spread
6 wooden cocktail sticks

For the savoury rice

50g white or brown rice – either long grain or basmati
1 medium onion – peeled and finely chopped
1 red or green pepper – de-seeded and finely chopped
25g button mushrooms – washed and thinly sliced
3 tbsp frozen or canned sweetcorn OR peas
Salt and ground black pepper
2 tbsp oil

Method

Stuffed chicken breasts:

1. Preheat the oven to gas 5/190°C.

2. Prepare the stuffing: For each chicken breast, place two basil leaves between two slices of mozzarella cheese, then wrap tightly in one slice of ham.

3. Spread the bottom of an ovenproof dish with the butter or vegetable fat spread.

4. Place the chicken breasts, skin side up, on to a chopping board.

5. Using the tip of a sharp knife, cut a horizontal slot along the whole side length of each chicken breast, taking care not to cut all the way through. Open each chicken breast, like opening a book.

6. Season with ground black pepper.

7. Place the ham, mozzarella and basil stuffing onto each chicken breast, close them up and pin the edges together with three wooden cocktail sticks in each chicken breast.

8. Put the chicken breast, skin side up, in the baking dish. Season with pepper, and place some aluminium foil over the dish.

9. Bake in the oven for 20 minutes, then carefully remove the foil and bake for another 10 minutes so that the chicken skin becomes crisp.

10. Remove the cocktail sticks. Place each chicken breast on a bed of savoury rice and serve with a basil leaf on top.

Savoury rice:

1. Place the rice in boiling water in a pan – cook white rice for 5–7 minutes. Brown rice takes 20–25 minutes.

2. Melt the oil in a frying pan and add the onions, pepper and mushrooms and sauté until they are softened.

3. Add the peas or sweetcorn and cook for another 5 minutes.

4. Drain the rice; mix with the vegetables and season with salt and pepper.

5. Arrange neatly on a plate with the cooked chicken on top.

Chicken curry
Serves 4 people

Ingredients

1 tbsp masala spice mix (see recipe below)
500g chicken breast, thighs or legs*
2 tbsp vegetable oil
1 onion
4cm (approx.) piece of fresh ginger root – peeled
4 garlic cloves
1 can (450g) chopped tomatoes
50ml double cream
120g spinach – washed and dried – **optional**
¼ tsp salt
¼ tsp dried hot chilli pepper flakes OR 1 fresh chilli – **optional**
2 tbsp chopped fresh coriander

* this recipe can be made with other commodities: e.g. 500g boneless leg of lamb, OR 500g lean beef OR 500g large raw or cooked prawns (raw prawns need to be de-veined) OR 500g chopped mixed vegetables such as sweet potato, courgette, carrot, beans, potato, leek.

This recipe uses:

Commodities
Poultry – chicken or meat
Vegetables
Spices
Cream

Techniques
Chopping
Peeling
Slicing
Grinding spices

Cooking methods
Frying – sautéing
Dry frying

Method

1. Cut the meat or vegetables into even, bite-sized pieces. Mix the meat or vegetables in the masala spice mix.

2. In a large, heavy saucepan, heat the oil over a medium heat and sauté the onion until softened.

3. Add the finely chopped or grated ginger root, the crushed garlic and the meat or vegetables. Fry gently for approximately 10 minutes, stirring the mixture.

4. Add the tomatoes and simmer for 20 minutes. If you are using raw (blue/grey) prawns, stir them in after 10 minutes.

5. Stir in the spinach, chopped chilli, and seasoning, simmer for 1 minute once the spinach is cooked. If you are using cooked (pink) prawns, stir them in 5 minutes before you serve the curry.

6. Add extra masala if desired. Add the cream. Simmer for 1 minute.

7. Serve the curry sprinkled with the chopped fresh coriander.

Masala (dried spice mixture)

This makes enough for several curries. It can be stored in an air tight jar in the refrigerator for 1 month.

4 tbsp cumin seeds
2 tbsp coriander seeds
1 tbsp black peppercorns
The small seeds from 12 cardamom pods
1 tsp fenugreek seeds

Tip the dry spices into a thick-based frying pan over a medium heat, and heat the spices, stirring, for 2–3 minutes or until they are a few shades darker and smell fragrant. Be careful not to let them burn.

In a mortar with a pestle or an electric grinder, grind the spices to a powder and transfer the powder to a jar with a tight-fitting lid. The masala can be used straightaway.

Commodity: Meat

Moroccan lamb tagine (or beef or chicken)
Serves 4–6 people

This recipe uses:

Commodities

Meat
Vegetables
Spices
Dried fruits

Techniques

Chopping
Peeling
Slicing

Cooking methods

Frying – sautéing
Braising

Ingredients

500g meat e.g. lamb, lean stewing beef or chicken – trimmed and cut into 5cm chunks
½ tsp cayenne pepper
1 tsp ground black pepper
½ tbsp paprika
½ tbsp ground ginger
½ tbsp turmeric
1 tsp ground cinnamon
1 large onion, peeled and finely chopped
1 tbsp olive oil
2 cloves garlic, crushed
280ml tomato passata (sieved tomatoes)
1 × 400g can of chopped tomatoes
50g dried apricots, cut in half
30g dates, cut in half (stones removed)
30g sultanas or raisins
40g flaked almonds
300ml lamb stock (you can use a stock cube)
½ tbsp clear honey
1 tbsp fresh coriander, roughly chopped
1 tbsp flat leaf parsley, roughly chopped

A medium/large ovenproof dish (approximately 30 × 20cm)

Method

1. Heat the oven to gas 4/180°C (170°C for a fan oven).

2. Place the cayenne, black pepper, paprika, ginger, turmeric and cinnamon into a bowl and mix to combine. Place the lamb in a large bowl and mix together with half of the spice mix. Cover and leave to marinate, preferably overnight in the refrigerator – if not, leave for at least 10 minutes.

3. Heat 1 tbsp olive oil in a large frying pan. Add the grated onion and the remaining spice mix and sauté over a gentle heat for 10 minutes so that the onions are soft but not coloured. Add the crushed garlic for the final 3 minutes.

4. Put the onions into an ovenproof casserole dish/tagine. A tagine is a traditional ceramic cooking dish with a tall, conical lid.

5. In the frying pan, heat the remaining oil and brown the cubes of lamb on all sides then add the browned meat to the casserole dish/tagine. De-glaze the frying pan (add a liquid to dissolve the residues left in the pan) with 80ml of the lamb stock and add these juices to the pan.

6. Add the passata, chopped tomatoes, apricots, dates, raisins or sultanas, flaked almonds, remaining lamb stock and honey to the casserole dish. Cover with a fitted lid, place in the oven and braise for 2–2½ hours or until the meat is very tender.

7. Place the lamb in a large serving dish and sprinkle over the chopped herbs. Serve.

Lasagne
Serves 4–6 people

Ingredients

1 tbsp olive oil
1 large onion, finely chopped
500g lean minced lamb or beef
3 cloves garlic, peeled and chopped
1 × 400g can of chopped tomatoes
1 small can tomato purée
1 tsp mixed dried herbs
175ml brown (beef or lamb) stock – use 1 stock cube
Freshly ground black pepper

For the topping
8 lasagne sheets – fresh or dried (the type that do not require cooking beforehand)
50g butter
50g plain flour
500ml milk
50g Parmesan cheese, grated
75g Cheddar cheese grated
¼ tsp grated nutmeg

A medium/large ovenproof dish (approximately 30 × 20cm)

This recipe uses:

Commodities

Meat
Vegetables
Dried herbs and spices
Dairy foods: milk, butter, cheese
Cereals: pasta

Techniques

Chopping
Peeling
Sauce making

Cooking methods

Frying – sautéing
Simmering
Boiling
Baking

Method

1. Pre-heat the oven to gas 4/180°C (170°C for a fan oven).

2. **Meat sauce**: Heat the olive oil in a large saucepan. Add the onion and sauté gently until the onion is soft but not coloured.

3. Brown the lamb/beef in the pan. Add the garlic and break up the meat with a fork until it has a loose texture.

4. Stir the chopped tomatoes, tomato purée and mixed herbs into the pan. Put the lid on and simmer the mixture for approximately 20 minutes.

5. **Béchamel sauce**: Melt the butter in a small pan and stir in the flour. Cook for 1 minute, stirring all the time. **Take off the heat** and gradually stir in the milk to produce a smooth liquid. Return the pan to the heat and stir continuously until the sauce boils and thickens. Simmer over a gentle heat for 1–2 minutes. Remove from the heat, stir in approximately ¾ of the Parmesan and ¾ of the Cheddar cheese and season with the nutmeg and pepper.

6. **Assemble the lasagne**: Cover the base of the ovenproof dish with half of the meat sauce then cover with half the pasta sheets. Repeat these two layers, ending in the pasta sheets, then pour over the cheese sauce. Sprinkle over the remaining Parmesan and Cheddar cheeses. Bake in the preheated oven for 40–50 minutes, until bubbling and golden. Allow the lasagne to settle for 5 minutes before cutting into squares and serving.

7. Serve the lasagne with a chunky tomato, cucumber, parsley and fresh mint salad and crusty garlic bread.

Beef burgers
Serves 4 people

This recipe uses:

Commodities

Meat
Vegetables
Dairy foods: cheese

Techniques

Chopping
Shaping

Cooking methods

Grilling

Ingredients

500g lean minced beef
25g (a handful) chopped fresh coriander
1 onion, finely chopped
1 tbsp Dijon mustard
1 medium egg
1 tbsp olive oil
Salt and freshly ground black pepper

To serve the burgers (optional)

4 slices mature Cheddar cheese
2 tbsp mayonnaise
¼ iceberg lettuce, shredded
4 ciabatta or ordinary bread rolls
1 small red onion, thinly sliced
1 large tomato, sliced

Method

1. Place all the burger ingredients in a mixing bowl and mix thoroughly with a fork (or with your clean hands) to combine (or use a food processor and process for a few seconds). Using your hands, shape the mixture into four equal-sized burgers.

2. Preheat the grill to hot. Cook the burgers under the grill for a total of 20 minutes, turning them every 5 minutes, until they are cooked right through.

3. Top each burger with a slice of cheese towards the end of the cooking time.

4. Before serving, mix together the mayonnaise and lettuce. Cut the bread rolls in half and toast them under the grill on both sides.

5. Top the bottom halves of the bread rolls with the, onion, lettuce and mayonnaise, followed by a slice of tomato. Place the cooked burger and cheese on top of the tomato and add the rest of the bread roll.

Commodity: Fish

Filleting a whole fish

A whole fish can be filleted to remove most of the bones and leave a piece of fish that can be used in a variety of recipes. Here are the instructions for a round fish, such as sea bass, bream, salmon, mackerel and trout – look at the images to help you.

1. If you can, use a blue chopping board, to prevent cross-contamination.

2. Using a sharp pair of kitchen scissors, trim the fins on the top and underside of the fish.

3. Remove the head of the fish by putting the knife behind the pectoral fin on the side of the fish behind the head and then cutting towards the back of the head.

4. Turn the fish over and repeat on the other side and then cut the head off. Dispose of the head on a paper towel.

6. With the tail towards you, run the knife down the spine from where the head was, towards the tail in a gentle slicing action. If the fish is slippery on the board, lay it on a paper towel to keep it still. You can also use a piece of paper towel to grip the tail firmly with your fingers.

5. Make a small cut 2cm from the base of the tail, stop when you feel the bone.

7. Continue until the fillet begins to come away. Keep as close to the bone as you can. When you get to the rib bones, gently let the knife follow the shape of the fish and slice over the bones.

9. Now remove the pin bones. Use tweezers to get a good grip and extract each pin bone with a firm tug. Wipe your tweezers on the board or a paper towel to remove the bone.

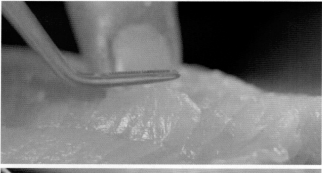

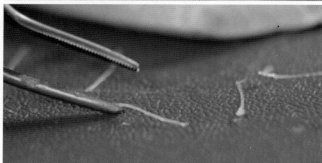

8. Remove the fillet. When both fillets are removed, trim the skin around the fillets to neaten them. Trim the tail..

10. Once you have done this, the filleting process is complete, and the fillets are ready to cook.

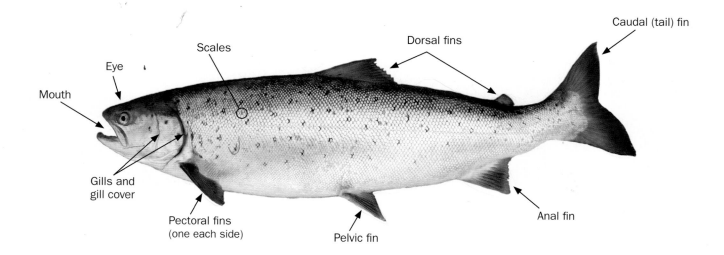

Baked fish in creamy lemon sauce
Serves 2 people

Ingredients

2 × fish fillets, from which the skin and bones have been removed (e.g. sea bass, sea bream)
25g unsalted butter
150ml double cream
1–2 garlic cloves – finely chopped
½ tbsp Dijon mustard
1 tbsp lemon juice
1 tsp finely grated lemon zest
Salt and pepper
2 spring onions – finely chopped
Fresh parsley and lemon slices to serve

Method

1. Preheat the oven to gas 5/200°C (190°C for a fan oven).

2. Place the fish fillets in a greased ovenproof baking dish. Season with salt and pepper.

3. Place the butter, cream, garlic, mustard, lemon juice and lemon zest in a microwave-proof jug or bowl. Microwave for 20 seconds, then stir. Repeat until the butter has melted and then stir until the sauce is smooth. Season with pepper and salt.

4. Sprinkle the fish with the finely chopped spring onion, then pour over the sauce.

5. Cover the baking dish with foil or baking parchment and bake for 12–15 minutes, or until the fish is just cooked.

6. Remove the fish from the oven and transfer it to a serving plate. Spoon over the sauce, and garnish with parsley and lemon wedges.

This recipe uses:

Commodities

White fish
Fruit: lemons
Vegetables: spring onions, garlic
Dairy foods: cream, butter

Techniques

Filleting a fish
Sauce making

Cooking methods

Microwaving
Baking

Pan-fried mackerel in oatmeal
Serves 2 people

This recipe uses:

Commodities

Oily fish
Cereals: rolled oats

Techniques

Filleting a fish
Coating

Cooking methods

Frying – shallow

Ingredients

2 fresh mackerel fillets (or trout)
A little plain flour – seasoned with ground black pepper
1 egg
50g rolled oats
4 tbsp oil to fry
Balsamic vinegar to serve

Method

1. Coat the mackerel fillets in the flour and shake off the excess.

2. Beat the egg in a shallow dish and dip the fillets into it, making sure they are well coated.

3. Dip the fillets into the rolled oats and press them on so that the fillets are coated well.

4. Heat the oil in a frying pan until a few rolled oats dropped into it start to bubble straightaway.

5. Carefully place the fish into the pan and adjust the heat so that it is frying gently. To avoid the fish sticking to the frying pan, you can place some silicone coated baking paper (**not** greaseproof paper) into the frying pan before you add the oil, and throw it away after you have cooked the fish.

6. Turn the fish over after 3–4 minutes and cook it on the other side for another 3–4 minutes. Repeat until the fish is cooked through.

7. Remove the fish from the pan and drain it on some kitchen paper.

8. Serve on a plate with a little balsamic vinegar drizzled over it, a fresh salad and some crusty bread.

Commodity: Eggs

Eggs are used in many different ways in cooking because they are so versatile (have lots of uses).
Here are a few recipes that demonstrate some of those uses.

Roasted Mediterranean vegetable flan
Serves 6–8 people

Ingredients

Pastry

150g plain wholemeal flour, or white flour or half
wholemeal and half white flour (75g + 75g)
75g butter or vegetable fat spread
8–10 tsp cold water

You will need a 20–23cm ovenproof loose-based flan dish or tin

Filling

1 small aubergine or butternut squash or sweet potato
1 red pepper
1 courgette
1 small onion   2 medium eggs
3 tbsp olive oil   150ml double cream
1 clove garlic   150g grated Cheddar cheese
A few basil leaves   Ground black pepper

Method:

1. Pre-heat the oven to gas 6/200°C (190°C for a fan oven).

2. Wash and chop the aubergine/squash/potato, onion and courgette into small dice.

3. Wash and chop the pepper into small pieces.

4. Mix the vegetables in a bowl with the oil, crushed garlic and black pepper.

5. Arrange the vegetables on a baking tray and roast in oven for 25–30 minutes until they are lightly browned and tender. Stir occasionally.

6. **Pastry base:** Prepare the pastry by hand or in a food processor. See pages 241–242 for shortcrust pastry recipe.

7. Knead the dough until it is smooth, then roll it out on a lightly floured worktop and line the flan dish or tin. Trim the edges to neaten them.

8. Bake the pastry blind for 15 minutes at the same oven temperature as the vegetables.

9. Remove from oven, take out baking paper and baking beans and place half of the grated cheese in the pastry case.

10. Place the roasted vegetables on top of the cheese and add the roughly chopped basil leaves.

11. Mix the eggs and cream together and pour over the vegetables.

12. Top with the rest of the cheese and bake at gas 5/190°C (180°C for a fan oven) for 25 minutes until the filling is set.

13. Serve warm with a fresh crisp salad.

This recipe uses:

Commodities

Flour – pastry
Dairy foods – cream, cheese, butter
Eggs
Vegetables

Techniques

Dough making
Shaping
Chopping
Peeling
Slicing

Cooking methods

Roasting
Baking
Baking blind

Eggs are used for:

Coagulation – setting the mixture

Eggs Benedict
Serves 2 people

Ingredients
2 eggs
2 rashers of lean bacon
1 English muffin – sliced in two and toasted

Hollandaise sauce
50g unsalted butter
1 egg yolk
½ tbsp. lemon juice
½ tsp mustard powder
Ground black pepper

This recipe uses:

Commodities

Eggs
Dairy foods – butter
Meat – bacon
Cereals – English muffin

Techniques

Sauce making
Use of bain-marie

Cooking methods

Toasting
Poaching

Eggs are used for:

Emulsification – making the Hollandaise sauce smooth and thick
Coagulation – in the sauce and poached eggs

Method

1. Grill or dry fry the bacon until crispy – keep it warm.

2. Toast the muffin slices and keep them warm.

3. **Hollandaise sauce:** Melt the butter in a small pan on the hob or a bowl in the microwave. When it is melted, transfer it to a measuring jug.

   – Beat the egg yolk in a heatproof bowl and place it over a pan of gently simmering water.

   – Add the lemon juice and mustard powder.

   – Whisk the ingredients briskly, using a balloon whisk or an electric hand whisk.

   – This will thoroughly mix the acid in the lemon juice with the egg yolk and help the development of an oil-in-water emulsion. The mustard powder acts as a stabiliser, to help prevent the emulsion from splitting.

   – Gradually add small amounts (approximately 1 tsp at a time) of the melted butter to the egg yolk, whisking very well after each addition.

   – Continue adding the butter in stages, whisking well each time, until all the butter has been incorporated into the egg mixture. It is very important that this process is done slowly to allow the emulsion to form and to prevent the sauce from splitting. Whisking the egg and butter mixture over simmering water allows the gentle coagulation of the egg yolk and this helps to stabilise the emulsion as the butter is added.

   – When all the butter is added, the sauce should be smooth and thickened. If it is too thick, add a little white wine vinegar and whisk until the sauce is the right consistency. The finished sauce should be thick and not separated, split or curdled. Season with pepper.

   – If you notice that the mixture is starting to split, you can **either**: Remove it from the heat, drop in an ice cube and whisk it in. The ice cube cools the sauce down and allows the mixture to stabilise. **Or:**

   – Add a tablespoon of boiling water and whisk vigorously. The boiling water will coagulate the egg yolk and stabilise the emulsion

4. **Poach the eggs:** half fill a small saucepan with water and heat it until it boils. Carefully crack open the eggs one at a time and drop them into the boiling water. Turn off the heat (carefully move the pan off the electric ring or burner) and place the lid on the pan. Leave the pan alone and time the eggs for 4 minutes. They should be nicely poached. Carefully remove them from the water.

5. Place the toasted muffin slice on the plate and spread some butter on it if wanted. Place the bacon on top, then a poached egg, then finally coat with the Hollandaise sauce.

Lemon meringue pie
Serves 6–8 people

Ingredients

Pastry
200g plain flour – white or wholemeal
100g butter or vegetable fat spread
10 tsp cold water

For the filling
150ml water
2 rounded tbsp cornflour
75g caster sugar
5 medium or 4 large eggs (separated into whites and yolks)
MAKE SURE THERE IS NO EGG YOLK IN THE EGG WHITES OR THEY WILL NOT WHISK
3 medium or 2 large lemons (finely grated zest of one lemon and juice of all)

For the meringue topping
Egg whites
200g caster sugar

You will need a 20–23cm flan dish or tin

Method

1. Preheat the oven to gas 6/200°C.

2. **Pastry base:** Prepare the pastry by hand or in a food processor.

3. Knead the pastry lightly until smooth on a lightly floured worktop.

4. Roll out the dough slightly larger than the flan dish/tin.

5. Line the baking dish/tin with the pastry – try not to stretch it. Trim the edge to neaten it.

6. Fill the pastry with baking paper and put some baking beans on top.

7. Blind bake the pastry for 15 minutes – remove the baking beans and bake for a few more minutes if necessary until the middle is crisp.

8. Turn the oven down to gas 1/140°C.

9. **Make the filling:** In a small pan, carefully blend the cornflour, water, sugar, egg yolks, lemon zest and juice together so that there are no lumps.

10. Heat the filling and stir all the time until the mixture boils and thickens.

11. Pour the filling slowly into the baked pastry case and leave to cool while you make the meringue.

12. **Make the meringue:** Place the egg whites in a clean, dry, grease-free bowl.

13. Whisk the egg whites until very stiff.

14. Whisk the caster sugar in a tablespoon at a time until the mixture is thick and glossy.

15. Pile the meringue on top of the lemon filling.

16. Place the pie in the oven for approximately 30 minutes to 1 hour until the meringue is lightly browned and crisp. Check it regularly to make sure it is cooking evenly.

This recipe uses:

Commodities
Flour – pastry
Dairy foods – butter
Fruit
Eggs

Techniques
Dough making
Shaping
Whisking
Sauce making
Meringue making

Cooking methods
Boiling
Baking

Eggs are used for:
Setting the filling (coagulation)
Meringue – trapping air to produce a foam

Commodity: Dairy products

Savoury buttermilk scone round
Makes 8 portions

This recipe uses:

Commodities

Dairy foods: buttermilk, cheese, butter
Cereals: flour

Techniques

Rubbing in
Dough making
Shaping

Cooking methods

Baking

Ingredients

225g self-raising flour – either wholemeal flour, OR white flour,
OR approximately half wholemeal and half white flour (112g + 113g)
½ tsp baking powder
¼ tsp cayenne pepper
50g strong flavoured Cheddar cheese *or* 50g Parmesan cheese – grated
25g pumpkin seeds *or* sunflower seeds **(optional)**
50g butter
150ml buttermilk (*or* cow's milk *or* goat's/soya/rice/oat milk)

Method

1. Preheat the oven to gas 6/200°C (190°C for a fan oven).

2. Sieve the flour, baking powder and cayenne pepper together into a bowl.

3. Rub in the butter with your fingertips to a breadcrumb mixture.

4. Stir in ¾ of the cheese and the seeds if you are using them.

5. Make a well in the centre and add the buttermilk/milk.

6. Stir the mixture together with a spoon until it forms a soft dough.

7. Knead the dough lightly on a floured worktop and shape into a round, about 2.5cm thick and 18cm diameter.

8. Grease a baking sheet and place the scone round on it.

9. With a knife, mark the scone round into 8 pieces.

10. Brush the top with milk and sprinkle with the remaining grated cheese.

11. Bake the scone round for 20 minutes until golden, well-risen, spongy to the touch, but not doughy in the middle – check with a skewer.

12. Cool the scone round on a wire rack and cut it into 8 pieces where you marked it before baking.

13. Serve warm with soup or cheese/ham and pickles.

Variations

Sweet scone

Leave out the cheese, seeds and cayenne pepper. Add 50g caster sugar. Serve with whipped cream and jam.

Fruit scone

Leave out the cheese, seeds and cayenne pepper. Add 25g caster sugar and 75g dried fruit, e.g. sultanas, raisins, chopped dried apricots, glacé cherries. Serve with butter.

Baked lemon and vanilla cheesecake
Serves 8–10 people

Ingredients

250g plain digestive biscuits
90g butter – melted
500g mascarpone cheese
250g caster sugar
3 eggs – beaten
165ml double cream
Zest and juice of 1 lemon
½ tsp vanilla essence

A 20–23cm spring clip round baking tin

Method

1. Pre-heat the oven to gas 3/150°C (140°C for a fan oven).

2. Crush the biscuits and add the melted butter.
    Press the mixture into the greased and lined spring clip tin.

3. In a large bowl or food processor, beat cheese with the sugar until thick, and then add the eggs.

4. Add the cream, vanilla, lemon zest and lemon juice and mix thoroughly.

5. Pour the mixture on top of the biscuit base, then bake the cheesecake in the pre-heated oven for 1 hour.

6. Turn off the oven and leave the cheesecake inside it for 15 minutes, then remove it and leave it to cool.

7. Serve the cheesecake with fresh fruits and strawberry, blackcurrant or raspberry coulis.

This recipe uses:

Commodities

Dairy foods: mascarpone cheese, cream, butter
Eggs
Cereals: digestive biscuits
Fruit: lemon

Techniques

Biscuit base

Cooking methods

Baking

Panna cotta
Serves 4 people

This recipe uses:

Commodities

Dairy foods: whole milk, cream
Fruit: berries

Techniques

Using gelatine to set a mixture
Chilling

Cooking methods

Simmering the milk

Ingredients

250ml whole milk
250ml double cream
3 gelatine leaves
1 tsp vanilla bean paste or vanilla extract
25g caster sugar

4 ramekin dishes, each holding 150ml

Method

1. Place the gelatine leaves in a bowl of cold water and leave them to soak for at least 15 minutes. They should be soft when ready.

2. Pour the milk and cream into a medium-sized saucepan and add the vanilla and sugar.

3. Heat the milk mixture until it is just simmering – remove the saucepan from the heat.

4. Squeeze the water out of the gelatine leaves.

5. Add the gelatine leaves to the milk mixture and stir well to allow them to dissolve.

6. Divide the mixture equally between the ramekin dishes and allow it to cool. Place the ramekins in the refrigerator until the mixture has set – about 1–1½ hours.

7. Turn the panna cotta out of the ramekins onto a plate. Serve it with fresh fruits and fruit coulis.

Classic kedgeree
Serves 4 people

Ingredients

350g smoked haddock
2 hard-boiled eggs
25g butter
1 medium onion
½ tsp curry powder
175g basmati rice
3 tbsp chopped parsley
1 tbsp lemon juice
Ground black pepper

Method

1. Place the eggs in a pan of cold water, bring to the boil then boil for 10 minutes. Remove from the heat and place the eggs in a bowl of cold water.

2. Remove the skin from the fish using a sharp knife. Put the fish in a pan and cover with 600ml of cold water. Heat until just under boiling point and poach for 8–10 minutes. When it is cooked, the fish should be opaque in appearance and break up easily.

3. Remove the fish and **save the liquid** it was cooked in.

4. Remove the shells from the hard-boiled eggs and chop them into quarters.

5. Peel and chop the onion into small dice.

6. Melt the butter in a large frying pan and sauté the chopped onion over a low heat for 4–5 minutes until it is softened.

7. Stir in the curry powder and the rice. Cook for a further minute, coating the rice in the butter.

8. Add the saved fish liquid to the rice mixture, cover with a lid or aluminium foil and simmer over a low heat for 15 minutes, or until the rice is cooked. Stir the mixture occasionally.

9. Break up the fish and stir it into the cooked rice along with the eggs, parsley, lemon juice and black pepper.

10. Cover and cook for a further 5 minutes.

11. Serve with vegetables, e.g. peas, broccoli

This recipe uses:

Commodities

Fish – haddock
Rice
Dairy foods – butter
Eggs
Vegetables

Techniques

Skinning the fish
Chopping
Peeling
Slicing

Cooking methods

Boiling
Poaching
Simmering
Frying – sautéing

Chicken Jambalaya
Serves 4

This recipe uses:

Commodities

Poultry – Chicken
Chorizo sausage
Rice
Oil
Vegetables

Techniques

Knife skills – chicken
Peeling
Chopping

Cooking methods

Frying – sautéing, pan frying
Boiling
Simmering

Ingredients

1 or 2 chicken breasts
60g chorizo sausage **(optional)**
2 cloves garlic
175g long grain rice – white or brown (wholegrain)
1 red and 1 yellow pepper
1 large onion – finely chopped
1 stick celery – finely chopped
1 tbsp oil
1 tsp dried thyme
1 tsp paprika
1 tsp Tabasco sauce
300ml chicken stock (you can use a stock cube – dissolve it in 300ml boiling water)
400g can of chopped tomatoes

Method

1. Cut the chicken and sausage into bite-sized pieces.

2. Peel and crush garlic. De-seed and slice the peppers.

3. Heat the oil in a large saucepan. Fry the chicken on a medium heat for 5 minutes or until browned all over. Remove from the pan and set aside in a clean bowl.

4. Fry the chopped onion, celery, garlic and peppers for 5 minutes.

5. Stir in the rice and fry it for 1 minute, until the rice is coated in oil.

6. Stir in the thyme, paprika and Tabasco sauce.

7. Add the chicken, sausage, chicken stock and tomatoes and bring to the boil.

8. Reduce the heat and simmer for 20 minutes, stirring frequently until all the liquid has been absorbed and the rice is cooked. Brown rice may take a few minutes longer to cook.

9. Serve with a crisp salad.

Zarda

(a sweet rice dessert from the Indian sub-continent)
Serves 4–6 people

Ingredients

350g uncooked white rice – either long or round grain
1 tbsp oil
175g sugar
5 whole cardamom pods
½ tsp yellow liquid food colouring (if a concentrated food colouring paste is used, use barely a ¼ tsp)
2 tbsp double cream
1 tbsp raisins
1 tbsp chopped almonds
1 tbsp chopped walnuts
Finely grated zest of 1 orange

This recipe uses:

Commodities

Rice
Sugar
Dairy foods – double cream
Dried fruits

Techniques

Zesting
Chopping

Cooking methods

Boiling

Method

1. Put the rice into a saucepan of boiling water with the cardamom pods and food colouring. Simmer the rice until it is tender. Stir it occasionally.

2. Put the oil into a large pan.

3. Drain the rice and tip it into the pan containing the oil. Heat the pan and add the sugar. Cook for a few minutes.

4. Turn off the heat and add the cream, raisins, nuts and orange zest. Stir well.

Commodity: Cereals – pasta

Basic pasta recipe

Ingredients
200g 00 grade pasta flour
1 egg
1 egg yolk

Method

1. Put 200g of '00' flour into a mixing bowl and make a small well.

2. Add the egg and the egg yolk.

3. With clean hands, or using a fork or knife, begin to fold the eggs into the flour; continue mixing until the mixture forms a soft dough.

4. Tip the dough onto a floured surface and knead it for about a minute to form into a ball shape.

5. Wrap the dough in cling film and leave to rest in a fridge for 20 minutes before using.

6. Cut the dough into two pieces.

Ravioli

Ingredients for ravioli filling

100g spinach leaves – cooked in a little boiling water, drained thoroughly and chopped
100g ricotta or feta cheese – grated
100g fresh breadcrumbs
1 egg yolk
1 whole egg
¼ teaspoon grated nutmeg
Seasoning

Method

1. Put a pasta sheet on the floured work surface and place heaped teaspoons of the filing mixture at equal intervals along and across the pasta.

2. Brush a little beaten egg around each heap of filling.

3. Lay another pasta sheet in top and carefully press down around each filling ball to remove any air.

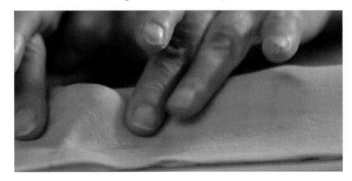

7. Flatten one piece until it's about 10mm thick.

8. Start with the pasta machine at its widest setting and pass the dough through the rollers.

9. Repeat this process, decreasing the roller setting down grade by grade with each pass until you reach the second to thinnest setting.

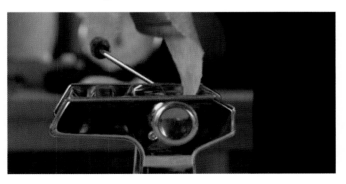

4. Use a cookie cutter to cut into circles, then dust with semolina flour and set aside until you have made all the ravioli.

5. Drop the ravioli into a pan of boiling water and cook until they float to the surface.

6. When they are cooked, drain the ravioli and place on a plate.

7. Pour a sauce over the ravioli and add a sprinkling of chopped parsley, basil or grated cheese.

Variations

Pasta dough can be flavoured and coloured using different ingredients, e.g.:

Herb pasta: add 1 handful of finely chopped fresh herbs (any mixture) to the flour and proceed as for the basic recipe.

Beetroot pasta: leave out the egg yolk and replace it with 50g peeled, cooked and puréed beetroot – proceed as for the basic recipe. A little more flour may be needed according to how much water was in the beetroot.

Spinach pasta (pasta verdi): leave out the egg yolk and ½ a cup of cooked and puréed spinach. Make sure that the spinach was squeezed to remove water from it after cooking. Proceed as for the basic recipe – a little more flour may be needed according to how much water was in the spinach.

Pepper pasta: add 1 level tbsp freshly ground black pepper. Proceed as for the basic recipe.
You could add a little chilli or paprika pepper if desired.

Tomato pasta: add 1 tbsp concentrated tomato purée. Proceed as for the basic recipe. You may need to add a little more flour to the dough.

Commodity: Cereals – wheat flour

Basic bread recipe

Ingredients

450g strong plain white bread flour
OR wholemeal bread flour
OR 225g of white and 225g of wholemeal bread flour
½ level teaspoon salt **(optional)**
285ml warm water (add an extra 15ml if you are using wholemeal flour)
10g fresh yeast OR 1 tsp dried yeast OR 1 tsp fast-acting yeast
1 tsp sugar

Method

1. Set the oven: gas 7/220°C (200°C for a fan oven).

2. Yeast: If you are using:

    Fresh yeast or dried yeast – dissolve it in the warm water and add 1 tsp sugar. Leave in a warm place for a few minutes to activate and produce bubbles of gas.

    Fast acting dried yeast – add the yeast directly to the flour. Do not add sugar.

3. Add the salt to the flour and stir well. Then add the yeast liquid/water to the flour and stir well with a wooden spoon until mixed to a dough.

4. Knead the dough on a lightly floured worktop for at least 5 minutes. The dough should be stretchy and smooth. Do not add too much flour as the dough will dry out and not rise properly.

5. *Traditional method*: leave the dough in a covered mixing bowl in a warm place to prove (rise) for at least 1 hour, until doubled in size. Tip the dough out onto the worktop and knead thoroughly for a few minutes. Cut and shape the dough into rolls or a loaf and leave in a warm place to rise again for 15 minutes before baking.

    Quick method: Either – cut and shape the dough into 8 bread rolls and leave on a greased or lined baking tray in a warm place for 15 minutes.

    Or – shape the dough into a loaf and leave on a greased or lined baking tray or loaf tin in a warm place for 15 minutes.

6. Glaze with beaten egg, milk or oil and sprinkle with poppy, sesame seeds, pumpkin seeds or oats if wanted.

7. Rolls: Bake for 15–20 minutes until well risen and golden brown. The cooked rolls should sound hollow when you tap them underneath with your fingers.

    Loaf: Bake for 20 minutes then turn the oven down to gas 5/ 190°C (180°C fan ovens) for a further 15 minutes. The cooked loaf should sound hollow when you tap it underneath with your fingers.

This recipe uses:

Commodities
Flour
Yeast

Techniques
Dough making
Kneading
Shaping

Cooking methods
Baking

Knot

Kaiser

Bloomer

Plait

Round

Snail/coil

Vienna/almond

Cob

Enriched yeast dough

This recipe uses:

Commodities

Flour
Yeast
Eggs
Dairy foods – butter, milk
Sugar

Techniques

Dough making
Kneading
Shaping

Cooking methods

Baking

Ingredients

450g strong plain white bread flour
20g fresh yeast OR 2 tsp dried yeast OR 2 tsp fast acting yeast
50g caster sugar
50g butter
2 eggs
Approx. 250ml warm milk (you need 300ml liquid altogether including the eggs)

This dough is used to make:

Chelsea bun

Iced buns

Doughnuts

Hot cross buns

Method

1. Warm the milk until it feels comfortably warm when you dip your finger into it.

2. Yeast: If you are using:

    Fresh yeast or dried yeast – dissolve it in the warm milk and add 1 tsp sugar. Leave in a warm place for a few minutes to activate and produce bubbles of gas.

    Fast-acting dried yeast – add the yeast directly to the flour. Do not add sugar.

3. Rub the butter into the flour and add the sugar.

4. Add the beaten eggs and milk/yeast liquid. Mix to a soft dough.

5. Knead for 5 minutes and leave in a warm place in a covered bowl to rise for 1½–2 hours, until doubled in size.

6. Knead again.

7. Shape into round or finger-shaped buns and leave to rise for another 10 minutes.

8. Bake at gas 6/200°C for 15 minutes until well risen and golden.

Shortcrust pastry

Ingredients

100g plain flour
50g butter (you can use block (hard) vegetable fat spread instead)
25ml cold water
NB: the *proportions* of the ingredients are always the same, i.e.:
half fat to flour, e.g. 100g butter to 200g flour
25ml of cold water to every 100g flour, e.g. 75ml cold water to 300g flour

This recipe uses:

Commodities

Flour
Dairy foods – butter

Techniques

Dough making
Kneading
Shaping

Cooking methods

Baking

Method – for best results make sure that all the ingredients are cold

1. Add the plain flour to a mixing bowl.

2. Cut the chilled, hard fat into the flour and distribute it evenly.

3. Rub the fat into the flour, using your fingertips as lightly and gently as possible.

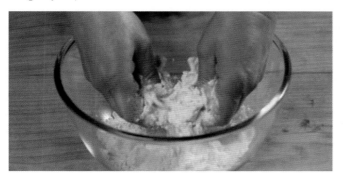

4. If you shake the bowl, any large pieces of fat will come to the surface.

5. When the fat has been rubbed in, make a well in the centre and add the cold water. Then use a palette knife to mix in the water.

6. Bring the dough together, cutting and turning, so it starts to combine.

7. Then bring it all together with your fingertips making a firm, smooth dough.

8. Remove the dough and knead it very lightly on a lightly floured work surface until it becomes smooth.

9. When the dough is ready, cover it and leave in the refrigerator for about 30 minutes.

10. Once rested, the pastry is ready to be rolled out and used as needed, for example, to line a pastry case or make pies or pasties.

Uses

Pies, tarts, flans, pasties, sausage rolls, etc.

Variations

- Add grated cheese to make cheese pastry (50g strong Cheddar cheese for every 100g flour)
- Pâté sucrée (sweet shortcrust pastry) – 200g plain flour, 90g butter, 60g caster sugar, 3 egg yolks (no water added)

Tip – shortcrust pastry must be handled very gently, otherwise it will become tough and very hard to roll out. If your hands are hot, the fat will melt, which will also make the pastry difficult to handle. To avoid these problems, make the pastry in a food processor, which only takes a few seconds and handle it carefully when you roll it out.

Puff pastry

Ingredients

225g strong white plain flour
150g butter or block vegetable fat spread (refrigerated and hard).
DO NOT USE soft vegetable fat spread or soft butter spread.
9 tbsp (135ml) cold water

For best results make sure that all the ingredients are cold

Method

1. Rub ¼ of the butter or block vegetable fat spread into the flour.

2. Chop the rest of the butter or block vegetable fat spread into small pieces about 1 cm³ and stir them into the flour.

3. Add the water and stir in to form a soft, stretchy, elastic dough that will be lumpy in texture because of the cubes of fat.

4. Carefully roll and fold the pastry (see diagrams) at least 4 times, allowing the pastry to rest in the refrigerator (covered) for at least 5 minutes each time after rolling and folding it.

5. Rest the pastry in the refrigerator before you use it.

6. The pastry must be cooked in a hot oven – gas 6/200°C (190°C for a fan oven) – to allow the fat to be absorbed by the starch in the flour and the air and steam to expand and raise the pastry.

7. Instructions for rolling and folding the pastry:

Rolling and folding a dough to create layers

The baked texture of some doughs, e.g. flaky or puff pastry, Danish pastries, get their texture from the dough being rolled out and folded several times. This process traps air, and along with the steam and layers of fat form light, crisp and thin layers of pastry to develop in the oven. This is what happens.

1. The dough is formed by rubbing some of the fat into the flour until it looks like breadcrumbs, then adding the rest of the fat cut up into small dice and the water. A lumpy, stretchy dough is formed as the gluten in the flour develops into long, stretchy molecules. The lumps are the pieces of diced fat.

2. The dough is rolled into a rectangle, three times as long as it is wide (use your hands as a measure). The rolling starts to squash the diced fat.

3. The dough is then folded into three and sealed at the edges and allowed to rest in the refrigerator for a few minutes to allow the gluten molecules to relax.

   Steps 2 to 3 are repeated at least 3 times.

This recipe uses:

Commodities
Flour
Dairy foods – butter

Techniques
Dough making
Kneading
Shaping

Cooking methods
Baking

Uses
Savoury plait
Vol au vents
Fruit mille feuilles
Cream horns
Pie toppings
Pasties
Sausage rolls
Mince pie toppings
Eccles cakes
Cream slices
Fruit turnovers
Etc.

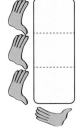
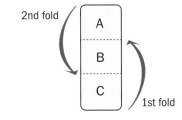

2nd fold

A

B

C

1st fold

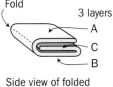

Fold

3 layers
A
C
B

Side view of folded pastry showing layers

Seal the edges with a rolling pin

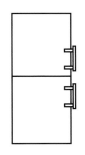

Rest the pastry in the fridge

Choux pastry
Eclairs – serves 10 people
Profiteroles – serves 6 people

Ingredients

Choux pastry – basic mixture:
150ml water
50g butter or block vegetable fat spread
60g flour (strong plain bread flour is best)
2 medium eggs

For chocolate eclairs, in addition to the basic choux mixture, you need:

Filling
200ml double or whipping cream whipped until thick
To make Chantilly cream, add ½ tsp vanilla essence and 2 tbsp caster sugar after the cream is whipped

Topping
150g plain cooking chocolate – melted in a bowl over a pan of simmering water

For profiteroles, in addition to the basic choux mixture, you need:
200ml double or whipping cream – whipped until thick

Chocolate sauce
150ml milk
1½ tbsp cocoa powder
1 tbsp sugar
1 tbsp golden syrup
10g butter or vegetable fat spread

For savoury eclairs, in addition to the basic choux mixture, you need:
75g strong flavoured Cheddar cheese or Parmesan cheese – grated and added to the choux mixture before adding the eggs
120g cream cheese mixed together with 1 tbsp chopped fresh herbs, mixed together for the filling

Storage instructions: Best eaten on the day they are made OR cover and store in a refrigerator in an airtight tin or box for up to 2 days.

The eclairs can be frozen for up to 3 months, either as just the pastry shells or filled.

Method

Making the choux pastry

1.   Heat the oven to gas 6/200°C (190°C for a fan oven), you will need to use the top shelf in a gas oven.

2.   Bring the water and butter (or vegetable fat spread) to the boil in a saucepan – make sure all the fat has melted.

3.   **Turn off the heat** and, straightaway, add the sieved flour and carefully mix it in with a wooden spoon and then beat it until a ball of **choux paste** is formed in the pan (you are developing the gluten strands when you beat it, which will help the choux pastry stretch when it rises).

4.   Allow the choux paste to cool for a few minutes.

5.   **Gradually** add the beaten egg, a little at a time – *you may not need it all* – beating the mixture well. The paste should be a dropping consistency, it must not be runny.

This recipe uses:

Commodities
Flour
Dairy foods – butter, cream, milk, cheese
Chocolate

Techniques
Choux paste preparation
Shaping/piping
Coating
Sauce making

Cooking methods
Boiling
Baking

Piping the mixture

For the eclairs:

1. Pipe the mixture into eclair shapes onto a greased or lined baking tray. Allow some room for them to expand.

For the profiteroles

2. Pipe the mixture into small, regular shaped mounds onto a greased or lined baking tray. Allow some room for them to expand.

For the savoury eclairs

3. Add the grated cheese to the mixture and beat well. Pipe the mixture into eclair shapes onto a greased or lined baking tray. Leave some room for them to expand.

Baking the choux pastry

4. Bake for 15 minutes, then turn the temperature down to gas 5/190°C (180°C if you are using a fan oven) for another 10 minutes – DO NOT OPEN THE OVEN DOOR WHILE THE ECLAIRS ARE BAKING, OTHERWISE THEY WILL COLLAPSE, BECAUSE THEY ONLY SET IN THE LAST FEW MINUTES OF BAKING.

5. The eclairs should be crisp and well risen – make a slit along the length of each eclair at the side and let it cool. Carefully scrape out and any doughy bits that are inside.

Baking the profiteroles

6. Bake for 15 minutes until well risen and crisp and make a slit in the side of each one and allow to cool.

Finishing the éclairs

7. Fill each with whipped cream, either with a teaspoon or by piping the cream.

8. Melt the chocolate in a bowl over a pan of simmering water and dip the eclairs into it and leave them to set on a cooling tray.

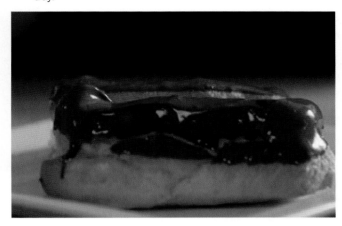

Finishing the profiteroles

9. Make the chocolate sauce. Put all the ingredients into a medium saucepan and heat gently until the butter has melted. Bring to the boil, then simmer gently for approx. 15–20 minutes to reduce the sauce until it is thick and glossy.

10. Carefully arrange 4–5 profiteroles into a serving bowl, then pour over a quantity of chocolate sauce and serve.

Finishing the savoury eclairs

11. Fill each eclair with a mixture of cream cheese and fresh chopped herbs or another filling of your choice.

Cake making: Whisked sponge

This recipe uses:

Commodities

Flour
Eggs
Sugar
Jam

Techniques

Whisking method
Rolling

Cooking methods

Baking

Ingredients

3 eggs
75g caster sugar
75g plain flour

Variations

A whisked sponge mixture can be made into a layered gateau containing fruit and cream or into sponge finger biscuits.

Method

1. Heat the oven – gas 6/200°C (190°C for a fan oven).

2. Grease and line a Swiss roll tin.

3. Place the eggs and sugar in a bowl and whisk at medium speed until the mixture is light, thick and creamy, and leaves a visible trail for at least 5 seconds when the whisk is removed.

4. Sieve the flour twice and fold it very gently into the mixture with a metal spoon in a figure of 8 movement, until there is no visible flour – do not eat it in or use a whisk, as the air will come out.

5. Pour the mixture into the tin and tip it until the mixture goes evenly into the corners.

6. Bake for 10–12 minutes until the Swiss roll is well risen, spongy to the touch and starting to shrink away from the edges of the tin.

7. Remove from the oven and STRAIGHTAWAY tip the sponge away from you onto a sheet of non-stick paper.

8. Carefully remove the paper that lined the tin.

9. Trim a little off the edges of the sponge with a sharp knife (they are crisp and may stop the sponge rolling up properly) and spread the softened jam (stir it with a spoon) over the sponge.

10. Roll up the sponge tightly and leave to cool.

All-in-one chocolate and orange cake

Ingredients

Basic cake mix:

225g self-raising flour

50g cocoa powder (not drinking chocolate)

1 tsp baking powder

225g softened butter or vegetable fat spread

175g caster sugar

3 large eggs

2 tbsp milk

Grated zest of an orange **(optional)**

Frosting

175g icing sugar

25g cocoa

70g butter or vegetable fat spread (softened)

Juice of the orange

Decorations: e.g. grated chocolate, chocolate leaves, orange glace slices, finely chopped pistachio nuts or almonds

You will need a 20–23 cm cake tin

Storage instructions

Store the cake in an airtight tin or box at room temperature for up to 5 days

Freezer: Can be frozen for up to 6 months but must be well wrapped and protected from drying out and being damaged in the freezer

Variations

Instead of using cocoa powder and orange zest in the cake and frosting, the following flavourings could be used:

For the cake:

Vanilla – add 1 tsp vanilla extract

Lemon drizzle – add the finely grated zest of 2 lemons to the mixture. To make the drizzle, squeeze the juice of the lemons and stir it into 2 tbsp icing or caster sugar, and pour over the top of the cakes as soon as they come out of the oven (make a few holes in the top of the cakes with a skewer first).

Method

1. Basic cake mix – place all the ingredients for the basic cake mix into a mixing bowl and whisk at medium speed with an electronic whisk, or beat well with a wooden spoon until well mixed and light in texture and colour.

2. Divide the mixture evenly between two 20cm sandwich cake tins, which have been greased or lined with non-stick paper.

3. Spread the mixture out evenly using a palate knife or the back of a spoon.

4. Bake at gas 4/190°C (180°C for a fan oven) for 20–25 minutes until the cakes are well risen and spongy to the touch.

This recipe uses:

Commodities

Flour

Eggs

Sugar

Dairy foods: milk, butter,

Cocoa

Fruit: orange

Techniques

All-in-one cake making methods

Decorating

Cooking methods

Baking

5. Turn the cakes out onto a cooling rack and allow them to cool.

6. Frosting: whisk or beat together the sieved icing sugar, cocoa and softened butter or vegetable fat spread until well mixed – it may be a bit dry at this stage but that is quite normal. Add the orange juice, a teaspoonful at a time, until the mixture is smooth, creamy and easy to spread.

7. Spread some of the frosting onto one of the cooled cakes and sandwich both of the cakes together.

8. Spread more frosting on the top of the cake and, if you have enough left, you can then pipe it onto the top of the cake with a star nozzle and piping bag to decorate.

9. Add your other decorations to finish the cake.

This cake can also be coated and decorated with chocolate ganache.

Chocolate ganache

For a cake filling or for a thick glaze to go on the top of a cake, equal quantities of chocolate and double cream are needed, e.g. 300g of double cream and 300g of dark chocolate (70–75% cocoa solids is best).

1. Chop the chocolate into small pieces.

2. Pour the cream into a pan and heat it gently on a low heat on the hob for a few minutes. It is important not to overheat the cream – it only needs to be warm enough to melt the chocolate. Carefully test – it should feel comfortably warm.

3. Remove the cream from the hob. Add the chocolate to the cream. Stir it gently then leave it for several minutes to give the chocolate time to melt.

4. Stir the ganache with a balloon whisk or wooden spoon, until it all looks the same colour and consistency.

5. The longer it is allowed to cool, the thicker the ganache will get.

6. For piping decorations on to a cake, the ganache needs to be completely cold, Give it a thorough stir before you use it for piping.

Spicy lentil and tomato soup
Serves 4–6 people

This recipe uses:

Ingredients

100g orange lentils
1 tbsp oil
2 garlic cloves
1 carrot
1 onion or 1 leek
½ tsp dried chilli powder **(optional)**
2 tsp ground cumin
1 tsp dried oregano
2 tbsp tomato purée
600ml water
1 small vegetable stock cube
Ground black pepper

Commodities

Oil
Spices, herbs
Vegetables – lentils, carrot, onion, garlic

Techniques

Chopping
Peeling
Slicing

Cooking methods

Boiling
Simmering
Frying – sautéing

Method

1. Peel and chop the carrot and onion or leek into small pieces. Peel and crush the garlic.

2. Heat the oil in a large saucepan; add the chopped onion or leek and sauté on a low heat for about 5 minutes with the pan lid on.

3. Add the garlic, chopped carrots, chilli powder, oregano and cumin, and then cook for 2 minutes with the pan lid on.

4. Stir in the lentils, tomato purée, the water and the stock cube.

5. Bring to the boil, and then simmer gently for approximately 20 minutes, stirring occasionally.

6. Blend the soup with an electric hand blender, taste, and adjust the seasoning with some ground black pepper.

7. Serve the soup with crusty bread or croutons (toasted or fried squares of bread) or a savoury cheese scone.

8. Garnish (decorate) the soup with finely chopped parsley or coriander.

Vegetable stir fry
Serves 2–3 people

This recipe uses:

Commodities

Oil
Vegetables
Fresh spices – ginger, garlic
Cereals – noodles

Techniques

Chopping
Peeling
Slicing
Blending (sauce)

Cooking methods

Frying – stir frying

Ingredients

50g dry noodles *OR* a packet of straight-to-wok noodles (pre-cooked)

Approximately 450g of a mixture of vegetables, e.g. red, green or yellow peppers, courgette, spring onions, mushrooms, mangetout, sweetcorn, carrots, bean sprouts, green beans, broccoli, celery, sweet potato, pak choi, cauliflower, snow peas

50g nuts (without shells) e.g. almonds, pistachios, cashews **(optional)**

2 tbsp oil

3–4 cloves garlic, crushed

1 piece of fresh ginger – approx. 2cm long, peeled and finely chopped or grated

Sauce

2 tbsp soy sauce

1 tbsp honey

1 tsp sesame oil

2 tsp corn flour

80ml water

Method

1. Prepare all the vegetables by cutting them into thin strips, sticks or slices, or breaking them into small pieces, e.g. broccoli florets. Set aside in a bowl.

2. In another bowl, soak the noodles in boiling water until soft (leave them in the hot water in the bowl while you are cooking the rest of the ingredients).

3. In a wok, gently heat the oil and add the nuts. Stir fry for 5 minutes, stirring constantly until the nuts start to brown.

4. Add all the vegetables and the garlic and ginger to the wok.

5. Stir fry for another 5 minutes on a medium heat, stirring constantly. If the mixture starts to become dry or it is sticking to the pan, add a little cold water (a few tablespoons is enough) rather than more oil.

6. **Sauce:** Blend the corn flour with the water, honey, sesame oil and soy sauce and add to the wok and cook for 5 minutes.

7. Drain the noodles and add them to the wok. Mix well.

8. Serve with rice.

Summer puddings
Serves 4 people

Ingredients

250g sliced brioche loaf
800g mixed summer fruits (frozen fruits work very well)
2 level tbsp caster sugar

4 non-metallic pudding moulds or ramekins, about 150ml each

Method

1. Remove the crusts from the brioche.

2. Line four 150ml (¼ pint) non-metallic pudding moulds, e.g. ramekin dishes with most of the bread, reserving enough slices to make a lid for each one.

3. Place the fruit in a large pan with the sugar.

4. Poach the fruit gently on a low heat, stirring, for 2–3 minutes or until the fruit has released its juices and the sugar has dissolved.

5. Fill the lined pudding moulds or ramekins with three-quarters of the fruit, top with the reserved slices of bread, then cover with cling-film.

6. Weigh down the puddings with weights or cans and refrigerate overnight.

7. Un-mould the summer puddings and spoon the remaining fruit on top to serve.

This recipe uses:

Commodities
Fruit
Cereals – brioche

Techniques
Lining a ramekin

Cooking methods
Poaching

Spiced apple trifle
Serves 6–8 people

This recipe uses:

Commodities

Fruit – cooking apples
Cereals – bread
Dairy foods – cream,
butter

Techniques

Peeling, slicing
Chopping
Stewing fruit
Frying breadcrumbs
Whipping cream
Piping

Cooking methods

Stewing
Shallow frying

Ingredients

450g Bramley cooking apples – peeled, cored and sliced
2 tbsp water
200g fresh wholemeal breadcrumbs (not from a packet)
75g butter
50g Demerara sugar
1 level tsp mixed spice

Chantilly cream
300ml whipping cream
½ tsp vanilla extract
25g caster sugar

Decoration
30g grated plain chocolate or 30g chopped pistachio or pecan nuts
Orange zest

To serve – 1 large or 6 individual glass dishes

Method

1. Stew the apples in the water in a covered
    pan on a low heat until they are soft and
    pulped. Stir regularly. Cool the apple pulp.

2. Melt the butter in a frying pan and add the
    breadcrumbs – fry on a medium heat until
    they are crisp, turning them frequently to
    prevent them from burning.

3. Mix the sugar and spice together and add
    to the breadcrumbs. Cook them for another
    5 minutes, then leave them to cool.

4. Whip the cream until fairly stiff and save
    some for decoration.

5. In the serving bowl, put a layer of cooled
    apple, followed by breadcrumbs, then
    cream, and repeat, finishing with a layer of
    cream.

6. Use the saved cream for piping a
    decoration on top. Add grated chocolate,
    chopped nuts or orange zest for decoration.

Chocolate mousse

Ingredients

1 pack (approximately 340g) of silken tofu (not regular, firm or smoked tofu)
120g dark chocolate – broken into pieces
3 tbsp maple syrup
½ tsp vanilla extract

4 glasses/ramekins for serving

Method

1. Melt the chocolate in a heatproof bowl over a pan of simmering water.

2. Put the tofu, maple syrup and vanilla into a food processor and process until smooth.

3. Pour in the melted chocolate and process until well combined.

4. Pour the mousse into individual glasses/ramekins and leave to chill in the refrigerator.

5. Decorate with soft fruits, e.g. raspberries, strawberries, blueberries or grated chocolate.

This recipe uses:

Commodities

Soya – silken tofu
Chocolate
Fruits – soft fruits

Techniques

Use of food processor
Use of bain-marie
Decorating

Cooking methods

Melting chocolate
Chilling

Variation

Fruit mousse

Leave out the chocolate.

Add: 150g frozen berry fruits, e.g. raspberries, strawberries, blackberries.

Put all the ingredients in the food processor and process until smooth. Then pour into dishes and refrigerate. This mousse may have a softer texture than the chocolate version.

Edamame (soya) bean salad

Commodities

Vegetables – beans, onion, pepper, Herbs and spices Fruit – lime

Techniques

Peeling
Chopping
Zesting

Cooking methods

Frying – sautéing

Ingredients

1 onion
1 small red pepper
1 tbsp oil
100g sweetcorn kernels – frozen or canned
100g canned black beans
100g canned kidney beans
150g frozen edamame (soya) beans
1 tsp cumin seeds
1 small handful of fresh coriander – finely chopped
1 lime
Seasoning

Method

1. Peel and finely chop the onion.

2. De-seed and finely chop the pepper.

3. Sauté the onion and pepper in the oil until softened.

4. Add the cumin seeds, all the beans and some seasoning.

5. Sauté for 5 minutes, then remove from heat.

6. Stir in the finely grated zest and juice from the lime.

7. Stir in the finely chopped coriander.

8. Serve warm or cold.

Variations

Other ingredients can be added to the salad, e.g. chopped avocado pear, chick peas, green peas, chopped cucumber, courgette, celery or apple, mushrooms.

Other recipe suggestions

Poultry – chicken, turkey, duck, goose

- Sweet and sour chicken
- Thai chicken soup
- Home-made chicken/turkey nuggets and burgers
- Roasted chicken with lemon, rosemary and garlic
- Chicken Caesar salad
- Small chicken pies with hot water crust pastry

Meat – beef, lamb, mutton, pork, bacon, ham

- Cottage pie
- Cornish pasties
- Moussaka
- Meat casserole
- Meatballs in tomato sauce
- Meat and vegetable kebabs

Fish – white fish, oily fish, seafood

- Fish pie
- Fish stew
- Seafood risotto/paella
- Fish chowder
- Fish cakes
- Fish pâté

Eggs

- Scotch eggs
- Omelette
- Spanish tortilla
- Egg custard tarts
- Frittata
- Egg fried rice
- Crème caramel/crème brulee

Dairy foods – milk, cheese, butter, cream, yogurt, buttermilk

- Bread and butter pudding
- Pancakes
- Ice cream
- Frozen yogurt dessert
- Shortbread
- Banoffee pie
- Fruit and chocolate mousse
- Fruit fool
- Crème Anglaise (custard)
- Savoury dips using yogurt as the base

Rice

- Risotto
- Paella
- Rice pudding
- Rice salad
- Pilaf
- Fried rice
- Rice and peas
- Sushi

Vegetables

- Roasted root vegetables
- Root vegetable mash
- Salads
- Vegetable moussaka
- Vegetable spring rolls
- Tempura (battered and fried) vegetables
- Potato/sweet potato/squash curry/saag aloo
- Lentil dhal
- Vegetable quiche
- Salsa

Fruit

- Fruit pies
- Crumbles
- Poached pears
- Banana bread
- Fruit cake
- Fruit fool
- Fruit trifle
- Fruit salad
- Sorbets and ice creams

Soya

- Stir fries
- TVP in curries, cottage pie, pasties, etc.
- Nut roasts
- Curries

Cereals

Flour – biscuits

- Shortbread
- Viennese whirls/fingers
- Ginger biscuits
- Cookies

Flour – cake making

All-in-one/creamed:
- Muffin variations:
  - chocolate chip
  - blueberry,
  - lemon drizzle
  - raspberry and white chocolate chip
  - ginger and lime
  - spiced apple
- Loaf cake variations
  - spiced apple
  - lemon and blueberry
  - banana
  - orange and apricot

Chapter 28

Unit 2 Assessment

What will I learn?

This chapter will cover the different stages for planning and carrying out the Unit 2 assessment, which is assessed through a **Controlled (supervised) Assessment Task (CAT)** in the form of a **Learner Assignment Brief (LAB)**. The CAT is carried out internally (at school/college), and is designed to allow you to demonstrate your knowledge, skills and understanding of the Hospitality and Catering industry. Your response to the LAB will be measured against the **Learning Outcomes (LOs)** and **Assessment Criteria (AC)**, which are set out in the course specification (see below).

Key terms

- **Assessment Criteria (AC)** – what you need to do to demonstrate your knowledge and understanding

- **Controlled Assessment Task (CAT)** – controlled assessment is a form of internal assessment, which includes control levels at three points:
  Task setting
  Task taking
  Task marking

- **Learner Assignment Brief (LAB)** – a piece of information that will describe a fictional hospitality and catering business or scenario that you will be asked to plan dishes for to meet the needs of customers

- **Learning Outcome (LO)** – what you need to know and understand

What you need to do to complete Unit 2

Below is a flow chart that sets out all the **stages** you need to complete for the Unit 2 assessment:

1 Carefully read the LAB provided by the examination board

2 Analyse the LAB making notes of key words and key hospitality and catering information, e.g.:
- Specified groups or customers
- Type and location of venue
- Staff numbers required

3 Task 1: Produce a written proposal
LO1 Understanding the importance of nutrition in planning a menu
Complete all the assessment criteria: AC1.1, AC1.2, AC1.3 and AC1.4

4 Task 1: Produce a written proposal
LO2 Understanding menu planning
Complete all the assessment criteria: AC2.1, AC2.2 and AC2.3

5 Propose dishes for the hospitality and catering provision specified in the LAB

6 Choose dishes that demonstrate different types of skills, techniques and cooking methods

7 Task 2: Plan the production of dishes for a menu
LO2 Understanding menu planning
Complete all the assessment criteria: AC2.1, AC2.2 and AC2.3

8 Task 2: Produce an annotated and dovetailed time plan for your chosen dishes
LO2 Understanding menu planning
AC2.4 Plan the production of the dishes including accompaniments

9 Task 3: Include teacher observation records/photographs
LO3 Be able to cook dishes
Complete all the assessment criteria: AC3.1, AC3.2, AC3.3, AC3.4 and AC3.5

Learner Outcomes (LOs) and Assessment Criteria (AC)

The three tasks in the LAB are broken down into AC that must all be completed, as shown in the chart below:

Task	Assessment Criteria	What you have to produce
1	**Task 1:** There are **4 parts** to Assessment Criteria 1: **AC1.1 Describe** functions of **nutrients** in the human body **AC1.2 Compare** nutritional needs of **specific groups** **AC1.3 Explain** characteristics of **unsatisfactory nutritional intake** **AC1.4 Explain** how **cooking methods** impact on nutritional value **Task 1:** There are **3 parts** to Assessment Criteria 2: **AC2.1 Explain** factors to consider when **proposing dishes** for menus **AC2.2 Explain** how dishes on a menu address **environmental issues** **AC2.3 Explain** how menu dishes meet **customer needs**	**Written proposal** (The proposal is a formal way of presenting your answers and ideas linked to the ACs and the LAB)
2	**Task 2:** **AC2.4 Plan** production of dishes for a menu	**Annotated plan** (A detailed time plan for the production of the dishes that you will make)
3	**Task 3:** **AC3.1** Use **techniques** in preparation of **commodities** **AC3.2** Assure **quality** of commodities to be used in food preparation **AC3.3** Use **techniques** in cooking of commodities **AC3.4** Complete dishes using **presentation techniques** **AC3.5** Use **food safety** practices	**Observation record; photographs** (Evidence of how you carried out your practical work and photographs of the finished results)

Each AC has performance bands attached. The example below is for AC 1.1 – 1.4. The performance bands charts range from Level 1 Pass (D–G level at GCSE) through to Level 2 Distinction (A grade at GCSE). *You should have the performance bands charts available to refer to throughout the whole time you are working on the Unit 2 assessment.* More information about performance bands is given on pages 260–261 and 265–267.

Performance bands					
Learning outcome	Assessment criteria	Level 1 pass	Level 2 pass	Level 2 merit	Level 2 distinction
LO1 Understand the importance of nutrition in planning menus	**AC1.1** Describe functions of nutrients in the human body	Outlines the functions of a limited range of nutrients in the human body.	Describes functions of a range of nutrients in the human body.	Describes clearly functions of a range of nutrients in the human body.	
	AC1.2 Compare nutritional needs of specific groups	Outlines nutritional needs of two specific groups. Comparison may be implied.	Compares nutritional needs of two specific groups giving some reasons for similarities and differences.	Compares nutritional needs of two specific groups giving clear reasons for similarities and differences	Compares nutritional needs of two specific groups giving clear and in-depth reasons for similarities and differences
	AC1.3 Explain characteristics of unsatisfactory nutritional intake	Outlines key characteristics of unsatisfactory nutritional intake. Evidence is mainly descriptive with limited reasoning.	Explains characteristics of unsatisfactory nutritional intake. There is evidence of reasoning and relating characteristics to specific groups.	Explains with clear reasoning characteristics of unsatisfactory intake of a range of nutrients. Explanations are related to specific groups.	
	AC1.4 Explain how cooking methods impact on nutritional value	Outlines how cooking methods impact on nutritional value. Evidence is mainly descriptive with limited reasoning.	Explains how a range of cooking methods impact on nutritional value. Reasoned statements are presented.		

Study tip

Before you start your assignment:

- Read through the LAB very carefully and several times.

- Highlight key words. Key words could be, for example, the type of venue the brief has described, the type of clients or customers, or the size of the venue.

- Understand what the LAB is asking you to do to be able to complete the tasks – check with your teacher if you are not sure what you have to do.

- Make sure you have class notes or teacher's notes. Your teacher will check these before the assessment starts.

- Have a copy of the LOs, AC, performance bands chart and mark record sheet to refer to throughout the assessment. *Your teacher should give you these before you read the brief.*

This is **Task 1**
Proposal

This is **Task 2**
Annotated plan

This is **Task 3**
Observation record:
Photographs
Annotated plan

Example Learner Assignment Brief

In this chapter, we are going to work through each stage of the Unit 2 assessment, using an example LAB, so that you can see what is involved.

In this section, you will learn:

- How to extract (pick-out) the key words and key points from the brief you will be given.

- How to cover the Assessment Criteria in each of the Learning Outcomes.

- What the different terminology means in the tasks and AC.

- The different styles you can use to present the evidence for your assignment.

- How to choose dishes that will meet the requirements of the LAB and the AC grading.

- The skill levels of dishes that could be prepared and made to meet the requirements of the LAB and AC.

Stage 1: Read the LAB

The LAB will be a scenario that will describe, for example, a fictional catering company and who their main customers are, what types of food they provide and how many people work there. You might be asked to plan dishes to meet the needs of the customers.

Set out below is an **example** LAB, which has a similar layout to the one you will complete for your CAT in Unit 2:

Edgerton is a small and **stylish village** just **outside London**. Edgerton has become very popular in the last 10 years with **young professionals** and the **retired generation**. Its main attraction is the countryside, peaceful, quiet surroundings and its good **transport links to London**.

Edgerton's population is mainly composed of **professional working people** with **young children** and **retired people**, many of whom have sold their homes in London and relocated to the countryside.

Edgerton already has a **number of upmarket pubs, two coffee shops and a sushi bar** with take away and delivery service.

'Gold Lilly' is a popular hospitality and catering company that have several restaurants in and around the London area. The company have acquired the old library building in Edgerton and have now completed a refurbishment and transformed it into a **classic and stylish restaurant** (the Gold Lilly restaurant), with an open-kitchen plan and **10 tables with availability to seat up to 40 customers**.

The business owners of Gold Lilly have employed a new catering manager, **four highly skilled chefs, a trainee chef and eight assistants** who will support front and back of house.

The catering manager and chef want the **menu to meet the diverse needs** of the local population and visitors to Edgerton.

You have been asked to propose **four** dishes for the new menu. The dishes can be **starters, main courses or desserts**. The trainee chef must be able to prepare and cook at least two of those dishes. You therefore need to ensure that the dishes allow them to demonstrate three skills in cooking and three in preparation. To help the trainee chef you also need to produce a plan that he/she can follow to **cook two** of the dishes. To make sure your plan works you should also prepare and cook the two dishes.

Stage 2: Analyse the LAB

Highlight key words, key points and key hospitality and catering information. In the example LAB, these have been highlighted for you.

Activity 28.1

1. List **three** important points that the LAB is asking you to do.

2. Discuss your answers with your peers.

As you can see, the example LAB is clearly stating the types of customers who will be eating at the Gold Lilly restaurant. Reading the brief helps you imagine the types of customer that you will need to cater for in the menu:

Gold Lilly's customers:

Professional working people with young children

Retired people

Here is a summary of the key words, points and hospitality and catering information that the example LAB is asking you to consider and do:

- Customers: Professional families with young children and retired people
- Venue: A classic and stylish restaurant
- Staff: 4 skilled chefs, trainee chef and 8 assistants to work front and back of house
- Propose 4 dishes: Starter, main or desserts.
- The dishes must demonstrate 3 skills in cooking and 3 in preparation
- Produce a plan for the trainee chef to follow.
- Prepare and cook the 2 dishes, to make sure the plans work.

Stage 3: TASK 1: Produce a written proposal

Now that you have a clear idea of what the example LAB is asking you to do, let us take a look at the Assessment Criteria to see what you need to include in your answer and how it could be structured.

You will learn:

- What the **performance descriptors** mean in each performance band.
- Details of each AC and what you need to do to for each one to achieve your best level.
- Different styles in which you could present your work.

Performance descriptors are the words and phrases used in the AC that tell you what you need to do to reach the standard required to be awarded a Level 1 or 2 pass, a Level 2 merit or a Level 2 distinction.

The performance descriptors have been colour coded: from **red** (higher level – where students give more detailed information, with examples and explanations) through to **green** (lower level – where students give more basic information):

Performance descriptors	Meaning
In-depth	To write about all the major points, giving detailed and thorough explanations and examples that demonstrate knowledge and understanding.
Independently	On your own, without help.
Credible	With evidence or justification to back up something that has been written, e.g. a book reference, an interview, the results of a survey, etc.
Clear/clearly	Easy to understand. To the point. In way that is easy to see or understand. Covering most of the main information.
Compare	Identifies similarities and differences between things.
Describe clearly	To write about the features and characteristics of a topic, place, activity, item or person, in a clear and detailed way.
A range	A variety; not everything.
Some	Adverb: a small amount; not everything included.
Outline	Set out the main types, features or characteristics of something. This could be presented as a simple list.
Explain	To write about something in a clear way, giving the purpose of it, or reasons for it. Using examples to illustrate your answer, to show that you understand what you are writing about.
Limited range	Without fullness/scope. Only covering limited parts of the assessment criteria.
Describe	To write about the features and characteristics of a topic, place, activity, item or person in a simple way without much detail.

Examples of performance descriptors:

To show you what to look for and see how to progress in the performance band chart, some performance descriptors for AC1.2 have been highlighted and colour coded in the chart below to match the previous chart:

Learning Outcome	Assessment Criteria	Level 1 Pass	Level 2 Pass	Level 2 Merit	Level 2 Distinction
LO1 Understand the importance of nutrition in planning menus	AC1.2 Compare nutritional needs of specific groups	Outlines nutritional needs of two specific groups. Comparison may be implied.	Compares nutritional needs of two specific groups giving some reasons for similarities and differences.	Compares nutritional needs of two specific groups giving clear reasons for similarity and differences.	Compares nutritional needs of two specific groups giving clear and in-depth reasons for similarity and differences.

Activity 28.2

Highlight and colour code the performance descriptors for all the Assessment Criteria in LO1, LO2 and LO3 on the performance bands chart you have been given by your teacher. This will help you identify and understand what you need to do to achieve your best result in the Unit 2 Assessment.

How to present your evidence for AC1.1

This is what you have to do for AC1.1

Learning Outcome	Assessment Criteria	Level 1 Pass	Level 2 Pass	Level 2 Merit	Level 2 Distinction
LO1 Understand the importance of nutrition in planning menus	AC1.1 Describe functions of nutrients in the human body	Outlines the functions of a limited range of nutrients in the human body.	Describes functions of a range of nutrients in the human body.	Describes clearly functions of a range of nutrients in the human body.	NB: AC1.1 does not go up to a distinction and will be blank on your performance band chart.

You can display your evidence for AC1.1 in a number of different styles:

- Poster
- Leaflet
- Chart/table
- PowerPoint
- Talk/discussion, which has video evidence.

Draw your own poster describing clearly all the functions of nutrients in the human body

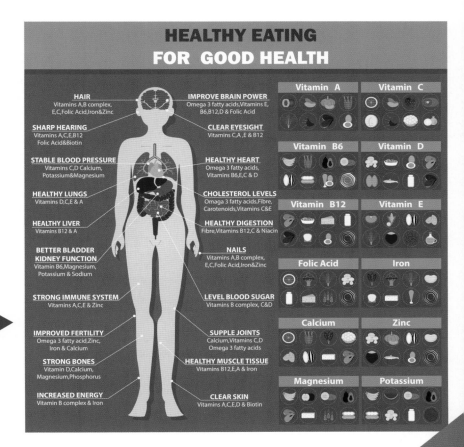

OR

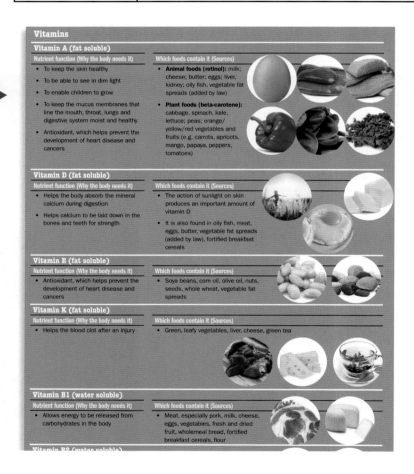

Prepare a chart that shows the specific nutrients that would be found in the proposed dishes

Proposed dish 1	Nutrients in proposed dish
Fresh pasta and chicken salad with a medley of vegetables	Fresh pasta: wholemeal starchy carbohydrate for energy and fibre, which is good for the digestive system Green pepper: contains vitamin C, which is good for healthy skin, absorbing iron and an antioxidant Chicken: high in protein, so good for repairing the body and growth Tomatoes: good amounts of fibre, vitamins A and C to protect from infections Kale: vitamin K, helps the blood clot when injured, vitamin C, good for skin, immune system and absorbing iron

OR

Include a chart covering all the nutrients in the body similar to the ones on pages 125–130

Activity 28.3 Poster challenge

Set out on the next page is an example of an answer that has been awarded a Level 1 Pass. Take a look at this and the teacher feedback alongside.

Discuss the poster with your peers, then design a new poster for AC1.1 to see if you can improve on the example provided to achieve a Level 2 Pass or Level 2 Merit.

AC1.1 Example poster – Level 1 Pass

Dietary fibre is a type of carbohydrate that can't be digested by our body. It keeps the gut healthy and is important to keep the risk of diseases low.

Carbohydrates are needed for our main source of energy.

*There is not enough **detail about the function** of carbohydrates.*

Water makes up to 75% of body mass. It is essential in removing waste, digestion and temperature control.

Fat is an essential nutrient that can provide energy, boost absorption of some vitamins and keeps you warm.

Vitamins the main vitamins are A, C, D, E, K, and B vitamins. Each vitamin has its own role to play in the body. All are needed to maintain optimal health. Vitamins are essential nutrients as they perform hundreds of roles. They help heal wounds, strengthen bones, help the immune system repair, and convert food.

*There is not enough **detail about the functions of nutrients and water**. The student could have added more detail to **all** the functions.*

Example:
Water: All cells and body tissue contain water. All body fluids contain water. Body temperature is controlled by removing heat from the body during sweating. Water is needed for the digestion of food and the absorption of nutrients from the small intestine into the body. Water removes waste products from the body. It helps keep skin moist and healthy. Water keeps the lining of the digestive system, mucous membranes and the lungs healthy and moist.

The student has only covered a limited range of nutrients. More detail could be included on the following:

- ✓ *Protein*
- ✓ *Fat*
- ✓ *Carbohydrate*
- ✓ *Vitamins*
- ✓ *Minerals*
- ✓ *Dietary fibre (NSP)*
- ✓ *Water*

To add more detail, this student could have included the following information for the function of carbohydrates:

The two groups of carbohydrates are complex carbohydrates (which includes starch) and sugars. Whole food carbohydrates, e.g. wholemeal flour, rice and pasta, are better for you as they contain other nutrients, e.g. calcium, fibre, iron and vitamin B complex. Carbohydrates give the body its main source of energy and regulate blood sugar levels. During digestion, they are broken down into glucose, which is absorbed into the blood stream, where it enters the body's cells with the help of insulin.

How to achieve a Level 2 Merit in AC1.1

To be awarded a **Level 2 Merit** all the information about the following nutrients in the human body should be described clearly: protein, fats, carbohydrates, vitamins and minerals, dietary fibre (NSP) and water.

Poster challenge – peer review

You were asked to design a *new* poster for AC1.1. Your poster must meet **Level 2 Pass** or **Level 2 Merit**.

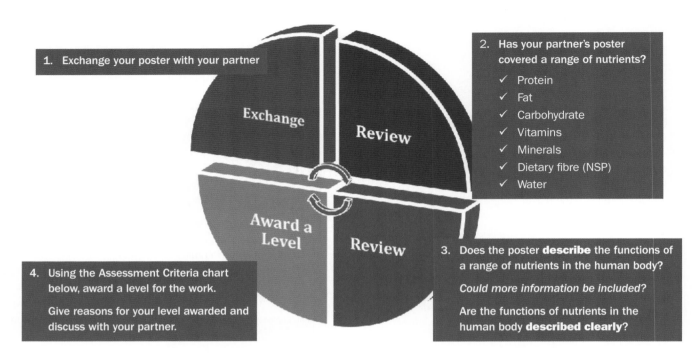

1. Exchange your poster with your partner

2. Has your partner's poster covered a range of nutrients?
   - ✓ Protein
   - ✓ Fat
   - ✓ Carbohydrate
   - ✓ Vitamins
   - ✓ Minerals
   - ✓ Dietary fibre (NSP)
   - ✓ Water

3. Does the poster **describe** the functions of a range of nutrients in the human body?

   Could more information be included?

   Are the functions of nutrients in the human body **described clearly**?

4. Using the Assessment Criteria chart below, award a level for the work.

   Give reasons for your level awarded and discuss with your partner.

Level	Brief description of each performance bands for AC1.1 *(WJEC information from: Guide to teaching)*	Tick if met
Level 1 Pass	Limited range: without fullness/not all mentioned/lacks detail	
Level 2 Pass	Describe: identify distinctive features and give descriptive, factual detail. Not all 'content' needs to be covered to meet Pass standard.	
Level 2 Merit	Describe clearly: identify distinctive features and give clear descriptive, factual detail.	

How to present your evidence for AC1.2

The LO for AC1.2 remains the same as AC1.1, however, a different response is required by you. Note the new performance descriptors for AC1.2, which were given in the example on page 261:

Learning Outcome	Assessment Criteria	Level 1 Pass	Level 2 Pass	Level 2 Merit	Level 2 Distinction
LO1 Understand the importance of nutrition in planning menus	AC1.2 Compare nutritional needs of specific groups	Outlines nutritional needs of two specific groups. Comparison may be implied.	Compares nutritional needs of two specific groups giving some reasons for similarities and differences.	Compares nutritional needs of two specific groups giving clear reasons for similarity and differences.	Compares nutritional needs of two specific groups giving clear and in-depth reasons for similarity and differences.

AC1.2 is asking you to compare the nutritional needs of *specific groups*. The *specific groups* can be found within the information given in the LAB. In the example brief we are using here, the specific groups are:

> 'Edgerton's population is mainly composed of **professional working people** with **young children** and **retired people**, who have sold their homes in London and relocated to the countryside.'

On the next pages are some example answers for the different performance bands for AC1.2, so you can compare the type and amount of detail required for each level. Each level has been annotated to show how it meets the AC1.2 requirements.

Remember that when you present this work, it should be clearly set out and easy to follow and read. You could make use of diagrams to help illustrate and explain what you are writing about.

AC 1.2 Compare nutritional needs of specific groups: Retired people and Children.

Example answers for different performance bands.

Level 1 Pass

Outlines nutritional needs of two specific groups. Comparison may be implied.

Only a brief and basic outline given for nutritional needs of both groups.

Information about the need to limit children's sugar intake could have been given here.

Implied comparison but no details to show knowledge and understanding.

Retired people need to have lots of nutrients – protein, fat, carbohydrate, vitamins and minerals, so they stay healthy because they are getting older and their body is gradually getting weaker. Retired people need energy like children do, so they need carbohydrate. They must not have too much sugar or fat though, because they might put on weight which could lead to problems with their heart. Children need all the nutrients because they are growing and very active.

Children need to grow strong bones so they will need minerals, but retired people's bones get weaker.

When people get older, they might lose their appetite so food needs to have seasoning like salt and pepper, but they must not eat too much salt.

Implied comparison of energy needs between the two groups, but no detail given; e.g. children would need more energy because they are growing and very active, and retired people need less as their metabolic rate slows down as they get older.

Information about the need to limit children's salt intake could have been given here as well as the need to encourage children to try new foods and flavours.

Level 2 Pass

Compares nutritional needs of two specific groups, giving some reasons for similarities and differences.

General comparison given about total nutrient intake between the two groups. Limited range of nutrients compared. No mention of water requirements.

Retired people are getting older, so they are slowing down and their body does not need as much of each nutrient as it did when they were younger. This is especially true for fat and carbohydrate (especially sugar), which will make them put on weight if they eat a lot and do not use all of these for energy, because they are not very active. Older people might be more at risk of developing Type 2 diabetes too, although more children are getting this too. They need to eat wholegrain foods to provide fibre and prevent constipation, which can happen if you are not very active.

Children are very active and growing, so they need plenty of all the nutrients, otherwise they will not grow properly. They need fat and carbohydrate for energy, but it is important to encourage them to eat carbohydrate foods that do not contain much sugar, e.g. wholemeal bread, wholegrain rice and pasta, so that they will get other vitamins and minerals as well as energy and fibre.

Quite good comparison of vitamin D and calcium requirements, showing the differences between the two groups.

Retired people need vitamins, such as vitamin D to help them absorb calcium to prevent their bones becoming very weak, which often happens in older people. Children's bones are growing and becoming strong, so they need these nutrients in their diet as well as being active, which helps bones to become strong.

Retired people need protein to repair their body if they have an injury and maintain their skin and body functions such as digestion. Children also need lots of protein to grow, which retired people do not.

Some good information comparing carbohydrate intake given for both groups, especially the risks of too much sugar in the diet for both groups.

General comparison of protein requirements, showing the differences between the two groups. Lacks detail.

Level 2 Merit

Compares nutritional needs of two specific groups, giving clear reasons for similarity and differences.

Clear and well thought-out comparison of general nutritional needs for both groups, with reference to the Eatwell Guide. Comparison clearly highlights similarities and differences between the needs of the body in both age groups.

As people get older, their body starts to slow down and they often become less active. They may have a smaller appetite, and sometimes lose their sense of smell and taste. Retired people need a balanced diet and should follow the Eatwell Guide to make sure they have a wide variety of foods and nutrients to maintain their health and their body.

Children's bodies are doing the opposite to older people. They are growing and developing and children are usually very physically active, which means they need lots of protein and energy. They should also follow the Eatwell Guide to make sure that they develop a taste for trying and eating a variety of foods, which will give them plenty of different nutrients.

Both children and retired people need carbohydrate and fat for energy, but should limit the amount of sugar they have in their diet. This is because excess sugar can lead to weight gain in older people and tooth decay and weight gain in children. Children will also develop a preference for sweet foods, which may lead to health problems as they get older. The same applies to salt, because many snack foods and takeaways have a lot of salt in them and children like the taste. Too much salt can lead to problems with high blood pressure and kidney problems in both children and older people. Older people must be careful not to eat more than 6g of salt a day.

Good, clear comparison of sugar intake and the potential problems associated with excess intake in both groups.

Good, clear comparison of salt intake and the potential problems associated with excess intake in both groups. The recommended maximum daily intake for children could have been given.

Vitamin D and calcium are important nutrients for both groups. For children, their bones are growing and they need calcium to be absorbed and laid down in their bones and teeth to make them strong and dense, so that when they are older, their bones do not break very easily. For retired people, these nutrients are needed to maintain the strength of the bones and make sure that they do not weaken too rapidly during the natural aging process.

Good comparison of the needs for vitamin D and calcium clearly showing differences in the two age groups as to why these nutrients are important.

Good comparison for iron and vitamin C requirements, clearly showing the differences in requirement for both age groups.

Vitamin C is needed by both groups to absorb iron and make connective tissue. Iron will prevent anaemia, which can be common in retired people and makes them feel very tired. As they get older, the skin becomes thinner and muscles weaken, so it is important to make connective tissue to slow down this process. For children, iron is needed to carry oxygen round the body, so they can get plenty of energy, because they are so active.

Both groups need to drink plenty of water, to make sure they are properly hydrated. Dehydration is a common problem in the elderly and can put a strain on their kidneys. Children should be encouraged to drink water, because they often choose sweet fizzy drinks rather than water, and this can lead to weight gain and tooth decay.

Dietary fibre is important for both groups and they should eat plenty of wholegrain foods and fresh fruit and vegetables to make sure they have enough. In retired people, and some children, constipation is a common problem and can lead to diseases of the intestines.

Clear comparison for water requirements between the two groups, highlighting similarities and differences. The same applies to dietary fibre.

Level 2 Distinction

Compares nutritional needs of two specific groups, giving clear and in-depth reasons for similarity and differences.

Clear and in-depth comparison of similarities and differences between both groups in terms of bodily changes and general nutritional needs.

As people become older, their body goes through a number of changes. Their metabolic rate slows down, which means that they need less energy from food, and they often develop a smaller appetite. Their body systems, such as digestion and blood circulation, start to slow down and work less efficiently, which means they may not absorb or be able to use nutrients from food as well as they used to. Many older people gradually become less physically active because their muscles weaken, or they may develop conditions such as arthritis, which means that walking is difficult. Older people need a wide variety of nutrients to help maintain their body as it goes through these changes and to keep them healthy and as active as possible. If they have too much fat and carbohydrate (especially free sugars) in their diet, they may gain weight, which can lead to problems such as obesity, heart disease, high blood pressure, Type 2 diabetes and cancer. This also applies to children, and recent research shows that an increasing percentage of young children in the UK are becoming obese and developing Type 2 diabetes, because they eat too many energy-dense foods.

Good use of terminology and clear and in-depth comparison of the dangers of excess intake of energy-dense foods for both groups.

In children, their bodies and all the systems in it are growing, developing and changing rapidly and they need a constant supply of a wide range of nutrients and energy from foods to allow this to happen properly and to keep them healthy. Both groups should follow the Eatwell Guide.

Clear awareness of how nutrients work together in the body and very good, in-depth detail of how antioxidants help prevent the development of cancer. More emphasis on older people than on children.

In children, adolescents and younger adults, calcium and vitamin D are essential nutrients because as the skeleton grows and develops, minerals (mainly calcium) are laid down in the bones until the skeleton reaches peak bone mass, when it is at its strongest. It is important that children and adults are physically active to help in this process. After this, the natural aging process means that the bones gradually start to lose minerals and weaken. In older people, this can develop into a painful condition called osteoporosis, in which the weakened bones easily deform and break. They need to ensure they have enough vitamin D and calcium to slow down this process.

Vitamin C and iron are both essential for children and older people. Vitamin C helps iron to be absorbed, so that it can carry oxygen around the body as part of the process that releases energy from carbohydrates in body cells. Vitamin C is also involved in the production of connective tissue that surrounds bundles of muscles and binds cells together in tissues and organs. This is essential to enable children to develop strong muscles, organs and tissues.

Very good, clear and in-depth detail of how calcium and vitamin D function in the body, clearly showing how and why the two groups differ in their requirements, and how these change as the body develops and ages.

Very clear and in-depth explanations of vitamin C and iron requirements, comparing how the absorption and function of these nutrients change as the body develops and ages.

A fairly common problem in older people is to develop anaemia, because the body does not absorb iron as well as it did, and they may not have enough vitamin C in their diet, which can speed up the weakening of their muscles and also lead to a condition called scurvy.

Vitamins A, C and E are involved in the health and development of the eyes. As people get older, there is a risk of developing age-related eye conditions, so it is important to maintain the intake of these vitamins. They are also important antioxidants, which have been shown to reduce the risk of developing diseases such as cancer, by preventing substances called free radicals from harming body cells. This is especially important for older people as the risk of developing cancer rises as people get older.

The B group of vitamins are involved in the function of the brain and nervous system, and in children this is important as they develop skills such as language, mathematics, understanding, etc. In retired adults, having sufficient B vitamins in the diet and keeping the brain active and alert is important to help prevent conditions such as dementia.

Good, general information on how B vitamins help brain function in the two age groups.

General information on the dangers of excess salt intake applied to both groups. A good range of nutrients have been covered by this student.

Children should be discouraged from eating lots of salt and salty foods because it can lead to problems with blood pressure and the kidneys. This also applies to retired people, especially as when they get older, the kidneys can stop working as well as they did.

How to present your evidence for AC1.3

You can see that the LO is the same, but AC1.3 is asking for new information and the performance bands, including the performance indicators, have changed.

Learning Outcome	Assessment Criteria	Level 1 Pass	Level 2 Pass	Level 2 Merit	Level 2 Distinction
LO1 Understand the importance of nutrition in planning menus	AC1.3 Explain characteristics of unsatisfactory nutritional intake	Outlines key characteristics of unsatisfactory nutritional intake. Evidence is mainly descriptive with limited reasoning.	Explains characteristics of unsatisfactory nutritional intake. There is evidence of reasoning and relating characteristics to specific groups.	Explains with clear reasoning characteristics of unsatisfactory intake of a range of nutrients. Explanations are related to specific groups.	NB: AC1.3 does not go up to a distinction and will be blank on your performance band chart.

Activity 28.4

Below and on the following pages are some example answers for the different performance bands for AC1.3. Compare the type and amount of detail that has been given for each level.

With your peers, discuss why each answer has been awarded the level it has been given.

AC 1.3 Explain characteristics of unsatisfactory nutritional intake related to specific groups: Retired people and children.

Example answers for different performance bands.

Level 1 Pass

Outlines key characteristics of unsatisfactory nutritional intake. Evidence is mainly descriptive with limited reasoning.

If people don't have enough protein they do not grow properly, their hair gets thin and they get weak nails.

If they have too much protein, they may put on weight.

Too much fat and carbohydrate can make people put on weight and get diseases such as heart attacks, obesity and Type 2 diabetes. Their liver may become very fatty and not work properly. If they do not have enough fat they will lose weight and feel cold. If they do not have enough carbohydrate they will not have enough energy.

People can suffer if they do not have enough vitamins, e.g. children will not grow properly without enough vitamin A and they may go blind, and if they do not have enough vitamin D, their bones will be weak and will bend because they have not got enough calcium in them. A lack of vitamin C will lead to scurvy and a lack of vitamin B_1 will lead to beriberi.

If people do not have enough minerals, they could get diseases, e.g. not enough calcium will lead to weak bones, not enough iron will give them anaemia and not enough fluoride will make their teeth weak.

People can also suffer if they have too much of some nutrients, e.g. too much sodium may give them high blood pressure, too much iron and vitamin A is poisonous, and too much fluoride can make their teeth go brown.

Level 2 Pass

Explains characteristics of unsatisfactory nutritional intake. There is evidence of reasoning and relating characteristics to specific groups.

Children are growing and developing fast, so if they do not have enough protein, they will not grow properly and their hair and nails will become weak because they are made of protein. Retired people still need protein to maintain and repair their body, so if they are short of protein, they may get infections more easily and not be able to digest their food properly. If they have too much protein, it may put a strain on their kidneys.

If people have too much fat and carbohydrate, they may gain weight and this could lead to other health problems such as obesity, Type 2 diabetes and heart disease. Children should be discouraged from eating too much sugar and refined carbohydrates as they are likely to gain weight, which will continue as they become adults. Retired people are often less active than they used to be and as their body gradually slows down they will be more likely to gain weight if they eat too much fat and carbohydrate.

It is quite rare for people not to have enough vitamins and minerals in the UK, but some groups of people may show signs of these deficiencies. For example, older people who have smaller appetites and may not eat a wide range of foods may develop the early signs of vitamin C deficiency (scurvy), e.g. red spots under the skin, and dry, spilt nails and anaemia (tiredness

and no energy) because of a lack of iron. They may also develop sores round their mouth or be unable to think or remember things properly, because of a lack of some B vitamins.

Children may develop the early stages of vitamin D deficiency (rickets) if they do not go out in the sunshine very much and do not have enough calcium in their diet. This may also happen in older adults and speed up the natural aging process where the bones lose their minerals.

Children are also likely to develop night blindness then full blindness if they do not have enough vitamin A, which is a problem in many countries, but not so common in the UK. Eyesight gradually becomes weaker in many older people, so they need to make sure they have enough vitamins to keep their eyes as healthy as possible.

One thing that health professionals are concerned about is people in the UK having too much salt (sodium) in their diet, which can lead to a strain on their kidneys and to high blood pressure. Children may eat too much salt in snack foods, e.g. crisps, takeaway foods and ready meals. Retired older people who may have started to lose their sense of taste may add more salt to their food to make it tastier and because they are older, they may develop high blood pressure and kidney problems.

Level 2 Merit

Explains with clear reasoning characteristics of unsatisfactory intake of a range of nutrients. Explanations are related to specific groups.

Children are especially vulnerable to deficiencies of nutrients because their body is growing and developing fast and therefore needs a constant supply of nutrients. This is very obvious when children do not have enough protein – they do not grow properly and the natural processes in their body that need a lot of protein, such as digesting food, growing hair and developing an immune system to fight infections are all affected, which makes them very ill.

Although retired people have stopped growing and developing, they still need a regular supply of protein to maintain all their body processes and repair it if they are ill or injured.

If children (especially babies) or retired people have too much protein, which is quite common in developed countries, such as the UK, that eat a lot of meat and dairy foods, this can put a strain on their kidneys and liver, which can be especially dangerous for babies and little children. It is also a problem for older adults who may have kidneys that do not work as well as they used to.

As people grow older, they need to make sure that they do not have too many foods that contain a lot of carbohydrate (especially free sugars) or fat in their diet. This is because these foods are

energy dense and if the energy they contain is not all used up in physical exercise and activity, it is stored as body fat. This can be a problem for older people as it can lead to other health problems such as obesity, heart disease and Type 2 diabetes. Obesity is also becoming a major problem in young children and teenagers and has been linked to having too much sugar, refined carbohydrates and fat in their diet from an early age, and not being active enough. Many children are also developing Type 2 diabetes, which is linked to their diet, weight gain and lack of activity.

Both children and retired people need to have enough dietary fibre in their diet to enable them to get rid of waste products from the body and prevent constipation and other intestinal diseases such as bowel cancer and diverticular disease.

Vitamin and mineral deficiencies are unusual to see in the UK, but they do happen. For example, some groups of children have developed rickets due to a lack of vitamin D (and exposure to sunlight to make vitamin D under the skin) and calcium in their diet. Research also shows that many adults do not have enough vitamin D in their bodies to enable them to absorb enough calcium, and this could be a problem as they become older.

Older adults lose minerals from their bones as part of the natural aging process. If their bones are already weakened due to lack of vitamin D when they were younger, then their bones will lose minerals and become weak more quickly, which can lead to bone fractures and pain.

Sometimes older adults develop the early signs of scurvy, because they do not eat enough fresh fruit and vegetables, which means they do not have enough vitamin C in their diet. Red spots that you can see under the skin, means that blood is leaking from blood vessels, because there is not enough vitamin C to make connective tissue to stop the blood leaking through the weak blood vessel walls. This will also mean that they do not absorb enough iron and are likely to develop anaemia as well.

In many countries, many people, especially children, go blind due to lack of vitamin A and children do not grow properly. People who take vitamin supplements must be careful not to have too much vitamin A because it is poisonous. In older age, eyesight starts to deteriorate, so it is important to make sure that they have enough vitamin A, C and E to help maintain the health of the eyes.

A deficiency of B vitamins is rare in the UK, but sometimes older people can develop some deficiency signs if they have a very limited diet, e.g. a sore mouth and tongue, a form of anaemia or not being able to think or remember things properly. If children are brought up on a vegan diet, their parents need to make sure they get enough vitamin B_{12}, as it is not easily found in plant foods and it is needed to make red blood cells and nerve cells in the brain and nervous system, which are developing fast.

Both children and older adults need to limit the amount of salt (sodium) they have in their diet. Children learn to like the taste of salt if they are regularly given foods such as crisps and other fried snacks, processed meats, takeaway foods and ready meals, many of which have a high salt content. Too much salt causes high blood pressure and puts a strain on the heart and kidneys. In children, the kidneys are still developing, so this is dangerous and in older adults, the kidneys may be starting to weaken due to the aging process and high blood pressure will lead to problems with their heart and other organs.

How to present your evidence for AC1.4

Again, the LO is the same, but AC1.4 is asking for new information and the performance bands, including the performance indicators have changed. In this AC, only Level 1 Pass and Level 2 Pass are awarded.

Learning Outcome	Assessment Criteria	Level 1 Pass	Level 2 Pass	Level 2 Merit	Level 2 Distinction
LO1 Understand the importance of nutrition in planning menus	AC1.4 Explain how cooking methods impact on nutritional value	Outlines how cooking methods impact on nutritional value. Evidence is mainly descriptive with limited reasoning.	Explains how a range of cooking methods impact on nutritional value. Reasoned statements are presented.	NB: AC1.4 does not go up to a merit and will be blank on your performance band chart.	NB: AC1.4 does not go up to a distinction and will be blank on your performance band chart.

Activity 28.5

Create an A4 page of information to explain how cooking methods impact on nutritional value.

- The information could include images of the cooking methods described and it must meet the requirements of a Level 2 Pass.
- Information on cooking methods and the impact they have on nutrients can be located on pages 146–147.
- Your teacher can mark this piece of work and show you areas to improve if required.

Now that you have finished AC 1.1–1.4, the next step is to complete AC 2.1–2.3. Once these are finished, you will have completed Task 1.

Stage 4: How to present your evidence for AC2.1

Learning outcome	Assessment Criteria	Level 1 Pass	Level 2 Pass	Level 2 Merit	Level 2 Distinction
LO2 Understand menu planning	AC2.1 Explain factors to consider when proposing dishes for menus	Outlines factors to consider when proposing dishes for menus. There may be some omissions.	Explains factors to consider when proposing dishes for menus. Explanation has some reasoning.	Explain factors to consider when proposing dishes for menus. Explanations are clear and well-reasoned.	NB: AC2.1 does not go up to a distinction and will be blank on your performance band chart.

Note: *The learning outcome has changed and is labelled* **LO2**

The AC is now labelled 2. This highlights the move to Assessment Criteria 2.

There are a number of factors to consider when proposing dishes for a menu:

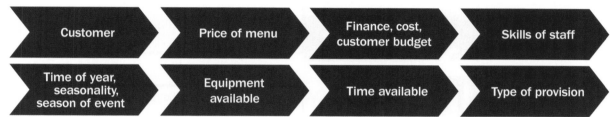

Customer   Price of menu   Finance, cost, customer budget   Skills of staff

Time of year, seasonality, season of event   Equipment available   Time available   Type of provision

You could present your evidence as a chart, as shown below, or a PowerPoint presentation.

For the example LAB, these factors are shown in the chart below:

Customer

Working families with children – small portions for children need to be available plus high chairs. Menus should reflect current concerns over sugar and salt intake.

Retired people – smaller portions should be available on request.

Price of menu

Fish & Chips £7⁹⁵
Sausage & Mash £6⁵⁰
Steak and Ale Pie £7²⁵
Veggie Lasagne £5⁹⁵
Braised Beef £8²⁵
with leeks in red wine sauce

Range of prices needs to be available in the menu to suit different income ranges and needs of customers.

Finance, cost, customer budget

*KIDS EAT FREE Sun-Thurs *from kids menu until 7pm * Terms & conditions apply

Menus may be priced so that children's meals are cheaper or part of a deal, e.g. children eat for free at certain times, in order to attract families with limited budgets.

Special deals for people with pensions may be offered on certain days or time of day.

Skills of staff

Menu production needs to be within the capabilities of the staff. The four highly skilled staff employed at the Gold Lilly restaurant will be able to produce a varied menu. The open-plan kitchen in the restaurant will enable them to be seen at work, which will attract customers.

The trainee chef must be able to prepare and cook at least two of the dishes proposed for the menu.

Time of year, seasonality, season of event

Edgerton's semi-rural location will mean that the Gold Lilly restaurant can buy seasonal ingredients from local farms and producers.

Seasonal events will attract many visitors to the village and the menu should be planned to cater for these events.

Equipment available

The menu will need to be matched to the availability of equipment, e.g. if the chefs want to make speciality ice creams using local ingredients, there need to be enough ice cream makers and freezer space available to store the ice creams to meet demand.

Time available

The restaurant wants to cater for the diverse needs of the population and visitors to Edgerton, so will need to be able to provide meals throughout the day, as well as the evening. This will require careful planning so that there are always enough chefs on duty throughout the day and evening to produce the meals in time, and enough storage facilities to allow ingredients to be prepared in advance and stored safely.

Type of provision

The menu provided by Gold Lilly restaurant needs to be varied and diverse to cater for the range of customers it is likely to have. It will be a good idea to have several menus planned that are rotated, e.g. every week, in order to be able to offer variations on a regular basis, plus some 'signature' dishes that identify the style of the restaurant and the chefs and become well-known by customers as, e.g. the 'Gold Lilly Pie', the 'Gold Lilly Curry', etc. This unique selling point (USP) will attract new and returning customers.

How to present your evidence for AC2.2

There is a great deal of information that you could write about in regard to how the dishes on a menu address environmental issues. However, the highest level you can achieve in AC2.2 is a **Level 2 Pass**. You should take this into account when completing the task.

Learning Outcome	Assessment Criteria	Level 1 Pass	Level 2 Pass	Level 2 Merit	Level 2 Distinction
LO2 Understand menu planning	AC2.2 Explain how dishes on a menu address environmental issues	Outlines how dishes on a menu address environmental issues. There may be some errors.	Explains how dishes on a menu address environmental issues. Explanation includes reasoning.	NB: AC2.2 does not go up to a merit and will be blank on your performance band chart.	NB: AC2.2 does not go up to a distinction and will be blank on your performance band chart.

For the example LAB, the types of information you could write about are shown below in the form of a mini poster that could be inserted into the menu to inform customers about how the restaurant addresses environmental issues:.

Gold Lilly
and the environment

At Gold Lily restaurant, we are committed to minimising our impact on the environment. This is how we do it:

 When planning our menus, we carefully consider the provenance of our food. We buy most of our ingredients from local farmers and producers so that we can provide seasonal foods and reduce food miles and polluting emissions from transport and delivery vehicles. We buy and use misshapen vegetables and fruits to prevent them from being wasted. We grow many of our fresh herbs in our own kitchen garden.

 We have made the decision to reduce our use of plastics because of current and ongoing concerns over land and sea pollution:

- we only buy ingredients and materials from suppliers who use minimal or no plastic packaging
- we recycle plastic packaging and other items, e.g. bottles
- we do not use individually wrapped items such as seasonings, butter, sauces, jams
- we use ingredients such as spices, flavourings, sauces, etc., that come in refillable or recyclable catering-sized containers
- we buy cleaning fluids in bulk and decant them into reusable smaller bottles
- we use takeaway containers made from materials that can be recycled, e.g. aluminium foil, card
- we have replaced plastic drinking straws with those made from paper
- in our customer toilets, we have replaced paper towels with solar powered electric hand driers.

 We regularly check and maintain our refrigerators, freezers, preparation and cooking equipment to make sure that they all work efficiently and use minimal non-renewable energy.

Our chefs use preparation and cooking methods that use minimal non-renewable energy, e.g. they fill up ovens to make maximum use of them; they cook many items on the hob to avoid heating up a whole oven; they regularly use microwave cookers, induction hobs and slow cookers, they use quick cooking methods such as stir-frying and sautéing.

 We send some food waste to be composted so it can be used to grow more plants.

We send suitable left-over ingredients and foods to food banks and charities for people in need so that it is not wasted.

We recycle as many waste materials as possible.

Stages 5 and 6: How to present your evidence for AC2.3

Stage 5: It is at this point in Task 1 that you need to start thinking about which dishes you are going to propose and plan to make for the assessment. There is no set rule about when you should start to do this, but now would be a logical time, as it will help you to answer AC2.3.

Learning Outcome	Assessment Criteria	Level 1 Pass	Level 2 Pass	Level 2 Merit	Level 2 Distinction
LO2 Understand menu planning	AC2.3 Explain how menu dishes meet customer needs	Outlines how menu dishes meet customer needs in general terms. Evidence is mainly descriptive with limited reasoning.	Explains how menu dishes meet needs of specified customers. Some evidence may be in general terms and descriptive. Explanation includes reasoned statements.	Explains how menu dishes meet needs of specified customers. Explanations are comprehensive and credible.	NB: AC2.2 does not go up to a distinction and will be blank on your performance band chart.

Activity 28.6

For the example LAB, carry out the following activities:

- Carry out some research for recipes that would make suitable dishes for the two specified groups: young children and retired people.

- **Stage 6:**
  Choose four dishes, remembering that you need to ensure that the dishes demonstrate three skills in cooking and three in preparation (a reminder of the skills is shown on the right). The dishes can be starters, main courses or desserts.

- Explain clearly and in detail how the four dishes you have chosen meet the needs of the two specified groups. Use your class notes to help you.

Preparation skills and techniques	Cooking skills
Weighing and measuring	Boiling
Chopping	Blanching
Shaping	Poaching
Peeling	Braising
Whisking	Steaming
Melting	Baking
Rub-in	Roasting
Sieving	Grilling (griddling)
Segmenting	Frying
Slicing	Chilling
Hydrating	Cooling
Blending	Hot holding
Portion control	
Position on serving dish	
Garnish	
Creativity	

Here are some chosen dishes for the example LAB and the skills and cooking methods they demonstrate.

Dishes for young children

Salmon pesto tray bake with a mixture of roasted vegetables

How it meets the needs of young children

- Salmon is not too strong a flavour

- Salmon is easy for the child to eat (all bones must be removed)

- Roasted vegetables give variety of colours, flavours and textures

- The dish provides a good range of nutrients needed by young children

Prep. skills and techniques and cooking methods

Fish preparation
Skinning, de-boning

Pesto preparation
Using food processor

Vegetable preparation
Peeling, chopping, shaping

Baking

Roasting

Baked chicken strips served with broccoli florets and creamy mash made from butternut squash, potato and carrot

How it meets the needs of young children	**Prep. skills and techniques and cooking methods**

How it meets the needs of young children

- The chicken strips can easily be eaten by young children with cutlery or their fingers

- The mash provides a contrasting texture, with plenty of colour and flavour

- The chicken strips provide a crunchy texture as a contrast to the soft mash

- The broccoli 'trees' are enjoyed by many young children

- The meal provides a wide range of nutrients, especially protein, carbohydrate, fibre, vitamins A, B group, C, D and E, as well as a variety of minerals.

Prep. skills and techniques and cooking methods

Chicken preparation
Skinning, cutting, coating

Vegetable preparation
Peeling, chopping, mashing
Garnishing

Baking

Boiling

Steaming

Dishes for retired people

Cauliflower and sautéed vegetable au gratin served with coleslaw and Cajun potato wedges

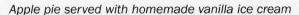

How it meets the needs of retired people

- Suitable for lacto vegetarians

- The meal provides a good variety of textures, flavours and colours so is therefore appealing to customers

- The meal provides a wide range of nutrients required by older adults, especially calcium and vitamin D, fibre, vitamin C and vitamins A, E and B group.

Prep. skills and techniques and cooking methods

Vegetable preparation
Peeling, chopping, shaping, grating, shredding

Béchamel sauce preparation and cooking

Garnishing

Steaming

Sautéing

Grilling

Roasting

Apple pie served with homemade vanilla ice cream

How it meets the needs of retired people

- The pie is a traditional dessert and enjoyed by many people from this generation

- The ice cream provides a good contrast with a different texture and complementary flavour

- The dish provides a range of nutrients, especially protein, carbohydrate, fat, fibre, vitamins A and D, B group, calcium and some iron.

Prep. skills and techniques and cooking methods

Shortcrust pastry preparation
Rolling, shaping, decorating

Apple preparation
Peeling, coring, chopping

Baking

Ice cream preparation
Making vanilla egg custard base
(crème Anglaise)

Freezing

Stages 7 and 8: Task 2: Plan the production of dishes for a menu

You must produce an **annotated and dovetailed timed production plan for your chosen dishes**, which should all be cooked within the same time frame.

Learning Outcome	Assessment Criteria	Level 1 Pass	Level 2 Pass	Level 2 Merit	Level 2 Distinction
LO2 Understand menu planning	AC2.4 Plan production of dishes for a menu	Plan outlines key actions required with some omissions and errors that require amendment. There is limited consideration of contingencies.	Plan has some detail and is mainly appropriate but may have some omissions and errors that require amendment. There is some consideration of contingencies.	Plan has detail with some minor omissions. Plan does not require changes to achieve planned outcome but would benefit from minor amendments. There are well considered contingencies.	Plan is comprehensive and detailed, incorporating well-considered contingencies for most situations.

For the example LAB, below is an example of an annotated and dovetailed timed production plan. The plan has been coloured coded to show which dish is being made and annotated to show the special points you need to remember when making the dishes.

For maximum marks, the annotated production plan must include all of the following:

- Quantities of commodities needed
- Equipment needed
- Mise en place
- Timing
- Sequencing (including dovetailing)
- Cooling
- Hot holding
- Completion
- Serving/presentation
- Removal of waste
- Contingencies
- Health, safety and hygiene points
- Quality points
- Storage

Production plan for: Baked chicken strips with creamy mash, peas and broccoli florets
Apple pie with home-made vanilla ice cream
Time: 09.15 – 12.00
Key: C = Contingency   HSH = Health, safety & hygiene point   QP = Quality point
Quantities of commodities needed:
Baked chicken strips (1 portion): 1 medium chicken breast, 2tbsp seasoned plain flour, 4tbsp breadcrumbs, seasoning, 1 egg
50g each of peeled and cubed potato, butternut squash and carrot, 25g butter, seasoning
50g trimmed broccoli florets
Apple pie (makes 8 portions): 450g plain flour, 225g butter (cubed), 110g (110ml) cold water, 2 cooking apples, 2 level tbsp. each of plain flour, water and sugar, milk or egg wash, icing sugar to dust finished pie
Vanilla ice cream (makes 10–12 portions): 4 egg yolks, 250ml whole milk, 250ml double cream, 100g caster sugar, 2 teaspoons vanilla extract, ice cubes

Equipment needed:

Baked chicken strips: meat knife, red chopping board, 3 small bowls, fork, tongs, lined baking tray, main oven, food probe

Mash: vegetable peeler, green chopping board, medium saucepan, masher, steamer for other vegetables

Apple pie: mixing bowl, knife, jug and scales to weigh/measure water, rolling pin, oven proof deep pie dish, vegetable peeler, apple corer, vegetable knife, mixing bowl, pastry brush

Vanilla ice cream: saucepan, hand whisk, wooden spoon, 2 medium mixing bowls, 1 large mixing bowl containing ice cubes, ice cream maker, a 1 litre capacity freezer box for ice cream.

Time	Activity	Notes (annotations)
09.15	Mis en place: line baking tray, weigh/measure ingredients, switch on ice cream maker to chill, process bread into breadcrumbs, organise other ingredients.	
09.30	Ice cream: place milk in pan and heat gently until nearly boiling. Meanwhile, whisk egg yolks and sugar until thick and light in colour in a medium mixing bowl. Remove the milk from the heat and pour it onto the egg yolk mixture, whisking it thoroughly. Pour the mixture back into the pan and heat gently, stirring all the time until the custard thickens – it should coat the back of the wooden spoon when it thickens. Remove from the heat. Place the custard in the other medium mixing bowl, and place it into the bowl containing ice, and leave the custard to cool. Stir it occasionally to keep it smooth.	**HSH** Wash hands thoroughly after handling raw eggs. **QP** Do not bring mixture to the boil to prevent the protein from coagulating too quickly and going lumpy. **C** If mixture does go lumpy, transfer it to an electric blender and blend until smooth.
09.50	Clear away and wash up. Throw away any rubbish and waste.	**HSH** Wash hands thoroughly after handling rubbish.
09.55	Pastry: Rub the butter into the flour until it resembles breadcrumbs. Add the cold water and mix to a dough. Knead the dough lightly until smooth. Leave the pastry (covered) in the refrigerator for at least 15 minutes for gluten to relax. Stir custard sauce.	Keep the mixture as cool as possible. **C** If your hands are very hot, use a food processor to make the pastry. **QP** Do not over-knead the pastry, otherwise it will become tough.
10.05	Prepare apples: peel, core and slice thinly into a bowl and sprinkle over the 2tbsp each of flour, sugar and water. Stir well to coat the apple slices. Place the apple slices into the pie dish in a domed pile.	Switch on the oven to gas 6/200°C.
10.20	Roll out the pastry to fit the pie dish, allowing for an extra strip of pastry to attach to the rim before placing on the pastry lid on the pie. Secure the pastry lid round the rim and trim and flute the edges. Leave a small hole in the centre to allow steam to escape. When decorated, brush the lid of the pastry with either milk or egg wash. Stir custard sauce.	Use the scraps of pastry to make decorations on the pastry lid. HSH Stand the pie dish on a baking tray to make it easy to put in and take out of the oven.
10.30	Bake pie for 20 minutes at pre-set temperature, then turn down to gas 5/190°C for a further 15 minutes to finish cooking the apples filling.	
10.32	Clear away and wash up. Throw away any rubbish and waste.	**HSH** Wash hands thoroughly after handling rubbish.

10.37	Check and stir cooled egg custard. Add the cream and the vanilla extract to the custard and mix well. Pour the mixture into the ice cream maker and switch it on.	C If there is no ice cream maker available, the mixture can be poured into a shallow tray and placed in the freezer. It must be stirred with a fork or hand whisk every 20 minutes to prevent large ice crystals from forming. This will take longer to freeze.
10.40	Remove skin from chicken breast and cut chicken breast into strips. Beat the eggs and place them in a bowl. Place seasoned flour and breadcrumbs in separate bowls. Dip and coat the chicken strips and place on the tray.	Organise work space so the chicken can be dipped into the flour, then the egg, then the breadcrumbs and finally placed on the lined baking tray. HSH Wash hands thoroughly after handling raw chicken.
10.50	Turn oven down for apple pie and time for a further 15 minutes.	
10.55	Place chicken strips in the refrigerator for baking later.	HSH Make sure raw chicken strips are covered and placed in refrigerator away from other foods to prevent cross-contamination.
10.56	Peel and cube the potato, butternut squash and carrot. Place in saucepan and bring to the boil. Boil gently for 15–20 minutes until all vegetables are soft.	To save time, heat the water in the saucepan whilst preparing the vegetables.
11.05	Remove apple pie from oven – test with a skewer to make sure the apples are soft in the centre. Keep the pie warm. Check progress of ice cream maker.	Do not switch off the oven as it will be needed later for the chicken strips at the same temperature.
11.25	Drain and mash the vegetables, seasoning well and adding the butter. Cover and keep hot. Prepare broccoli. Prepare a pan of boiling water for the steamer.	HSH They must be kept hot at a minimum core temperature of 63°C.
11.30	Clear away and wash up. Throw away any rubbish and waste.	HSH Wash hands thoroughly after handling rubbish.
11.35	Place the chicken strips in the oven for 15 minutes.	
11.37	Stop ice cream maker and transfer contents to the ice cream box. Place in freezer. Place broccoli in steamer once the water is boiling.	
11.50	Check progress of broccoli florets and remove from heat when tender. Keep hot. Check chicken strips with the food probe and remove from oven. Keep covered and hot.	QP Do not allow broccoli to overcook as it will lose a lot of vitamin C and will develop an unpalatable colour and flavour. HSH Cooked chicken must have a core temperature of a minimum of 70°C for 2 minutes. They must be kept hot at a minimum core temperature of 63°C.
11.55	Serve chicken strips with a neat mound of mashed vegetables and some broccoli florets.	QP Garnish with a little finely chopped parsley. Serve on a warm plate.
	Dust pastry crust of apple pie with a little icing sugar. Serve a slice of warm apple pie with two scoops of vanilla ice cream.	QP Decorate with a drizzle of honey or caramel sauce.
12.00	Final clear away and wash up. Throw away any rubbish and waste.	HSH Wash hands thoroughly after handling rubbish.

Once you have written your production plan, you will have completed Task 2.

Stage 9: Task 3 Prepare, cook and present your dishes

Task 3 is your opportunity to demonstrate your practical and creative skills by making the dishes you have chosen and written a production plan for. In order to achieve your best result, you need to be able to demonstrate that you can do all of the following:

- Use a range of **food preparation techniques** and **cooking methods** with **competence** (ability and skill), **confidence**, **precision** (care and accuracy) and **speed**

- Work **independently**

- Show good **food safety** and **hygiene** practices during **preparation, food storage, cooking, serving, washing up** and **waste disposal**

- Check the **quality** of the **commodities** you use throughout their **preparation, cooking** and **serving**

- Produce dishes that have a **high quality** for **flavour, texture, aroma, creativity** and **appearance**.

Here are the results of the two dishes made for the sample LAB:

Baked chicken strips with vegetable mash and broccoli

Apple pie and home-made vanilla ice cream

Activity 28.7

Here are some more examples of dishes prepared, cooked and presented by real students for Task 3.

Each dish demonstrates a number of different techniques in preparation and cooking to meet the AC for this Task.

Have a look at the dishes and discuss with your peers which techniques and cooking methods you think they have used.

Pancetta chicken stuffed with pesto mousse and winter stew.

Lemon sorbet, served with lemon mint cream.

Fillet of sea bass, basil snow and Italian herb salad, served with tomato coulis.

Baked raspberry cheesecake with coulis and meringue pieces.

Index

Picture credits

The authors and publisher wish to thank the following:

Jacqui Housely for her help with reviewing draft chapters

Scott Bradley, The Academy at Shotton Hall, **Jonathan Dix**, Dartford Science and Technology College and **Lydia Chattaway**, Heartlands Academy, for allowing us to use the images of students' finished dishes in Chapter 28.

Dedication

My thanks, as always, to Nick and the family for their support and encouragement throughout the writing of the book (Anita Tull)

Thank you to AC for the opportunity to work with her (Alison Palmer)

Acknowledgements

p19 Food Hygiene ratings, reproduced with the kind permission of the FSA; **p20** SRA sourcing, society and environment logos, Sustainable Restaurant Association logo, copyright © Sustainable Restaurant Association; **p23** City&Guilds logo, reproduced with the kind permission of City & Guilds; **p23** Future Chef photo, reproduced with the kind permission of Springboard's Future Chef; **p33** Green Key design, copyright © Green Key International; **p37** Challenge 25 poster, courtesy of the Scottish Beer and Pub Association; **p39** Trip Advisor logo, reproduced with the kind permission of Trip Advisor; **p39** World Food Travel Association logo, reproduced with kind permission of the World Food Travel Association; **p62** Prezzo allergen menu, reproduced with the kind permission of Prezzo; **p63** WAHL hairdryer instructions, reproduced by kind permission of Wahl UK Limited; **p66** Health and safety at work summary statistics for Great Britain 2017, reproduced with the kind permission of HSE; **p88** peanut death story – picture of David and Sarah Reading, reproduced with the kind permission of Emma Reading; **p101** Inspecting hotplate, courtesy of www.jasonlock.co.uk; **p101** inspecting under cooker, courtesy of Derby City Council; **p102** bins, reproduced with the kind permission of Egbert Taylor; **p134** Eatwell Guide, contains public sector information licensed under the Open Government Licence v3.0.; **p157** Soil Association logo, reproduced with the kind permission of the Soil Association; **p158** ReFill logo, reproduced with the kind permission of City to Sea; **p158** Water UK logo, reproduced with the kind permission of Water UK; **p160** Junk Food Project logo, © TRJFP Charitable Foundation 1160107; **p172** croissants box, reproduced with the kind permission of Ad Cart; **p172** Jus-Rol image, reproduced with the kind permission of Jus-Rol; **p187** double saucepan, reproduced with the kind permission of KitchenCraft; **p201** temperature gauge, reproduced with kind permission of Jim Chan, Health Inspector's Notebook www.chanchris.com; **p202** chef with open fridge, reproduced with the kind permission of Hengel; **p212** red spatula on plate and yellow spatula on plate, reproduced with kind permission of Mercer Culinary; **p213** Silikomart precision spoon, reproduced with the kind permission of Silikomart.

Reproduced with kind permission of Nisbets Plc: **p44** kitchen mixer, griddle, industrial toaster, meat slicer, industrial potato peeler, lincat dispenser; **p45** colour-coded boards, tongs, knives and labels; **p54 & 55** dumb waiter; **p70** fatigue mat ; **p72** plate dispenser ; **p75** plate dispenser; **p77** chopping boards; **p113** combi oven; **p172** blast chiller; **p187** peeler; **p212** white silicon plating wedge; **p213** precision spoon, fine tweezers, ring mould, plastic squeeze bottle for drizzling or dotting sauces onto a plate; **p214** metal chip scoop, plastic chip scoop

Published in 2018 by Illuminate Publishing Ltd,
P.O. Box 1160, Cheltenham, Gloucestershire GL50 9RW

Orders: Please visit www.illuminatepublishing.com
or email sales@illuminatepublishing.com

© Anita Tull and Alison Palmer

The moral rights of the authors have been asserted.

British Library Cataloguing in Publication Data

A catalogue record for this book is available from the British Library

ISBN 978-1-911208-64-8

Printed by Standartu Spaustuvė, Lithuania

09.18

The publisher's policy is to use papers that are natural, renewable and recyclable products made from wood grown in sustainable forests. The logging and manufacturing processes are expected to conform to the environmental regulations of the country of origin.

Every effort has been made to contact copyright holders of material produced in this book. Great care has been taken by the authors and publisher to ensure that either formal permission has been granted for the use of copyright material reproduced, or that copyright material has been used under the provision of fairdealing guidelines in the UK – specifically that it has been used sparingly, solely for the purpose of criticism and review, and has been properly acknowledged. If notified, the publisher will be pleased to rectify any errors or omissions at the earliest opportunity.

Publisher: Claire Hart

Editor: Geoff Tuttle

Design and layout: Nigel Harriss

You will find suggested answers to Activities, Practice questions and Stretch and challenge activities from the book, online:

www.illuminatepublishing.com/hosp&cateranswers